T0369042

EDUCATION AND CULTURAL POLITICS

Interrogating Idiotic Education

ivan hugh walters

iUniverse, Inc.
Bloomington

Education and Cultural Politics
Interrogating Idiotic Education

iUniverse books may be ordered through booksellers or by contacting:

iUniverse
1663 Liberty Drive
Bloomington, IN 47403
www.iuniverse.com
1-800-Authors (1-800-288-4677)

ISBN: 978-1-4401-7696-8 (sc)
ISBN: 978-1-4401-7695-1 (hc)
ISBN: 978-1-4401-7697-5 (e)

Printed in the United States of America

iUniverse rev. date: 10/12/12

TO MARGARET

AND

OUR THREE CHILDREN: VONRAD, IVAN, AND TATIANA

Contents

Acknoledgement

Education and Cultural Politics: Interrogating Idiotic Education evolved out of my studies in the Master of Education Program at Vermont College of Union Institute and University. I met many persons on this campus, the academic and administrative staff and my class mates who have enriched my life in one way or the other and I am greatly indebted to them. I speak in particular of Dr. Connie Krosney and Dr. Ken Bergstrom who were my supervisors. My comrades in the ministry of life: Rev. Dr. Walker-Walker and Rev. Dr. Raymond G. Wilson. I owe special debt of gratitude to my good friend, Dana Bennis. Dana and I discussed at length most if not all of the subject matters that are treated in this book. During our two years on the Master of Education Program I have had the benefit of his sharp, decisive, and critical mind.

They are truly the *sine qua non* that provided me with the upliftment and the courage to write this book. I love them and thank them for loving me.

I owe a debt of gratitude to my friend and colleague Jean Rosemary Butcher who read and edited the manuscript and made practical and intelligent suggestions for clarification of some of the issues that helped to shape this book into what it has become. Jean's sharp language and editorial skills were invaluable.

In writing this book, I have drawn on the works of many others who have written on the subject matters herein. I owe an enormous debt to them and I have acknowledged and credited them in my reference section.

I have written this book from the perspective of a particular form of transgressive oppositional cultural politics which I hope to develop further as my theoretical gnosis continues to evolve.

Introduction

Education and Cultural Politics: Interrogating Idiotic Education is the end product of my evolutionary processes up to the time of writing. I am sure that I will continue to evolve; into what, I do not know. I say evolution because I was not born into riches. I have a working class background. In fact, I grew up dirt poor but my life so far has gone through some exciting twists and turns somewhat like a winding staircase. I am not sure where it will take me but I am following the path it has opened for me. My previous experiences have shown that there appears to be invisible hands guiding my path. When I choose a path for my life, I am frequently buffeted by obstructions until I go in the direction that is apparently decreed for me. I have no doubt that I will continue to evolve; I hope into a better human being.

As a child I was always consciously aware that there are differences between the persons who lived in the ghetto and those who lived in the developed areas and attended the best schools in the Island. They were the *crime de la crime* of Antigua and Barbuda. These were the well-to-do, middle and upper classes. I was also aware that those persons who are of Caucasoid origin or of the lighter hue were better treated and received preferential attention. Class divisions were just as much a social fixture as was color, but it may have been more pernicious. The acculturated Blacks acquired the taste and posture of the White upper class. They held on to their middle class or near middle class status with tremendous zeal almost like a zealot. They gawked down the long, elongated pipe of their fake aquiline noses (much like an ant-eater) with great disdain for those of us who were from the ghetto with our rustic and often vulgar mannerism, gesticulation, and gyration.

I read somewhere a pithy comment on racial coloring to the effect that if you are White you are right, if you are brown you are near but if you are Black you are wrong. I believe this statement encapsulates the way in which I conceptualized my environment as a child. As a matter of fact my reputed father had an issue with my coloration – I guess the gametics did not work out too well for him. My childhood experiences made me very conscious and self-conscious about issues of race, color, and social class. But as I grew older I learned to accept myself as being just as good as any other even though I am from the ghetto. My love of me (without being narcissistic) was fostered by some of the black music of the 1960s such as James Browne: "Say it loud, I am black and I am proud". I was aware of the black power movement of the 1960s and what the movement was doing for the upliftment of Black people; I also heard about Martin Luther King, Jnr. and his movement to liberate Black people in America. I was saddened when he was assassinated. All the events of the 1960s brought home to me that there was something terribly wrong with the way Black people are treated in England, the United States of American and right here in the Caribbean.

My conviction springs from my life of marginalization in my youth. The father whom I have known was my mother. My experiences have cultivated in me a deep, abiding, fundamental resentment of the human tendency to treat persons who are different with degradation; to designate those who are cast as marginal as the *Other*. The subordination and devaluation of their human worth to my mind is legally and morally reprehensible. Through my experiences I have come to realize that I must focus my energies on particular forms of unjustified suffering across the board whether due to patriarchy, economic inequality, white supremacy, male supremacy, heterosexism, or religious bigotry. I believe a stout resistance to these axes of oppression is the only way that I can truly respond positively to my humanity and my sense of moral integrity. This is demanded of me through my calling to become what I am in the *Christos*. As a Christian, I am obliged to follow the dictates of my conscience even where it conflicts with dictates of the lords of the earth.

I believe that evil will thrive when good men and women do nothing to advance its eradication. Parker (2003) demonstrates that this is the point that is made so compellingly and cogently by the Protestant Pastor, Martin Niemoller when he was asked how the Nazis accomplished what they did: first taking over a state (Germany), then wreaking havoc on other states and engineering the holocaust. Similarly, the enslavement of African people was made possible because the moral integrity of the European mind was shrouded in the almighty dollar and man's rapacious greed.

I am well aware that to take on an unpopular position on the issue of discrimination and to challenge the oppression of those who are socially under- privileged will open a door to moral censorship, public odium, and opprobrium of me. But I will not deny the dictates of my conscience to scorn the beaten path: the path of popularity and acceptance. I must take my stance here in the interest of social justice and social transformation as the *Amicus* of the marginalized, for the *Other*, the undefended. I believe that I must identify with them for the purpose of counter balancing their *Otherization*. I take this stance with a large measure of trepidation however, because my detractors are powerful and can easily assassinate my character by accusing me of being motivated by self-interest. That is, the hurling of the big rock of identity politics at my vital parts. Be that as it may, here I take my stance in defiance of my detractors.

My reflections and theoretical perspectives which are written herein evolved out of my experiences as a child growing up in the ghetto, my attendance at primary and secondary schools, and at the tertiary institutions where I was temporarily incarcerated in the pursuit of gnosis, especially at the Seminary where my gaolers were holey men. My success at secondary school paved the way for my entrance into the Seminary where I served a four-year sentence from 1979 to 1983. During my four year sojourn at the Seminary, I spent my time hunting after truth and righteousness. It was in the Seminary that my faith was truly tested. Here I came to see the *men of the cloth* for what they really are: share rabid pretenders. At any rate most of them. After graduation my life followed a rocky path. I had undergone a transformation in those four years in the Seminary which made the hierarchy of the

Church negatively disposed towards me. Consequently, I was both prosecuted and persecuted by the then Archbishop Lindley Fokker and his henchmen to the full extent of their powers.

It is now thirty years since I entered that citadel of learning, that noble institution to test my vocation to the sacred ministry. And what a test that was. In the testing my pristine faith became a casualty. The result of that test has shown, according to the noble and wise Archbishop Fokker and his fawning band of rancid 'publicans', that I was not worthy of the priesthood and I was accordingly denied ordination to the sacred ministry. However, I believe I became unworthy of the priesthood in the eyes of the Church because I dared to challenge the hypocritical practices of the Church. I refused to surrender my will to the noble and wise Archbishop Fokker so that he and his holey men could mold me as they see fit. I further surmise that my lack of priestly worthiness and piety are derived from the fact that I have far too many wayward thoughts which are incongruent with and repugnant to the practices of 'good Anglicanism'. I had become seised with a radical liberal philosophy that was and is inimical to the mystique of the Church.

So by the time I graduated I had liberated my mind from the idiocy of the education which I had received at the Seminary. For these reasons the Church's dogmatic approach and I became incompatible and alienated. Consequently, I was unceremoniously kicked out of the Church on my posterior. I believe that I was rejected not so much because of my philosophy but because of who I am: a barefoot boy from the ghetto who has no pedigree and who dared to challenge the hierarchy of the Church in a way which was most offensive to them. So there was no *cake and ale* for me in the Holy Church. No consecration of me in the holy sanctuary. I was sent in the direction of Hades.

From this time onward I have experienced discrimination and victimization for one reason or the other whether because of race, social class, nationality, or personality. But I have learnt that above all things, I must be true to myself and my convictions even though my style and posture may be redolent with social danger.

In 1986/87 the Church having kicked me out of its fold brought a civil action against me for, as they claimed, breach of contract in the High Court of Antigua and Barbuda. The basis of the law suit was that I had breached my contract with the Church because I did not serve the Church for five years following my graduation from the Seminary. This was a curious law suit indeed because I never refused to honor my contract. The then Archbishop, Lord Fokker, refused to ordain me "indefinitely" because he was not convinced that I was fit to be a priest and hence my rejection. This erratic decision is strange because upon graduation I returned to Antigua and Barbuda and offered to serve the Church in accordance with the requirements of my contract (as opposed to my calling). But the good holey Archbishop Fokker did not want my service because I had become inveigled with a heretic philosophy and he was laboring under the (mis)apprehension that I would have caused spiritual mayhem in the congregation. That was the claim, but from what I can see in me, I was/am innocent. However, I will not dwell on this issue here since it is one of the topics in my second book: *No Sacred Place: Bad Faith, Lies and Illusions* to be published shortly. Suffice it to say that the learned judge in his wisdom ruled in favor of the Holey Church.

Following my departure from the Holey Church I re-entered the University of the West Indies, Cave Hill Campus in Barbados in the Caribbean from 1989 to 1992 where I studied law. I then went on to the Sir Hugh Wooding Law School in the Republic of Trinidad and Tobago from 1995 to 1997 where I studied for the Bar Examinations. I became a lawyer in 1997 and practiced mostly in civil matters. I was also employed as a tutor-in-law at the Barbados Community College from 1997 to 2007. In 2004 I embarked on a course of study at Union Institute and University, Vermont College for the Master of Education. This College is special to me because here I was able to develop my liberal philosophical perspectives along the path which I have chosen rather than along one that was dictated to me by the institution. Of the institutions where I have sojourned, Vermont College was the institution with which I was most comfortable and at home. The others cannot compare.

I am presently the Chief Magistrate of Antigua and Barbuda having been appointed to this position in June of 2008. My appointment as Chief Magistrate was greeted with a baptism of fire (the brimstones were not far behind) from some section of the society that had formed the view that I should not have been granted the appointment. My presence in this position continues to be to the displeasure of some persons on the basis of partisan politics and social class. I have been the object of much public ridicule and contempt not because I am unqualified, inexperienced, or inefficient but because I am not of the right social pedigree (you would have thought that I am some breed of canine) or because of a perceived wrong political disposition. However, my ascendancy to the position of Chief Magistrate was celebrated by right thinking persons in the society. Consequently, I was not moved, not even for a moment by the odium, the overt vilification, and the disparaging publications which were aimed at demonizing and belittling me in the eyes of right thinking men and women in the society. This is merely the reflection of the idiotic education with which my detractors have been and are inflicted and from which their redemption would augur well for the country. But when you get down to the nitty-gritty pound for pound and blow for blow none of my detractors can walk in my shoes or hold a candle to me. I therefore stand firm for truth, justice, and righteousness without hesitation and without fear. My background and experiences have cultivated me into the kind of man that I have become with my peculiar outlook and theoretical perspectives for which I make no apology whatsoever.

THE THEORETICAL PERSPECTIVES

The purpose of *Education and Cultural Politics: Interrogating Idiotic Education* is to conceptualize protest and resistance against the cultural politics of oppression/domination of peoples of African descent in the Caribbean and North America and to theorize the redemption of a people who have been victims of racism, classism, sexism, and heterosexism. I have combined the theoretical models of discrimination and oppression using the axes of racism, classism, sexism, and heterosexism to critically analyze the cultural politics of idiotic education in relation to Black people in the African Diaspora through the lens of a critical redemptive pedagogy which is shot through with an Africentric philosophy.

The word "idiotic" as used in current parlance means "stupid or mentally deficient". However, etymologically the word is derived from the ancient Greek word "*idios*" that shares the same root meaning as "idiom" and "idiosyncratic". Therefore, the word "idiotic" as used in this book means "egocentric", "selfish", or "self-centered". I believe this original meaning should be recaptured and rejuvenated in our language because it is an apt description of the kind of education that is provided in traditional schooling. I further believe that it pertinently describes the kind of self-centered, slavocratic mentality that was instilled in those of us who have been the victims of traditional schooling. The non-idiotic education which this book advocates seeks to create unity in diversity through an Africentric philosophy of multicultural reconstructionism, a critical redemptive pedagogy *ex pluribus unum* (out of many one). It is the forging of one people out of many peoples. In Christian sacramental theology, as represented in the liturgy, it is believed that "we are one because we all share in one bread – the *Christos.*

I believe that the lives of Black people were constructed by slavery and colonialism which have etched their mores into the Black psyche. I also believe that the slavocratic, colonial construction of our psyche is not indelible. I further believe that Black people's redemption lies in our being able to deconstruct our slavocratic, colonial psyche and reconstruct our psyche through a none-idiotic, liberatory education using the philosophy of critical redemptive pedagogy which has the potentiality to foster a genuine *koinonia* among Black communities and which can replace the current Black *nihilism* that is the legacy of our oppressive existence.

I have had this fire in my belly for many years. During both my undergraduate and graduate studies I have been constantly haunted and harassed by the moral question as to why the social evil of racism persists even in post-modern times despite the abundance of enlightenment and in the face of lauded democratic principles not to mention the two thousand years of Christian theology in Western societies. Through my studies, my personal reflection, and meditation I have become sensitively attuned to the ways which have shaped and constrained the possibilities of a democratic political life for Black folks with our background of the effect of protracted post traumatic slavery and colonialism that have impacted profoundly on our lives. It is this painful history that has shaped the societies in the Caribbean, England, and North America.

Our Ancestors were uprooted from their country of origin and brought across the Atlantic to work on sugar plantations in the Caribbean and the cotton plantations in North America. Under this system of oppression they were transformed into a species of sub-humans. As descendants of former African slaves, we are forced to negotiate in our society the different axes of identity, difference, discrimination and oppression. The many years of oppression and mis-education have contributed significantly to the Black *nihilism* which prevails in the inner cities in North America and the gangster thuggery in the ghettoes of the Caribbean.

But a strange irony prevails in the Caribbean where Blacks are the majority and where the leaders are Black, but the commanding heights of economic power are concentrated in the hands of few local Whites who are descendants of former slave masters, and expatriate Whites from North America and Europe; and people from the Middle East in some instances. From this perspective Black people though in the majority are still living in marginalized social and economic positions. This makes me wonder whether emancipation is a figment of our imagination. Perhaps we are just educated slaves, if I may call it that, on a different kind of plantation. In this regard Black people are yet to liberate themselves from the yokes of oppression which continue to postpone our economic enfranchisement.

The situation in the United States is not so incredulous given that Blacks are in the minority but it is profoundly amazing, if not astonishing given the democratic idealism of the United States that Blacks are still relegated to the bottom of the social pile. But maybe things are changing because Americans have recently shocked the world when they elected a Black President in November of 2008. But there is the saying that: "the more things change, the more they remain the same". The future will tell the tales.

Democratic politics which is practiced in these countries laud the most idyllic utopian dreams of the value of diversity, equality, and freedom. These ideals are integral to the right of self-determination (*kujichagulia*). The entrenchment of these fundamental rights in the constitutions of the Caribbean and United States of America insulate them against ordinary legislative power. However, these democratic ideals remain largely as elusive as phantoms in practice because *de facto* segregation and economic disenfranchisement are akin to resident evils which appear to be resistant to the most sophisticated form of exorcism. In these societies, the abundance of democratic possibilities co-mingled with some of the most notorious and egregious violations of social justice which is the lot of Black folks.

It is against this historical background that this book advocates the view that Black folks can be redeemed from this colossal of discrimination and oppression through an education that is non-idiotic and liberatory. Redemptive education creates democratic space for cultural and political discourse for the creation of new epistemology, greater participatory democracy, and social transformation.

Therefore, the main thrust of the book is to critically explore and examine the participation of idiotic education in the cultural politics of oppression/domination, and subordination of people of African descent in the Diaspora, women, and other marginalized peoples through the power of the various media of education. I advocate that oppressed peoples can turn their social circumstances upside down using the same media of education: redemptive education. Put simply, education enslaves and education can liberate. The critical focus then is a critical examination of the protracted impact of slavery, colonialism, Eurocentric patriarchy, heterosexism, sexism, classism, and racism on the lives of African people in the Caribbean and the United States. The book is theory grounded in the realities of notorious and egregious social injustice and seeks to interrogate them in order to expose them and call them by their real names.

In the pages of this book I challenge social injustice by advocating a theory of an Africentric philosophy of critical redemptive education. This is a transgressive theoretical discourse which seeks to unravel and explain human relationship and fear of difference without pretending to be the final and absolute truth, and which also seeks to foster love and generosity in a multicultural world. It is a humanism that seeks to redeem humankind from its worst excesses. In this book I critically reflect on and examine the causes of oppression and privilege by interrogating them.

I take the stance that resistance to oppression/domination is the path to redemption which will generate a new radical critical praxis that is the *amicus curiae* for the Other, the nobodies. In this book I have reduced to writing what I have been doing all my life: trying to make sense of life and seeking an abiding hope and peace for our fragile humanity. This is why I dare to speak for the *Other* who is the marginalized and the down trodden. This is an onerous burden for anyone who dares to be an amicus for the *Other*. Therefore, I must walk circumspectly with decorum and dignity as I seek to embrace truth, administer justice fairly to both the Meads and the Persians in the name of one law for all; and to stay focus on my quest for righteousness. A cardinal principle of Christian salvific theology is that we are a work in progress: we are saved, we are being saved, and we shall be saved (*sodzo, sodzi, sodzominous*).

> Lead, kindly Light, amidst the encircling gloom,
> Lead Thou me on; the night is dark, and I am far from home;
> Lead Thou me on. Keep Thou my feet; I do not ask to see
> The distant scene; one step enough for me (Hymns Ancient and
> Modern No. 266).

CHAPTER ONE

Educational Devolution in the Caribbean

> This book, which I now offer to those who are interested in this theme, is a decisive NO to an ideology that humiliates and denies our humanity (Freire, 1998(a), p.27).

This chapter examines the historical, social, political, economical, and educational development in the Caribbean to provide the context in which colonialism, slavery, and neo-colonialism impacted on the region when European culture collided with the cultures of native Amerindians and transplanted Africans. This is the context in which race relations were developed in the Caribbean and its subsequent impact on the evolution of all of the social institutions in the Islands. I will critically examine the negative effect which the advent of Europeans in the Caribbean had on the aboriginal people and the consequent wanton obliteration of the natives in several of the Islands. The last part of the chapter examines the persistent legacy of colonialism, slavery, and Black subordination through the persistence of White racist ideology in the social and economic arrangements in the region that is maintained by the descendants of the former white planters, the present beneficiaries of the plantation system. The present beneficiaries of the plantation system are able to maintain their strangle hold on the bulk of economic activities through the assistance of their faithful acculturated African descendants. The Eurocentric education system is the matrix that is used to maintain continued Black subordination in these post-emancipation societies.

THE HISTORICAL BACKGROUND

The Islands of the region form the archipelago known as the Caribbean. It is situate in the Caribbean Sea stretching from United States of America in the north to South American in the south. "The English speaking Islands of the Caribbean stretches for two thousand miles, from Trinidad in the South-East, including Guyana in South America and Belize in Central America, to Jamaica in the North" (Campbell,1985, p.154). The Islands were settled by England in the first half of the 17th century and many of them remained English colonies without changing hands during the wars that were fought in and over the region during the 18th century. Two of these Islands which remained tied to England throughout their colonial history are Antigua and Barbados. The Islands remained English colonies until they became independent. "These Islands have been bound together for three centuries through the British colonial office and the rivalry between French and British capitalism. Their specific identities have been molded by the experiences of slavery, indentureship, colonialism and white racism" (Campbell, 1985, p.154).

Most of the Islands, with the exception of Trinidad, Guyana, and Dominica retained the English Monarch as their nominal head of state. The Monarch is represented by a governor-general who is appointed by the Monarch on the advice of the prime minister. (Guyana is a South American country but it is historically and culturally connected to the Caribbean. Guyana was one of the first countries to abolish the Queen from its constitutional arrangement). The systems of governance are constitutional democracy tailored on the Westminster export model. The government is controlled by the descendants of former African slaves; and in Trinidad, Guyana and Jamaica a combination of descendants of former African slaves and East Indian indentured laborers make up the majority of the nationals. The leaders of the various countries are voted for in periodic general elections.

The region has a tropical climate with temperature between twenty and thirty degrees centigrade. The coast is strewn with long stretches of sandy beaches. The countries capitalize on this natural beauty in the promotion of its tourism product, the mainstay of many of the Islands' economies. These are small developing states with open market economies. The countries are heavily influenced by consumerism. Apart from tourism, other foreign exchange earners are manufacturing, banking, financial services sector, the sugar industry, and some other minor agricultural productions. The region generally enjoys a high quality of living and it is reputed to have a high standard of education. Some of the countries are densely populated. Barbados, for instance has a population of 250 010 persons and a density of 1,619.2 persons per square miles according to the 2000 Population Census as shown in Table 1. The larger countries of the region like Guyana, Trinidad, and Jamaica, have had some serious economic setbacks but are still managing to hold their own in the region.

THE EUROPEAN IMPACT ON THE ABORIGINAL PEOPLE

The advent of Christopher Columbus in the 17th century in the Caribbean brought two cultures together: that of the Amerindians and the Europeans. Christopher Columbus and his soldiers, priests, and colonists, paid no regard to the culture of the simple indigenous society which they found in the Caribbean Islands. The people of the region were still at the communal stage of development when they came into contact with the Europeans who had already advanced to the capitalist stage of economic development (Rodney, 1972). The life world of the indigenous people was irreparably disrupted and the people dispossessed of their lands and their possessions and forced into a system of hard labor

by the Spaniards. Almost immediately the aboriginal societies were fed
with heavy doses of the capitalist ethics of material production with
its concomitant evils, particularly the erosion of human values. This
was a well-timed invasion by the Europeans of a peaceful domain and
they raped, plundered, murdered, and subjugated the inhabitants with
consummate terror. Except in the islands of Dominica, St. Vincent, and
Jamaica the indigenous population of the region was soon obliterated
due to the terrible transformation of their life world by the imposition
of European culture, together with epidemics of European diseases such
as small pox and syphilis. Alleyne (2002) writes:

> It is well known that the indigenous peoples fared very badly.
> They were first of all enslaved, overworked and generally
> maltreated. Their forced interaction and intercourse with
> Europeans exposed them to new diseases which ravaged
> their populations. In a matter of decades their numbers
> were so drastically reduced in the Greater Antilles that they
> ceased very early to constitute groups that could preserve
> and transmit their ethnicity through generations (p.85).

This was the genocidal impact which the European invaders had on
the indigenous people wherever they were found in the Caribbean.
When the first European adventurers came to the Island of Barbados
the Amerindian people were not physically present, they had already
moved on up the Island chain. The archaeological finds suggest that
they were present on the Island many years before the Europeans came
(Hoyos, 1978). However, their presence was found in the other Islands
at the time of contact.

The European enslavement and brutal exploitation of the indigenous
people paved the way for the life of cruelty and inhumanity that became
the lot of the African slaves who were transplanted in the Caribbean
to provide cheap labor for the capitalist economy. Caribbean societies
therefore came to be characterized by the predominance of material gain
over human existence through the aggressive exploitation of both the
people and the natural resources of the countries. This relationship of

exploitation and subordination by the Caucasoid over the Amerindians and the Africans as established then still by and large characterize the societies today. The political, social, and economic structures which characterized the colonial society then still characterize the democratic societies today, albeit that some modifications to fit the changing times are evidenced today.

The Legacy of African Slavery and the Plantocracy

The extermination of the indigenous population by the Europeans gave way to the importation of West Africans and the creation of a slavocratic colonial society based on the plantocracy system. This system brought White Europeans who were planters to the Islands and Africans who were slaves to work on the sugar plantations that were established in the region (Beckford, 1972). The development of virgin land for agriculture required a cheap source of mass labor. West Africa was the pool from which this inexpensive labor could be obtained with ease because the African people, like the Amerindians in the Caribbean, were defenseless against European weapons of mass destruction, such as crossbows, swords, guns and canons. African slave labor was a crucial part of the capitalist machinery that was set up in the region. "The modern Negro slave trade was considered an economic necessity prior to the advent of the machine. This would last until the mid-nineteenth century" (Diop, 1955, p. 24).

As a result of the plantocracy system, the region's population was made up of White English planters and African slaves for most of its history. In recent times, however, people of other ethnic backgrounds from East India, China, Syria, and Mixed (African/European, European/East Indian, or African/East Indian) have taken up residence in the region. The present population of Barbados is an example of the introduction of other races into the region. At the present time 92.9% of the population is made up of the descendants of former African slaves.

The other 7.1% comprises persons of White, East Indian, Chinese, Syrian, and Mixed ancestry. This demographic structure is reflected in the 2000 Population and Housing Census as shown in Table 1.

TABLE 1
POPULATION COMPOSITION BY ETHNIC ORIGIN
Ethnic Origin (Both Sexes)

Population	Black	White	Chinese	E Indian	Arab	Mixed	Other	Total
250,010	232,507	7, 982	118	2,581	66	6,561	195	250,010

2000 Population and Housing Census.

The countries of Trinidad and Guyana have a greater population of East Indian descendants, and to a lesser extent Jamaica. The East Indians, as indicated above, were also brought to the Caribbean as laborers to work on the sugar plantation following the abolition of slavery as an institution.

The establishment of sugar as king in the Islands created an agricultural monoculture that required a massive labor force. The English colonists' quest to satisfy this labor demand led to the inhumane trafficking of humans across the Atlantic from Africa. Beckford (1972) points out that both Whites and Blacks were brought to the region solely for the purpose of producing sugar for export to Europe. "This means therefore, the structure of authority established for this exercise would influence the entire social order on the plantations" (p. 61). This emphasis on sugar production and authoritarianism created a rigid system of social stratification along the lines of race and color. This was a total caste system which did not permit any social mobility. African people were systematically stripped of their African culture and forcefully acculturated to White European culture (Beckford, 1972). This was a systematic destruction of African culture by unabashed racist alienation inflicted by White planters. In this situation "Colonial rule ensured its own perpetuation by destroying African family forms, oral traditions, customs, and belief systems, thereby inducing a form of cultural amnesia." (Brookfield, 2005, p.28) In this terrible situation

Africans' future was a life of subordination and degradation in a servile association with the White planters who dominated every aspect of their lives.

The slavocratic societies did not permit any form of education for the African slaves. In fact it was believed that this would be subversive of the plantation project. The Africans spoke different languages because they came from different locations in West Africa. This made communication difficult and many planters thought this was an advantage so as to keep them from plotting rebellion against them. Therefore, no education for the slaves was acceptable, apart from the skills that were necessary for the cultivation of sugar. However, the children of the planters were sent to England at the age of twelve years for their formal education. "This was a policy that enjoyed the approval of the planters as a whole and was condoned by the clergy of the Established Church" (Hoyos, 1978, p. 140).

The plantocracy system set the stage for the political, economical, social, and educational patterns that subsequently developed in the Island. The plantocracy determined the social value that was placed in the slavocratic society on things that are African and those that are European. "In this regime, power and knowledge combined to allow a small group of White Europeans to assign worth and status to other human beings on the basis of their phenotype" (people's facial features, hair texture, and skin pigmentation) Brookfield, 2005, p.288). This has had a lasting effect on the society even up to the present time.

THE PERSISTENT SLAVOCRATIC PSYCHE

Although Slavery was legally abolished in the region by the Emancipation Act of 1838, the basic structure of plantation society persists in the Islands with the small White section of the population, which has been reinforced by White investors from North America and Europe, who control and monopolize the bulk of the economic production in many of the countries. "And even to the present, the commanding heights of the economy in the Island have remained largely entrenched in White hands" United Nations Committee for The Elimination of all Forms of and Racial Discrimination (CERD Report, Barbados, 2005, p.5). These oligarchies are armed with hubris, greed, and bigotry in the same manner as their predecessors. Although the political directorate is constituted of descendants of former African slaves, there seems to be little that they can do about the situation of White folks' domination of the economic activities. The effects of Eurocentric ideology and hegemony still have a dominant sway over the lives of the citizenry and many unquestioningly accept and identify with them.

This is especially so because of the deeply entrenched Eurocentric acculturation throughout some of the societies especially among the better educated, as in Barbados. The main opportunity for social mobility is through education. But even this comes with a high price for the most part of denying black culture and assimilating Eurocentric cultural values. This historical situation created deep seated alienation for Africans and African descendants. In the current situation, the more Blacks try to mimic and ape European behaviors, appearance, and practices, the more acceptable and patronized they become. Campbell (1985) succinctly captures this Black colonial pathology where he states:

> Blacks were forced to deny a decisive part of their social being: to detest their faces, their color, the peculiarities of their culture, and their specific reactions in the face of life, love, death and art. All this was done so that they would idealize the color, history and culture of Europeans. (p.38)

White overt terrorism, violence, and brutality have been replaced with condescension and cultural genocide. Many people of African descent still carry the names of their former slave masters and practice the religion of Christianity of their former slave masters as they (Blacks) received it. This is the ultimate form of self-effacement.

Beckford (1972), points out that this creates the stage for a dynamic process through which Black people sought social mobility by aspiring continuously to become more and more Eurocentric. Barbados for example, 'Because of this the Island is often referred to as 'Little England' and for a long time, Barbadians have been regarded as more "British than the British" (Ellis, 2003, p. 9). This Eurocentric aspiration permeates and pervades all aspects of the society: education, residence, manner of speech and dress, religious beliefs and practices, social values and attitudes. Christianity, the religion of the former colonial masters is, ironically, the dominant religion in the Islands. "[T]here are powerful symbols of consensual values mainly of Eurocentric nature and origin to which all groups give some allegiance as a consequence of sharing a history of British colonialism and a common educational experience" (CERD Report, 2005, p.4). These, according to Beckford (1972), are the hallmarks of the Blacks who have "made it" from those who have not. Those who display an affinity for things African are frowned upon and spurned by the 'better educated'. Rodney (1969) poignantly describes Caribbean societies as laboratories of racism.

This state of affairs is not one for which one should feel complimented but rather it should ring an alarm because it is the manifest personification of a deep malady of self-hate from which many Black people suffer, despite our far removal from the days of slavery. One would have thought that in the post-emancipation era African descendants would have seized the opportunity to return to their roots, but no such progress is forthcoming except for the advancement made by Pan-Africanists and the Rastafarian Movement (Campbell, 1985). The Eurocentric educational system has played a significant role in transmitting the worthiness of things European and the damnation of things African. "Evidence is also provided to indicate that individuals have strong preferences for physical appearances that are close to the European model and have derogatory attitudes to those that are like African" (Beckford, 1972, p.69). This point is also emphasize by Fanon (1967) who shows that despite black pigmentation many people of African descent prefer to wear a white mask to hide their self hatred.

THE MALAISE OF THE EDUCATED NEGRO

The cultural alienation referred to here has a far greater impact on intellectuals of African descent than their ordinary brothers and sisters because their education has made them aware of world opinion about them, their people, and their culture. Interestingly, the Negro intellectuals have also been exposed to the civilizing role that Africans played in the world, but they have been so victimized by Eurocentric values in their early education that they are unable to appreciate Black culture (Diop, 1955). The word "Negro" is seldom used to describe Black people in Barbados, some may even find it highly offensive. "Individuals may on a purely personal level, asserts an African Identity and called themselves "African Jamaican", or "Afro-Cuban", and so on. In some territories, Barbados for example, such individuals are a rarity, and the term and concept "African Barbadian" virtually does not exist" (Alleyne, 2002, p.95). This self-hate and personal alienation are deeply entrenched in the psyche of Negro intellectuals. "Furthermore, the fundamental Black-White cleavage is reflected in the very limited degree of social interaction between these two groups" (CERD Report, 2005, p.4), in Barbadian society.

LACK OF RACIAL INTEGRATION

This social interaction is seen in the curious social arrangement in the society in that it exhibits both cultural pluralism and social integration at the same time. However, the social integration appears to be superficial mainly for the purpose of economic production wherein the Blacks provide the bulk of the labor force while the Whites are the managers and owners of the majority of the private corporations. There remains a social divide in terms of race and class because of the underlying inherent social and cultural differences and the continuous efforts by the dominant White group to maintain its strangle hold on the economic activities in Barbados. For example, "...the social structure of Barbados approximates to that of a "heterogeneous" society – a term which implies that the society remains segmented socially and culturally as a result of its long history of plantation slavery, involving European masters and African slaves" (CERD Report 2005, p. 4).

To expose this curious arrangement to public discourse and scrutiny is to tread on dangerous grounds and expose oneself to public odium because whenever the issue of Black marginalization is raised, vis-à-vis the economic activities of Barbados, the powerful White entrepreneurs, the descendants of the former European planters, and their acculturated Blacks come to the fore to counter the proponents of, as they see it, such idle imagination, because there is no racial segregation in the paradise of Barbados. West (1993) has ably shown how race matters in a similar context. Woodson (1933) aptly described this attitude when he says, "This is slightly dangerous ground here, however, for the Negro's mind has been all but perfectly enslaved in that he has been trained to think what is desired of him. The "highly educated" Negroes do not like to hear anything uttered against this procedure because they make their living in this way, and they feel they must defend the system" (p. 24). Black adherence to a social system that continues to alienate them from their roots and their own interest is the ultimate successful hegemonic work of the plantation system.

BLACK FREEDOM IN WHITE SHADOWS

Barbados (like most of the other Islands) as a former colonial society has not put in place any comprehensive anti-discriminatory legislation neither in the post-emancipation era nor in the post-independence era. Section 23 of the constitution makes discrimination on the grounds of race, creed, or origin illegal. However, this provision suffers from an inherent debility in that the constitution only provides remedies in public law for breaches by public administrators. Therefore, section 23 of the constitution has no application to discriminatory practices between private persons. This state of affairs prevails although Barbados is a signatory to the United Nations Convention on the Elimination of all forms of Racial Discrimination. Article 1 of the Convention defines racial discrimination as being the "exclusion, restriction or preference based on race, color, descent, or nationality or ethnic origin" which impacts negatively on any person.

However, the official policy of Barbados firmly opposes any policy that is based on racial discrimination, apartheid, xenophobia, and other forms of racial discrimination. This is the obvious and sensible position that any country that was formerly a slave society should take. As a former colonial country, there should be zero tolerance for racial and other forms of discrimination. To this end some of the legislation in Barbados has attempted, in a piece-meal manner, to address the matter of racial discrimination. The Shops Act makes it a criminal offence under section 21(1) to discriminate in some aspects of commerce on the basis of race, color, or creed: "No person shall on account of his race, color or creed be refused access to any shop; or opportunity to avail himself of any facility, service or amenity offered to the public." Furthermore, section 33 of the Public Order Act, Chapter 169A of the Laws of Barbados forbids incitement to racial hatred and disaffection: "A person is guilty of an offence if (a) knowingly he publishes or distributes written matter which is threatening, abusive, or insulting;" or if such conduct is done in public and is "likely to stir up hatred against any section of the public in Barbados distinguish by color, race, or creed." Further support for Barbados' non-discriminatory stance is found in the Barbados Community College Act that forbids selection of students on the basis of race, color, or creed.

These measures are worthy in and of themselves. However, a strong countervailing mind-set that holds up to public ridicule and contempt persons who raise the issue of racism in public discourse, has become a part of the general ethos of the society. The fact that there has not been in recent times any case brought before the high court for redress of racial discrimination is indicative of the acceptance of the current social arrangements. This is due to the disguise that is worn by racism in Barbados that has made it more covert rather than overt. Through the use of this mechanism, racism has become 'invisible'. This may be as a result of people's feelings of insecurity of the White minority group, but racist practices have been so ingrained and entrenched in the psyche of the Barbadian population that they are taken for granted, and even when they are overt, hardly any one complains against them.

This is ironic because the Black majority does not suffer from the kind of fear which racism has engendered in other countries like the United States in terms of racial profiling, racial violence, and pernicious racism under the apartheid regime in South Africa. Blacks in Barbados, due to their socialization, seem to be unable to detect the subtle form of racism because it is covert and is overlooked without objection because it is considered to be the natural order of things. The difficulty of this social phenomenon is that once it becomes a part of the psyche, people conduct themselves automatically within the framework of the discrimination without even realizing the racist nature of their thoughts and actions.

EUROCENTRIC IDEOLOGY

Eurocentric ideology is able to perpetuate itself in the society because it is disguised in ways that are various and clever. Through these disguises the Black majority is duped, subjugated and hoodwinked into accepting as normal the social and economic inequities that are to the advantage of the White descendants of the former slave masters and who are beneficiaries of their ancestors' exploitation and abuse of African peoples. This modus operandi coincides with Brookfield's (2005) definition of ideology as "...the broadly accepted set of values, beliefs, myths, explanations and justifications that appears self-evidently true, empirically accurate, personally relevant, and morally desirable to the majority of the populace" (p.41). In other words, Eurocentric ideology works in such a way that the subject people give free and voluntary consent to their own domination.

In the Caribbean context ideology is combined with Eurocentric hegemony to complete the circle of subtle control. Hegemony here means the consent of the majority of the people to their domination by a system of inequity that they think is in their best interest. Brookfield (2005) puts it this way: "Hegemony – the process by which people learn to live and love the dominant system of beliefs and practices – is not imposed on them so much as it is learned by them" (p.96). In other words, hegemony works well when people voluntarily internalize the beliefs and practices that actually work against their best interest. The dominant group does not normally have to proclaim its racism, sexism, or homophobia. It is done in a very subtle manner. So " … hegemony is lived out a thousand times a day in our intimate behaviors, glances, body posture, in the fleeting calculations that we make on how to look at and speak to each other, and in the continuous micro-decisions that coalesce into life" (Brookfield, 2005, p.96-97). Hegemony becomes intricately interwoven in the tapestry of daily living. It can only be observed by those who are aware and alert to its workings.

In the circumstances, the Caribbean continues to be dominated by its colonial legacies in its economic structures and ideology. The strange thing is that these socio-culture structures which originated in England in the eighteenth century for the most part have been laid to rest in England but still have current significance for and form an integral part of Caribbean cultural heritage and personal identity. Fisher (1985) makes the observation of Barbados that:

> Present-day Barbadian society is built on a history of racism and class divisiveness, two interconnected phenomena described by Lewis as "diseases" of comparable magnitude. Poor Barbadians experience history as a punishing mythology, one which makes it natural that they should forge their identities in ways that are both self-containing and supportive of the social order (p.35).

In other words, Black Barbadians find it difficult to tear themselves away from British colonialism. Blacks participate fully in their own self-effacement. The Queen of England is seen as an important nominal figurehead. Any attempt to sever the British umbilical cord would be seen as a serious national tragedy. Clarke (2003) in reflecting upon his own childhood days in Barbados refers to it as: "Growing up Stupid under the Union Jack." The continued rule of the White clan is a most problematic situation for the Black majority and they have the impudence and temerity to think that it is their God given right to own the resources of the country. Beckles (1993) describes in the situation in this way:

> [T]he overt display and articulation of these still virulent forces within contemporary society represent for many nothing short of an open attack upon the relevance and legitimacy of the African derived mindscape, and symbolize the unashamed promotion and institutionalization of minority eurocentricism" (p.528).

This chronic socio-cultural pathological situation was pellucidly articulated by Fisher (1985) when he states that "the emancipated Barbadian slave had little option but to remain in agricultural labour on the same plantation of his or her former enslavement" (p. 33). In other words, when the apprenticeship system came to an end in 1838 the ex-slaves remained tied to the plantation which was/is the source of their enslavement. This situation effectively continued the system of slavery. Negroes had neither interest in nor ownership of land. All the land in Barbados was owned by the planters. This gave them effective control over the ex-slaves and so continued the paternalistic dependence of Blacks on the generosity of the White minority. It would seem that emancipation did not make too great a difference to the ex-slaves in Barbados as it did in the cases of Trinidad, Guyana, and Jamaica where there were large tracks of Crown land on which the ex-slaves squatted away from the plantation and their former enslavement. Here on Crown land ex-slaves created the Black agricultural peasantry in free villages which made them independent of their former slave masters (Campbell, 1985). This independence resulted in serious labour shortages in these larger islands soon after emancipation. But in Barbados " the 'racial bullying and economic intimidation' of the black population has ensured white power remains 'pretty much the order of the day' ... This reality represents ... a severe indictment of independence in economic terms" (Beckles, 1993, p.528). In other words there is a real continuity of the social structures which remained undisturbed despite the apparent changed which supposedly occurred after 1838.

Apparently emancipation changed the legal status of the Negroes in the Caribbean but it did not give them freedom. The Negroes in Antigua and Barbados, for example, simply moved from one form of domination to another. Whether the Negroes in the Caribbean have entered fully into freedom is arguable. In fact the politico-cultural situation is aptly captured by Boland (1993) where he states:

> While not denying that the change in legal status of the majority of the population, and their subsequent attainment of some limited civil rights, constituted an important social event, it is nevertheless clear that the social condition of 'full freedom' was not, and arguably has not yet been achieved (p.119).

Boland's argument is that Negroes are yet to come into a state of full freedom. This argument may appear strange to many because we have bought into the Eurocentric hegemonic false antinomy that we live in a world in which we are either enslaved or we are a free people, as though the two extremes are mutually exclusive. He posits that:

> If we can emancipate ourselves from the slave/free antinomy we may better examine and understand the continuities (as well as the changes) in structures of social relationships, and in particular the continuities in the struggle of power, in the nineteenth century (Boland, 1993, p.119).

The point is that domination continues even though domination has changed or is changing from domination to domination. The continued dominance of White power in the Caribbean, the persistent poverty, powerlessness, and rightlessness of the working class people must be related to their particular racial identity and the dominant structure of White minority control of the bulk of the economic activities of the countries which is maintained by racist ideology.

POLITICAL INDEPENDENCE AND ECONOMIC DEPENDENCE

This state of affairs in the Caribbean leaves the majority Black population to live in the shadow of the White minority. The granting (as oppose to winning) of independence in the 1960s shifted political power only, to the Black majority, but the Whites in order to ensure their survival and their continued ownership of the economic resources in the post independence era, manoeuvred and manipulated the economic situation to their advantage with the assistance and complicity of Black Eurocentric acculturated leaders. The discourse of many intellectuals like Professor Beckles (1993) in relation to Barbados "shows that white in contemporary society, who constitute less than 5% of the island's population 'enjoy a life of privilege, ease, and comfort' based upon their dominant control of the corporate economy" (p.528-527). Because the Whites control the economic resources of the country that gives them a big say in the political decision-making process which they manipulate to their advantage.

The colonial education of the country's Black masses was so contrived and devised that it lends support to continued White economic domination through the acculturation of Black intellectuals from working class origins. Western style of government did not serve to liberate education but facilitates a new 'enslavement' of the minds of Black students. Blacks who were fortunate to go to school in the post-emancipation neo-colonial Caribbean were taught that the heroes of the society were the genocidal butcher Columbus, thieves and pirates like Drake, Hawkins, and Morgan.

The status of being middle class is seen as a big achievement and those who have achieved that status will not seek to change it because

for them this is the ideal social status for a Black person to possess.
Therefore:

> The Black middle class embraced the prevailing ideological
> system; many were proponents of Empire. The majority
> sought access to a system; they did not seek to destroy
> it. Status as a middle class and their dependency on the
> paternalism of the oligarch, and the colonial system,
> blunted the nationalist revolutionary spirit of black middle
> income groups and go a long way in explaining the recent
> political history of the island (Beckles, 1996, 536).

In other words, the middle class is unhelpful in effecting the kind of
meaningful social, educational, and transformational changes that
the Caribbean so deeply and richly needs and deserves. The political
leaders, civil servants, and educators are drawn from the middle class
but most of them come to their profession already acculturated into a
Eurocentric ideology and this does not facilitate the revolutionary quest
for change. Blacks in Barbados, for instance, continue to be dominated
by a handful of White Barbadian and foreign entrepreneurs.

MANIFESTATION OF CRYPTO-RACISM

As indicated above, the overt racism that was previously practiced
in the Caribbean during the colonial period does not exist anymore.
However, we must admit that domination persists even while the
relations of domination have changed and that the status of those who
are proclaimed to be legally free can be turned into various states of
dependency and unfreedom (Boland, 1993). The dominant ideology
perpetuates itself through the acceptable social practices in both
religious and civil behaviors. For example, in the religious practices
of practically all of the denominations in the Caribbean (with the
exception of Rastarianism), the perception or the assumption is that
God is White. There are very few Churches which keep Black images
of God or Jesus because this is taboo. In fact, some Churches even have

two congregations: a White congregation at the 6:00 a. m. service and a Black congregation at the forenoon service, albeit that a Black priest officiates at both services. The assumption that God is white shows that White ideology and hegemony still holds sway in Christian religious observances

The socio-cultural situation of Barbados in the post emancipation era has produced a species of racism that is not easily detectable. It is not overt, but invisible, subtle, and perhaps self-inflicted "crypto-racism" which prevents the co-mingling of the races except in the work place with Whites as owners/mangers and Blacks as wage earners, or in keeping up social appearances of racial cohesion. Crypto-racism is also seen in White retreat from predominantly White social activities, such as sports or in housing areas when the Blacks become dominant. It is not unusual when one visits some of the secondary schools to see the White children congregating among themselves to the exclusion of the Black children. This form of racism is far more difficult to dismantle than other types of racism such as apartheid.

Critical adult education can be an effective challenge to invisible racism through the careful preparation and organization of the academic curricula, the use of critical/dialogical methods of instruction, the establishment and support for greater research in cultural hegemony and ideological constructs which were/are used to victimize Black people, in human rights issues, racism, and racial discrimination, and African civilization. In other words, curricular reform must be centered on a radical paradigm of social and educational transformation to address invisible racism and continued White domination. Even more important is the urgent need for us to accept that White domination persists in the midst of apparent freedom. The need for critical vigilance cannot be overstated. "As the negation of slavery made way for a new form of domination, so the new system also generates the social conditions which provides for its eventual dialectical transcendence" (Boland, 1993, p.121).

In other words, social systems have evolutionary dynamics for self perpetuation which moves through thesis, to anti-thesis, to synthesis.

We must harness, and become seised of the evolutionary dynamics of the social system so as to weave a working class hegemony that will dominate the social structures and power relations in the society. In order to forge this new social structure, a post-secondary education that is nurtured in criticality is crucially important.

POST-SECONDARY EDUCATION IN THE POST-EMANCIPATION ERA

The Barbados Model.   There is the general view in Barbados that education is important for the country's development so the "Government has consistently invested more than 7% of its GDP (from 1993 to 2000) in the provision of educational services at the primary, secondary and tertiary levels" (CERD Report, 2005, p.11). Education is one of the media through which Eurocentric acculturation is transmitted to the Black populace, the majority of whom are from the working class and who invest heavily in education as a means of social mobility. In Barbados education is free and compulsory from the ages of 5-16 years and is available and accessible to all regardless of ethnic or racial background as provided in the Education Act. While education is free in Barbados there is no constitutional or other legal guarantee of a free education. It is a gift of prudential governance for the long term development of the country because its future economic development is in the tertiary industries and its primary source of labor for those industries is its people.

Post-secondary education, or for that matter education of slaves as indicated above, was not of any significance in the plantation society. The descendants of slaves, like their ancestors, were taught what they needed to know to work on the plantation in the production of sugar for export to Europe. No serious education system was developed during slavery and the early post-emancipation period. An education system was later developed which offered primary and to a lesser extent secondary education for the descents of the ex-slaves. The education system mirrored that of England.

Post-secondary education became a part of the educational system in Barbados with the founding of Codrington College in 1743. This was the first and only institution of post-secondary education in Barbados and in the Caribbean in general for over two hundred years. Its main concern was and is the training of Anglican priests. Codrington College "was the result of a benefaction left under the will of Christopher Codrington, a wealthy Barbadian plantation and slave owner, remained unique for nearly two hundred years. It was the only College offering higher education in the English-speaking Caribbean until 1921" (Cobley, 2000, p. 2). Christopher Codrington was once the Chief Governor of the Leeward Island. He died in 1710 and his will was admitted to probate in Barbados in 1711. The will contained a bequest of his two plantations in Barbados to the United Society for the Propagation of the Gospel. From 1745 until 1775, and 1789 to 1880 a grammar school was maintained by the Society as an institution of higher learning and students received instruction in theology and the classics. The desire of Codrington was to maintain at least three hundred Negroes on the plantations and a convenient number of professors and scholars under the vows of poverty, chastity, and obedience while they study and practice medicine and theology. In this way they will be able to attend to both the physical and spiritual needs of humanity (*Re Codrington, USPG v. Attorney General* (1970).

The scarcity of post-secondary education in the post-emancipation period was due to three main reasons: 1) those who had the resources preferred to pursue higher education in Britain or other European countries; 2) there were very few persons with qualifications in post-secondary education, and the few who had saw no urgency or advantage in creating institutions of higher learning; 3) both the planters and settlers were negatively disposed toward the education of Black people because they thought educating the majority of Black people was a dangerous thing (Cobley, 2000). The main efforts to bring about post-secondary education in Barbados were due to the work of religious organizations such as the Anglican Church, the Moravians, the Methodists, and the Baptists. These religious organizations did not seek to create possibilities for higher education gratuitously; they saw it as the vehicle through which the Christian Gospel could be propagated throughout the Black population in Barbados. Apart from the objective of proselytizing Black people, the colonial establishment came to the realization that commerce in Barbados and the other Anglophone Caribbean territories would become stagnant without well-trained employees. They saw it as a crucially important matter that the Blacks be trained for the job market.

BISHOP MITCHISON

Post-secondary education in Barbados was given a boost in 1876 when Bishop Mitchinson recommended the creation of Island scholarships that would be awarded by the Government of Barbados to one or two of its most outstanding citizens to pursue course of studies in England at the University of Oxford or Cambridge for undergraduate degrees. Although this development provided some Barbadians, exclusively male and mostly White at that time, with a higher education, it had the adverse effect of "… elevating an Oxbridge education to the status of Holy Grail for West Indian Students, and, by implication, tended to belittle the efforts of local institutions to offer quality education" (Cobley, 2000, p. 5). Barbadian intellectuals therefore imbibed British traditional educational philosophy. As a result, many of them, like so many others from the British colonial outposts, "became more British than the British" (Williams, 1987, p. 25).

Another important recommendation of Bishop Mitchinson was the broadening of the program at Codrington College: "Accordingly in 1878 the College began teaching a number of courses leading to degrees of the University of Durham" (Cobley, 2000, p. 10). Thus, the first institution in Barbados to offer post-secondary education was under the tutelage of a British university. This had serious political ramifications for governance and education in the Island: "By this means, indigenous elites would not only receive the training they required for effective leadership, they will remain intellectually and ideologically tied to Britain (Cobley, 2000, p. 10). This practice still continues in the Island up to the present time with some innovation in that persons who obtain a scholarship can study at the University of their choosing whether in the United States of American or Europe. However, hardly any Barbadian scholar would want to study in Africa or, African Civilization, as this has not been valued by the society.

THE UNIVERSITY COLLEGE OF THE WEST INDIES

Opportunity for post-secondary education was improved in 1948 with the establishment of the University College of the West Indies, and the Rawle Institute for the training of Educators, also part of the Christopher Codrington estate. The University College of the West Indies is the precursor to the University of the West Indies (UWI). The UWI is now the main tertiary institution in Barbados and the English speaking Caribbean. Post-secondary education has come a long way in Barbados. Today there are a number of institutions offering post-secondary certificates, diplomas and degrees. These institutions include: Barbados Vocational Training Board, the Barbados Youth Service, the Samuel Jackman Prescod Polytechnic, the Barbados Community College, and Erdistan Teachers' Training College.

I firmly believe that a radical transformation of these post-secondary institutions can bring about tremendous and creative critical counter-education in the interest of a greater participatory democracy and social justice fostered through a radical curricular paradigm. It is of grave concern that the statistical figures show that there is a greater interest in post-secondary education among minority groups than there is among the Black majority. This is the case although students have the opportunity to attend colleges and institutions without having to pay any economic cost. This may be an indication that the bulk of the Black majority in Barbados still does not appreciate the importance of post-secondary education in their own personal development and for their constructive participation in the running of the country. According to the statistical data that is shown in Table 2, the percentage of persons who have pursued post-secondary education in Barbados is greater across all minority groups than that of the Black population. 38.8% of White respondents have attended university or another tertiary institution; likewise 36.9% of Arabs, 22.4% of East Indians, 34.8% of Chinese, 26.9% of the Mixed population. The figure for Blacks is only 15.75%.

TABLE 2
POPULATION BY HIGHEST LEVEL OF
EDUCATION AND ETHNIC ORIGIN

Highest Education Level	Ethnic Origin							
	Black	White	Chinese	E Indian	Arab	Mixed	Other	Total
University	11 260	1 550	24	311	17	720	44	13 926
Other Tertiary	22 260	1 374	15	220	7	88	18	25 373
Other Institutions	2 020	124	3	51	2	69	8	2 277
None	410	8	1	21	-	12	3	455
Not Stated	4 388	128	21	60	4	97	7	4 705
Total	40388	3 184	64	663	30	986	80	46737

Barbados Statistical Department: Cross Tabulation of the 2000 Census.

CURRENT POST-SECONDARY EDUCATION POLICY: THE PHILOSOPHICAL UNDERPINS OF THE CURRICULUM

The philosophy of the post-secondary educational system is rooted and grounded in essentialism and perennialism, that is to say, in the traditional neo-conservative/neo-colonial acculturation. This is evident in the 1995 White Paper on Education Reform which purports to transform the post-secondary curriculum so as to prepare students for the twenty-first century. But its content and projections fall short of any radical transformation of the curriculum and merely tantamount to window dressing. The proposed reforms are very mild and simply reiterate the traditional core values of education and training for the marketplace. Indeed the White Paper enunciates that the purpose of tertiary education in Barbados is to make its citizens more marketable and to be able to make a worthwhile contribution to economic development, and "... provide education and training across the whole spectrum of post-secondary education from skills training, apprenticeship training and trades training to undergraduate and post-graduate university education, to meet developmental needs" (White Paper on Education Reform, 1995, p. 27).

This vision for post-secondary education without more is unsatisfactory. Post-secondary education must provide for a former colonial people much more than a 'conveyor belt education'. Education must go much further and deeper than lining up citizens for the job market. Citizens must be able to think and reflect critically on their society, the economy, the political system, the legal system, and more. Citizens must inquire whether education promotes social justice and struggles against neo-colonial domination. In other words, education is much more than a commodity for sale on the open market.

This traditional approach to education and the philosophy that underpin it see human persons as resources to be mobilized for the purpose of social, economical, and political growth and advancement. The emphasis appears to be on economic growth for competition in the market place in the light of globalization. The problem here is that when educational goals are so focused, it will "track people into particular economic and social roles within a market economy" which produce a kind of "schooling normalization, conformity, and docility, not a critically engaged and informed citizenry" (Kohli, 2000, p. 30). The emphasis on education for the job market amounts to a commodification of education with its attendant tunnel vision in students learning: "In a commodified world people develop their identity and calculate their sense of self-worth in pure economic terms" (Brookfield, 2005, p.70). The commodification of self is done to the detriment of humankind's higher ideals such as altruistic and spiritual pursuits. People's inner character becomes completely identified with economic value. People are not valued for their humanity, but for their economic value in the market place, their monetary value. The great fear in this regard is that when education becomes commodified, the next step, if it has not already been taken, is the commodification of the human person. This is a slippery slope to tread on for any government with a genuine interest in education for the transformation of the society.

As indicated above, the pedagogy of post-secondary education is informed and underpinned by the educational philosophies of essentialism and perennialism. "Essentialism is a theory that asserts that education properly involves the learning of the basic skills, arts, and science that have been useful in the past and are likely to remain useful in the future" (Gutek, 1997, p.264). Essentialists espouse the view that traditional and historical knowledge are timeless and valuable *ad infinitum* to humanity. These are traditional static principles of knowledge that do not encourage Black students to look their history in the face; that hide and obfuscate it by laying emphasis on the classical traditions in learning which are based on Eurocentric modules. Black students are not encouraged to remember the past violations as a way of eliminating their reoccurrence in the future. The proponents of this theory, such as Hirsch (1996), advocates that certain skills are essential and are the basic requirements in all educational endeavours which have contributed to human well being, such as reading, writing, and arithmetic. So he posits the view that:

> [T]he college curriculum should consist of both the liberal arts and science. By mastering these subjects that deal with the natural and social environments, students are prepared to participate effectively in the civilized society (Gutek, 1997, p. 264).

This philosophy is reflected in the 1995 White Paper on Educational Reform in Barbados which proclaims that:

> Core skills *must* (emphasis added) be strengthened at the primary level if the secondary and tertiary levels are to perform effectively. The bolstering of the primary system is informed by the Ministry's vision of having children who can: Read, Write, Be numerate, Reason, Deal with normal situations and those of conflict, Have high self esteem.(p. iii).

In other words, this is a call to a return to the basics. As seen "in the current debate over schooling, we hear again calls for the schools to return to their primary task of cultural transmission, the emphasis on core values and the basic knowledge that all our citizens need" (Stanley, 2000, p. 65). While nothing may be inherently wrong with the basic skill as they are important, it is arguable that students need much more than the basic skills to deal effectively with complex social living.

Essentialists argue that although schools are part of a societal context, they are most effective when they fulfil their primary academic function. Knowledge of the social context should help educators do their academic jobs more effectively and efficiently.

> However, the existence of social problems should not deter educators from performing their academic tasks, nor should these social issues be allowed to alter the primary function of the school. The Essentialist view is that large social problems are at base political, economic, and social issues that need to be addressed by agencies outside of the schools, whose functions are appropriate in dealing with these problems (Gutek, 1997, pp. 272-273).

The proper function of the school is to examine issues academically, not to solve them in the school. Indeed, the Essentialist is likely to argue that it is beyond the school's power to solve social problems And furthermore that the school does its job when it educates an intelligent citizenry and a competent work force by imparting the necessary skills and knowledge of subject matter (Gutek1997).

The essentialist educational philosophy is applied in tandem with the educational philosophy of perennialism. The perennialism theory holds that knowledge is constantly repeating itself and all that needs to be done is to pass on this time honoured knowledge to the young students. In this way society will remain constant by inculcating the same set of knowledge into each generation. Gutek (1997) provides a vivid description of the theory:

> The perennialists educational theory seeks to develop the intellectual and spiritual potentialities of the child to their fullest extent through a subject-matter curriculum based on such disciplines as history, language, mathematics, logic, literature, the humanities, and science (Gutek, 1997, p. 280).

In other words, these subject matters contain the perennial knowledge of humanity which each generation needs for the perpetuation of human civilization. This of course is coloured by Eurocentrism and excludes critical philosophies.

The background of the development of the philosophy of the essentialists and perennialists is rooted in Socratic/Platonic philosophy which underpins Western education systems and which Barbados has inherited from England as a former colonial territory. This is why the structures of post-secondary educational institutions take a traditional form. Such traditional educational structures, according to Spring (2000), follow the Socratic definition of schooling as being the inculcation of acceptable social behavior that each person can assume his/her rightful place in the society.

RADICAL APPROACH IN
EDUCATION METHODOLOGY

Within the last decade or two, education in Barbados' public schools has become a ferocious bone of contention. The controversy concerns single sex or co-ed schools, instructional methodology, the curricular content, and in particular the mechanism for the transfer of students from the primary to the secondary schools. The continued social divide between students who attend the older secondary schools (the elites) and students who attend the newer secondary schools (the underdogs) needs an urgent solution The radicals and reconstructionists are critical of the current educational practices because they have marginalized poor, disadvantaged, working class families many of whom are headed by single women. As far as the conservatives are concerned, education has abdicated its avowed purpose which is to serve the needs of capitalism and the market economy. The conservatives see the purpose of the educational system as being the development of the human resource for economic growth and teachers as "the providers of knowledge in the system" (White Paper, 1995, p.ii). This is a teacher-centred educational system, but liberatory educators argue for a system that is leaner-centred for students' intellectual advancement and challenges the students to take on the responsibility for their own education.

The Common Entrance Examination is the root of all this educational evil, but it is one of the Barbados' sacred cows which everyone knows has outlived its usefulness and ought to be laid to rest. But none of the politicians has been brave enough to put an end to this educational decadence. The frequently pontificate on the urgent need for the abolition of the system when they are in opposition, but when they form the ruling party they avoid the issue like the plague. This pusillanimous approach to educational reform is to the advantage of the conservatives.

The conservatives have maintained a stranglehold on education from time immemorial and have promulgated the traditional educational practices because its tenets ensure the political ascendancy of the dominant elite groups over the masses. Traditional education has fostered the artificial notion that knowledge is based on the principle of transference, referred to by Miller & Seller (1985) as "the transmission position". In this model educators are the repositories or the providers of knowledge over which they have arrogated to themselves the sole prerogative to dispense or transmit as they deem fit. The learners are seen as the "empty vessels" to be filled with the knowledge of the educator from his/her repository of great learning. Only that which the educator puts out is worthy of learning. Therefore, there is no need for the learners to ask questions or offer any challenge, since their position cannot be other than a passive receptacle of the knowledge which their educators possess (Freire, 1985).

The methodology that is used for instructional purposes can become a political instrument that either inculcates conservative docility and an unquestioning acceptance of the social order or the instrumentality for the liberation of the learner. This is education for political activism. Curriculum theorists see schools as using three basic methodologies for instructional purposes: transmission, transaction, or transformation (Miller and Seller, 1985) which determines the outcome of the education process. However, Freire (1985) sees the purpose of the educational process as having two arms: either to domesticate the learner or to liberate him/her. This is especially applicable in an economic environment in which the dominant class takes an unfair advantage of the oppressed group(s). Freire (1985) further states:

> It does not matter whether or not the educators are cognizant that they are following a domesticating practice, since the essential point is the manipulative direction between the educators and the learners, by which the latter are made passive objects of action by the former" (p.101).

Freire (1985) further explains the flipside of the role of the dominant educator as being the passive, subordinate position of the learner who contributes nothing to his/her learning experience:

> As passive individuals, learners are not invited to participate creatively in the process of their learning; instead they are filled by the educator's words. Within the cultural framework of this practice, the educators are presented as though the latter were separate from life, as though language-thoughts were possible without reality (p.101).

In other words, in a domesticating educational practice, the social structures are never discussed as a problem that needs to be challenged in the interest of social justice and equity. On the contrary, these structures are made out to be the ideal way of life for all right thinking people. The objectives of this kind of teaching are to reinforce the learner's "false consciousness" and dependency on the educator. The educator is the instrumentality of the dominant elitist interest that ensures that the curriculum and the hidden curriculum are adhered to. The educator also ensures that the student accepts his/her role as a passive receptacle for the transmission of the society's traditional values. The learner takes no active part in the learning process and takes no responsibility for his/her learning. The learner may be compared to a sponge that is expected to suck up all the knowledge that pours from the lips of the educator.

In this traditional context the aims of education are to protect and promote the interest of the dominant class. This is why the pitched battle in education is being fought vigorously and passionately on one hand by the conservatives who wish to maintain and perpetuate the *status quo* that gives them their identity and keep their power structures sacred. In this way the conservatives protect and preserve their vested interest in the social order., On the other hand there are the radicals and reconstructionists who are seeking to liberate the minds of the working class students who are dominated and oppressed by the conservatives. The radicals and reconstructionists believe that education has been hijacked by the conservatives so as to tailor it to their ulterior objectives. Radicals and reconstructionists have formed the considered opinion that education for liberation must come from below because the conservatives are not going to willingly furnish the oppressed people with the tools for critical reflection on the structures in the society which are responsible for their depressed circumstances and lack of progress. This would be self-defeating for the conservatives.

However, the seeds of education for liberation are unwittingly sown in the womb of conservative education; it is not an entity that is external to the system. Boland (1993) points out that the negation of slavery simply made way for a new kind of domination and this new system will eventually generate the social conditions for its own demise. This is a social dialectical reaction, the negation of a negation. Freire (1985) expresses the view that it would be extremely naïve to expect the dominant class to develop a type of education that would enable the subordinate class to perceive social injustice critically. That would be akin to a householder presenting the burglar with the tools to burglarise his/her home. The dominant group would not do so consciously, but they, through their domination of the working class sow the seeds of negation in bosom of their oppression.

The domesticating style of education has to function in the transmission methodology so as not to allow any elbow room for the learner to question the authority of the teacher or to have the mental acumen to reflect critically on his/her own social circumstances. This style of education is based on mimicry and regurgitation. This methodology makes such deep furrows in the minds and psyches of the learners that by the time they reach maturation they shall have become perfected mimic men and women, who would swear that they have received the best education since Columbus sailed the Atlantic Ocean. They are totally oblivious of their blissful ignorance. Obviously, in this position learners cannot participate fully in any sense as subjects in the learning process, but as empty vessels waiting to be enlightened by the teacher filling them up with his/her brilliance much like filling an empty bucket under a tap. This type of education is the premium for enslavement and further enslavement of the mind of the learner.

The antithesis or the antidote to the domesticating style of education of course is positive political education: education for political action, for growth and for personal development, to become somebody because education can create self-awareness that is transformative. Apple (1998) makes the point that what both identity politics and a politics of the self have in common is a new understanding of education as the ongoing process of 'becoming somebody'. This represents a radical challenge to traditional but still powerful notions of education as the transmission of knowledge to passive students, conceptualized as empty vessels waiting to be filled with official knowledge.

The counter hegemony of traditional transmissive education is learner-centred education which, *a fortiori*, seeks to bring about the liberation of the learner through the use of the language of critical analysis and the language of possibility. In other words, it is not sufficient for the educator who wishes to participate in transforming his/her learners to offer tools of critical analysis; he/she must go a step further to show the learners the possibilities of their liberation. To borrow a concept from the discipline of theology, it seeks the redemption of the politically illiterate. A redemptive pedagogy is what is most required for the development of critical, dialectical thinking at the post secondary level. Table 3 shows an example of a radical curricular module which is learner-centred. The educator has a duty to choose the material for the learning experience with care, the approach, and the kind of assessment which are conversant with the kind of transformation that is advocated in this study.

TABLE 3
RADICAL CURRICULAR ORIENTATION MODULE

Module	Description	Objective	Content	Perspective	Approach	Assessment
Multicultural Education	Critical/ Reflective Examination of race, class, and gender power	a) **Cognitive** to enhance knowledge and understanding of diverse cultures and ethnic backgrounds b) **Affective** to engender love for difference, faith, self-determination, reform society more equitably c) **Behavior** to enhance social skills, reduce prejudice and discrimination improve cooperatives and creativity	Must be accurate and complete Inclusive of various ethnic backgrounds, avoid historical inaccuracies, racial coloring, or motif Avoid tokenism History of Africa, Europe, slavery and colonialism in the Caribbean and USA Post-emancipation, segregation, racism, discrimination Civil Rights Movement Critical examination of Eurocentrism, malecentricism, heterosexual-centricism, classism Afro-Asiatic contributions	To be accurate, must be inclusive – from majority and minority Male – Female Heterosexual, gay, lesbians Critical examination of materials through various lenses	Learner-centered, engage students in the teaching and learning processes – make use of their experiences to facilitate the learning experience Cultivate critical thinking skills in students Encourage them to challenge the instructor's assumptions Make content and delivery relevant to students' development level	Curriculum must be frequently assessed for accuracy, biases, and relevance Have students provide feed back Have colleagues critique curriculum Multiple testing methods

Critical, dialectical thinking is brought about through the meeting of the minds (*ad idem*) of the educator and the educand. This counter hegemonic medium is radical education for liberation. The educator invites his/her students to go with the educator on a pilgrimage; only that on this occasion they are not going to visit any religious shrine, but they are making a visit to their inner selves for the purpose of doing some spring cleaning. The educator invites learners to recognize and unveil reality critically and to reject the false consciousness which has been insidiously imposed upon their psyche creating a facile adaptation to their reality. That is to say, while a domesticating educational practice seeks to impose its will on the learner, a liberatory educational practice which is based on a redemptive pedagogy cannot seek to impose freedom on the learners. The learners must come to the point where they recognize the need to repent of their previous political views. This is the point of *locus poenitentiae* for the learner – the repudiation of his/her domesticating education and the redemption of her/himself from his/her alienation. The practice of domesticating education creates a dichotomy between the manipulators and the manipulated – the expendable pawns on the political canvas. But may be on second thought they may not so expendable because through their political activism the dominating system would have created its own negation. According to Freire (1985), in an educational practice for liberation, there are no subjects who liberate or objects to be liberated, since there is no dichotomy between subject and object.

Both the educator and the learner must join in the struggle against oppression of whatever kind: the struggle against the oppression of the poor, of women, the struggle against racism, prejudice, bigotry, and sexism. It is no consolation for the poor and oppressed people that they will enjoy life in the hereafter in the 'Sweet by and by' while their labour, blood, sweat, and tears, and resources are being exploited here and now to make other people who oppress them rich, comfortable, and famous. This philosophical outlook is repudiated by redemptive pedagogy.

When the scales of domestication are removed from the eyes of the learner, she/he will see the shameful exploitation and cowardly victimization of those whom the oppressors consider not to be on their side. Both the liberated educator and the learner must surrender to the risks and dangers that face all who challenges the entrenched structures of power and domination which are supported by the invisible racism in the society and their acculturated Black educators. In this situation educational redemption can only be facilitated through a radical transformative paradigm.

CONCLUSION

I have discussed in this chapter the historical development of the Caribbean in several regards including the racialized cultural politics which were responsible for the victimization of African people and African culture. The enslavement of African people alienated them from their roots and placed them in a servile, degrading position in relation to White Europeans. The chapter also discussed the struggle for the establishment of post-secondary education in the post-emancipation era, and examined the traditional philosophical underpinnings of post-secondary education in the current system. I emphasized the fundamental importance of recognizing the contribution of African people to their civilization and to humanity; the need to develop a multicultural social system which will inform public discourse in the search for a solution to racism and other social ills. This chapter also advocates the possibility for educational liberation through a radical Africentric paradigm on the basis of a critical redemptive pedagogy. The chapter is an invitation to join me in the philosophical exploration of our alienation through the eyes of *critical redemptive pedagogy* as it is conceived in the following chapters. This is a journey that will take us to some of the more uncomfortable places of cultural politics' contrivances for the purposes of educational domestication of the minds of Black folks with object of dismantling them. The journey is psychologically rough but the reward is intellectual liberation for both the learner and the educator if they persevere to the end.

CHAPTER TWO

Theoretical Activism for Curricular Reform

The real issue centers on whether the field is moribund, both politically and ethically. Is the curriculum field in a state of arrest, incapable of developing either emancipatory intentions or new curricular possibilities? (Giroux, 1988, p.11)

This chapter critically examines the theoretical constructs which are most suitable for curricular reform and development for the transformation of post-secondary education for Black people in the African Diaspora. The theoretical constructs which are examined are critical theory, multiculturalism, social reconstructionism and critical pedagogy. These theoretical constructs are re-interpreted in the light of the socio-cultural, socio-psychological and educational situation of Black people of the neo-external/internal colonialism. This is done under an overarching radical transformative paradigm, on the basis of the six principles of an African world view, for the purpose of identifying a radical Africentric philosophy for post-secondary education.

The reinterpretation of the theoretical constructs that are used is important because they were constructed in the socio-cultural circumstances of the African Diaspora to bolster Eurocentric ideology. This reinterpretation in the light of radical transformation is crucial to this discourse which is seeking to find a way forward for the radical transformation of the post-secondary curricula using the concept of redemptive pedagogy. The view that is taken here of radical curricular transformation is that it can bring about meaningful social changes and the promotion of social justice. Education for radical curricular transformation is advocated in this chapter for the purpose of advancing an alternative critical discourse which has as its overarching focus, *inter alia*, the vicissitudes of racism, alienation, sexism, classism, and other social-ills which impact on the lives of Black people. Critical/dialectical analysis is used here because it provides the most useful framework for the examination of systems of domination and oppression and is therefore well suited in the context of the African Diaspora. This radical approach emphasizes Black pride and unity on the basis of the six principles of *Nguzo Saba*.

Redemptive Pedagogy: A Transformative Paradigm

Redemptive pedagogy advocates a philosophy that counters the ideological and hegemonic background of traditional market oriented education which sees the human person as a product to be cultivated and prepared for sale much like agricultural manufactured products. In this system education becomes commercial training which transform human beings into commodities. The counter philosophical vision herein relies on the principles of critical theory to effectively and efficaciously explicate the critical educational discourses in this thesis that are advocated for curricular transformation in the post-secondary educational system. This philosophical vision uses an educational program of counter-socialization to attenuate the indoctrination of students in the predominantly neo-conservative/neo-colonial educational system. The aim is to re-orient the curriculum from the

philosophy of the dominant neo-conservative/neo-colonial group
to pedagogy of redemption from below. The objective of this aim is
to create a more democratic cultural program in which the cultural
and historical backgrounds of all ethnic groups in the society are
represented. The post-secondary curriculum must be so "designed to
counteract the sociostructural and sociopsychological effects of racism"
(Colin and Guy, 1998, p.47). This is why I believe that the philosophy
of *Nguzo Saba* is important in the context of African Diaspora because
it emphasizes the importance of the human person in the community
and at the same time recognizes the right of the individual for self-
determination. *Nguzo Saba* focuses the economic activities of the
community as a work of cooperative endeavors. It also promotes
human dignity, unlike economic competition which creates profitable
circumstances for private investors and makes education the preserve
of the privileged elites.

The redemptive pedagogic approach is based on a reinterpretation
of the principles of critical theory to make them applicable to the
social situation of Black people. This reinterpretation is important
for an emancipatory philosophical approach which is rooted in
multiculturalism. Critical theory is being reinterpreted because as it
now stands it is a racialized philosophical concept. That is to say, the
concepts which are central to the discipline were created by White male
scholars who studied and write about the society of White middle class
adult men. So it must be reinterpreted in the light of a radical curricular
paradigm that is relevant to the people of the African Diaspora.

The principles of the concept of *Nguzo Saba* are at the heart of
the Africentric paradigm. This concept is based on seven principles
of Africentrism: Unity *(cumoja)*, self-determination *(kujichagulia)*,
collective work and responsibility *(ujima)*, cooperative economics
(ujamaa), purpose *(nia)*, creativity *(kuumba)*, and faith *(imani)* (Colin
& Guy, 1998). The principles of *Nguzo Saba* emphasize the importance
of the community. Colin & Guy (1998) express the opinion that the
emphasis on community and collective action is a critical departure
"from the traditional Eurocentric perspectives of individualism,

competition, and decision making" (p.50). Bishop Tutu (1999) in the South African paradigm emphasizes "ubuntu," that is, all human beings share a common humanity despite our phenotype. Bishop Tutu explains further:

> A person with ubuntu is open and available to others, affirming of others, does not feel threatened that others are able and good, for he or she has a proper self-assurance that comes from knowing that he or she belongs in a greater whole and is diminished when others are humiliated or diminished, when others are tortured and oppressed, or treated as if they were less than who they are (p.31).

In other words, the bond of common humanity forbids our mistreating our brother or sister, as well as encourages us to love and care for others. The community of humankind is what is in important in this philosophy. I believe this is why Belle (2000) also in the South African context stresses the importance of restorative justice over against punitive justice for the healing of the community. Lamming (2000) suggests:

> Race is the persistent legacy of the Admiral of the Ocean Sea. No one born or nurtured in this soil has escaped its scars, and although the contemporary Caribbean cannot be accurately described as a racist society, everyone – whatever their ancestral origin – is endowed with an acute racial consciousness (p. 39).

The descendants of those who were involved in the Congo genocide, both the perpetrators and the victims, co-exist in Barbados' society. Post-secondary education must focus on bringing upliftment and dignity to Black people and help White people to be brought to the realization that the inequities of the slavocratic colonial society cannot be perpetuated *ad infinitum*. Part of the solution to the problem of invisible racism is acceptance and appreciation of multiculturalism.

Critical theorists and social reconstructionists argue that both perennialism and essentialism are a reflection of the dominant Western

Eurocentric ideology and hegemony. They deny their claim that there are perennial basic "features of human nature reappearing in each generation regardless of time or place and that the funded human wisdom of the human race is recorded in certain classical works" (Gutek, 1997, p.290). Both essentialism and perennialism disregard cultural differences that are not European because they perceive them as vulgar and unworthy. "Both Reconstructionist and Critical Theorist also contend that the perennialists' alleged universality is really a culturally based theoretical support of historically dominant institutions" (Gutek, 1997, p.290). It is common knowledge that the traditional purpose of schooling is to promote the interest of the dominant class. Critical theory provides the means for a counter-socialization by "emphasizing the power of individuals to structure their own destiny and to ameliorate the oppressive nature of institutions in which they live" (deMarrais & Lecompte (1999, p.32).

The radical philosophical vision of counter-socialization seeks to provide adult learners, especially those of African descent, with a better, more balanced understanding of the world. Having understood the world from a critical perspective, they are better able to effectively change it through critical analytical reflection and practice (praxis). The principle of educational praxis here is to urge adult learners to become the architects of their own destiny in the world in which they live and have their being. That is to redeem themselves from alienation and oppression because only they can liberate themselves from these invisible bars of imprisonment. Through praxis adult learners are brought to the intellectual place where they are able to challenge their assumptions about school and the purpose of schooling. Brookfield (2005) has given an apt description of criticality to which I subscribe:

> After all critical theory and its contemporary educational applications such as critical pedagogy are grounded in an activist desire to fight oppression, injustice, and bigotry and create a fairer, more compassionate world. Central to this tradition is a concern with highly practical projects – the

> practice of penetrating ideology, countering hegemony,
> and working democratically (p. 10).

Given that racism is a behaviour that is learnt by cultural transmission through the agencies of socialization, chief among them being the educational system, careful, proper preparation of the schools' curriculum in social studies and history, and the use of critical/dialogical instructional methodologies could facilitate the cultivation of a critical consciousness and raise a high level of awareness of racism and racial discrimination to bring about meaningful social change.

Education is the instrumentality of change and development. It is also a process of enlightenment that equips the oppressed with the tools for reflection and to challenge the dominant culture which is the source of their oppression. Education is all-inclusive and cannot be confined to traditional educational institutions of schools, colleges, and universities, as noble as these may be. So education includes and moves beyond the notion of schooling. Schools represent only one important site where education takes place, where men and women both produce and are the product of specific social and pedagogical relations. Giroux (1985) states:

> Education represents in Freire's view both a struggle for
> meaning and a struggle over power relations. Its dynamic
> is forged in the dialectical relation between individuals and
> groups who live out their lives within specific historical
> conditions and structural constraints, on the one hand,
> and those cultural forms and ideologies that give rise to the
> contradictions and struggles that define the lived realities
> of various societies, on the other (p.xiii).

In other words, educational institutions are sites of continuous struggles for meaning and liberation. Here adult learners through reflective practice can come to grips with their questions, their personhood which is denied them by the dominant group, to throw off the shackles of alienation and discrimination that is to say:

> Education is that terrain where power and politics are given
> a fundamental expression, since it is where meaning, desire,
> language, and values engage and respond to the deeper
> beliefs about the very nature of what it means to be human,
> to dream, and to name and struggle for a particular future
> and way of life (Giroux, 1985, p.xiii).

A redemptive pedagogy is therefore the catalyst that brings about liberatory change through the development of a critical consciousness and politicisation of the sites of educational struggle for meaning and freedom which challenge oppression and the places where small people are dehumanized and commodified. This is why education is so crucial to the role of civic transformation. But it must be a non-idiotic education if it will meet the goals of liberatory education.

As a referent for change, education represents a form of action that emerges from a joining of the languages of critique and possibility. It represents the need for a passionate commitment by educators to make the political more pedagogical, that is, to make critical reflection and action a fundamental part of a social project that not only engages forms of oppression but also develops a deep and abiding faith in the struggle to humanize life itself (Giroux,1985, p.xiii).

Giroux has aptly conceptualized the political framework for liberatory struggle. Redemptive pedagogy teaches those who are oppressed to place an eternal value on themselves as good human beings regardless of any teachings to the contrary in their socio-cultural/ socio-political circumstances.

MULTICULTURALISM AND POST-SECONDARY EDUCATION

Redemptive pedagogy is a progressive approach to the transformation of the instrumentalities of good pedagogy: instruction, curriculum, and assessment. It critiques the current political and cultural hegemony and addresses its weaknesses, failings, and the promotion of discriminatory practices in education. It is founded and rooted in the ideals of social justice and educational equity, and is committed to the provision of educational experiences which reflect the concerns of diverse cultural groups so that students can reach their full potential as learners. Multiculturalism facilitates the objectives of redemptive pedagogy. Richards (1993) sees multiculturalism as honouring the various ethnic groups in the society as agents for the promotion of change by exposing the present deceit and omission in the knowledge base. This interpretation of multiculturalism is consistent with that given by Sleeter & Grant (1994) who identify five goals of multicultural education in the work of Gollnick (1980):

1.   Promoting the strength and value of cultural diversity,

2.   Promoting human rights and respect for those who are different from oneself,

3.   Promoting alternative life choices for people

4.   Promoting social justice and equal opportunity for all people

5.   Promoting equity in the distribution of power among groups. (p.167)

In addition to Gollinick's five goals, two others could be added: promoting equity in the distribution of economic activities, and promoting equity in the distribution of educational resources. The ideology of multiculturalism is to bridge the gap between what is and what ought to be. It has a strong working class ideology that reaches out tenaciously to achieve its objective, that is to say, genuine social changes in society, not simply integration into society of people who have been left out, deliberately or otherwise. That would be cosmetic surgery. Multicultural education aims to change the very social fabric of the neo-colonial society. This ideology has two main components: cultural pluralism and equal opportunity. This would remove the need for any feign or ostensible social integration that is both mock and superficial. It has an explicit commitment to the cultivation of greater democracy in a pluralistic society. The end products of multicultural education, unlike the current mono-cultural education which focuses on economics and training for the job market, are to inculcate and direct its subjects to self-determination and empowerment.

The Caribbean's multiculturalism is the result of its long history of plantation slavery whereby two cultures collided, with the result that the Eurocentric culture arrogated to itself paramountcy over African culture. Consequently, there is in Caribbean societies the predominance of Eurocentric hegemony. The same situation is obtained in North America and England. However, features of African culture persist and so have constituted them heterogeneous societies in which African cultural values are relegated to the bottom of the social ladder. The objective of a multicultural philosophy in this situation is not to create a socially cohesive ethnic society that can be described as homogenous. That would be a gross misrepresentation of the racial reality of each country. Multicultural philosophy accepts and encourages the various ethnic groups to retain their particular cultural patterns, *inter alia*, family life, religion, musical and artistic expressions, and their language. To do otherwise would mean that some authority would have to decide which aspect of a particular culture should be deleted to create homogeneity. No doubt such an authority would act arbitrarily. The existing cultural differences must continue as an integral part of the cultural matrix. In other words, multicultural philosophy promotes unity in diversity as advocated by Nieto (1992). This can be achieved through the proper structuring of the curriculum to reflect the stories of all of the ethnic groups in the society and in this way redeem the people from economic, political, and cultural alienation.

The philosophy of multiculturalism anathematizes the kind of superficial social integration which is prevalent in former colonial societies. The pretensions of the pseudo-integration in Barbados, for example, are rooted in the previous slavocratic society. Corporate Barbados is controlled by a small group of White descendants of the former English colonial planters who had owned the land and the African slaves, together with White investors from North America and Europe. People of African descent in North America and England are minorities who are still struggling to recover from the scars of rabid White racism. As stated above in relation to Barbados, this minority racial group although it constitutes less than 5% of the population controls the bulk of the commercial activities in the country. The ideology of this group is to maintain its control over the bulk of the economic activities of the country to preserve its power and privileged position. This state of affairs creates a serious challenge for Black entrepreneurs who are not allowed to make any serious inroads into the White controlled commercial sector, except in the running of small businesses which pale into insignificance when compared to White interest. Such small businesses do not pose any threat to White interest. In any case, these small businesses frequently depend on the largesse of big White businesses which are the importers and agents for many of the items which are consumed in the country.

The current post-secondary education is designed to maintain this Eurocentric hegemony in the commercial sector. Blacks are for the most part trained to manage White businesses for Whites and hardly to be entrepreneurs themselves. Furthermore, the country's main industry is tourism the mechanisms of which are controlled by the Government, but the bulk of the tourism infrastructure is owned by White interest. The tourism industry provides secondary jobs for Blacks, while the primary jobs are held by local and expatriate Whites. In these circumstances a multicultural philosophy seeks to bring about the liberation of the culturally disadvantaged Black majority in Barbados, in the same way as it seeks to liberate the Blacks in North American and England through personal transformation of the individual, education, and educational institutions to create equal opportunity which will have an exponential effect in the society. It challenges the educational practices directed towards race, culture, language, social class, gender and disability.

Multiculturalism in the context of the African Diaspora does not see racism as the only form of social injustice or inequality that needs redress. It also challenges classism, sexism, and homophobia, which are also matters of grave social concern. The legitimacy of these social ills must be challenged and exposed for their vacuity and deceptivity whether in the church, in commerce, in the law courts, or in the educational institutions. It is imperative that these be confronted head on because there is no social and/or educational sustainability in exchanging one form of bigotry, that is, slavery, for another.

Multiculturalism is crucial for the awakening of the people's conscience to the tremendous harm that is being done to people of colour, the poor, and dispossessed through discrimination and prejudice. It was shown above that section 23 of the constitution of Barbados and Article 1 of the Convention for the Elimination of all Forms of Racial Discrimination prohibit discrimination and prejudice based on race, colour, gender, age and creed. But the society continues to be plagued on the one hand by attitudes and behaviours that are derogatory to African culture, some ethnicity, social or national groups, and on the other hand by preferential treatment for others, especially those of Eurocentric origins on the basis of their sex, sexual orientation and the school which they attended. Unofficial inequality is alive and well, manifesting itself in crypto racism, ethnocentrism, prejudice, favoritism, discrimination, nepotism, cultural appropriation, and cultural hegemony. The same can be said for the United States of American when it belched into the rioting following the Rodney King trial. In England where Black people faced racism from all major institutions in the country resulted in the Notting Hill and Nottingham riots in 1958. "All British institutions had to adopt themselves in one form or another to the black presence, and this adaptation took very negative forms in the school system and in the coercive apparatus – courts, prisons and the police" (Campbell. 1985, p.184).

Multiculturalism requires an understanding of democracy that is based on social pluralism which is anti-racist, and anti-sexist, anti-homophobic. Post-secondary education in neo-colonial societies that is based on acculturation of Eurocentric monoculture does not fall within the purview of multiculturalism because it requires the giving up or sacrificing of one's African identity to become something artificial; multicultural education seeks to promote unity in diversity – no collective, no assimilation, but reconstructive pluralism. This is clearly illustrated by Worthis and Hall (1993) as being ultimately " to develop children's ability to function competently within multiple cultures" (p. 48). Multiculturalism is the ideology which seeks to unite peoples of various cultural backgrounds, views, life styles, and gender. The salient objective of multiculturalism therefore is to inculcate respect and appreciation for difference whether in culture, point of views, or life style in order to create a greater participatory democracy. It acknowledges and accepts the differences that exist in a democratic pluralistic society. The philosophy of multiculturalism is the golden thread that seeks to weave a multiplicity of cultures together for their redemption from alienation. The philosophy of Multiculturalism is consistent with the philosophical principles of *Nguzo Saba*.

Multiculturalism is one of the vehicles for the transmission of the ideology of redemptive education. It is through the creation of multicultural programs and the placing of these programs on the post-secondary curriculum, like the teaching African civilization, for example, that there can be the catalyst for changing human inter-racial relationship in the African Diaspora. The teaching of African civilization in the post-secondary curriculum will give rebirth to Black pride and devotion co-equal with White respectability, Black empowerment, and will challenge the anti-Black self-hate. African civilization as a taught subject can help to redeem Black minds from their slavocratic mental conditioning and enable them to continue the struggle for rescue and redemption. This educational posture is essential for the salvation of the Black race in a most literal sense (Diop, 1974). One of the biggest socio-cultural problems for Black people is the negative mental conditioning which we have 'inherited' from the negative social conditioning of our African ancestors who survived the degradation of slavery. As Alleyne (2002) states:

> Caribbean descendants of Africans have been struggling not
> only for political independence and economic survival but
> also for mental liberation. This was poignantly expressed

by Bob Marley in the well-known song lines: 'Emancipate yourselves from mental slavery / None but ourselves can free our minds' (p. 82).

I believe that the strength and greatness of the African people in the Diaspora and in Africa can be seen in how, in the face of what seemed to be the unleashing of all the forces of hell against the Black race, we were able to fight it all and survived to the twenty-first century. The question is, from whence cometh this Negro tenacity, this death-defying attitude? Williams (1987) describes this Black tenacity:

> This point is important. For one of the most remarkable chapters in the history of the Blacks is that dealing with those dauntless leaders and people who, having lost one state after another along with three-fourths of their kinsmen, nevertheless overrode all the forces of destruction and death and began to build, always once again, still another state(p.47).

The practice of racism is and was a moral disgrace. Racism is a cultural disease which is the progeny of Eurocentric hegemony and which has no place in a pluralistic democratic society. Until the society provides the opportunities for all citizens to achieve the good life on equal footing, it will continue to slip into a consuming abyss. This is why care must be taken that multicultural education is not viewed as vague policies and curricula add-ons. "Today's educators have the opportunities to be the agents of change and multicultural education can address "the structures of the inequity and challenge the status quo" (Richards, 1993, p.47). Education is an appropriate vehicle through which such a challenge to the status quo may be mounted. It must be remembered that slavery confirmed the absolute pejoration of all things African, including African people. African people need, *inter alia*, public and institutional affirmation and acceptance of things African and African people. African people need a redemptive pedagogy that teaches them to love themselves because they have goodness and beauty inherent in their Africentricity. It would teach African men and women that they can be good fathers/mothers, astute businesspersons, and good political leaders. Further, it would teach African women to love their woolly hair, their fleshy noses, to love their breast and their hips because these are gifts with which nature has endowed them and there is nothing that is inherently vulgar about them. This positive approach to things African can be actualized in education through a curriculum that has an Africentric orientation based on the philosophy of redemptive pedagogy.

SOCIAL RECONSTRUCTION AND POST-SECONDARY EDUCATION

Social Reconstructionism is another criticality that would have a great effect and impact on social oppression, social structural inequality based on race, social class, gender, and disability. It advocates a reasonable solution to social problems that is consistent with redemptive pedagogy. Social Reconstructionism is particularly important in the struggle of African people for socio-cultural affirmation and acceptance and also for curricular transformation. Socio-cultural reconstruction is important because African descendants in the Diaspora are unable to attach themselves to any old continuous African traditions. When the African ancestors were brought to the Caribbean they were savaged, humiliated, and forced to sever all connection with Africa. So the African ethnicity of Diaspora people would have to be reconstructed. Social Reconstructionism as an educational philosophy is suited to the temperament, the aims and objectives of curricular and instructional reform of the post-secondary education system in the Caribbean, North America, and England that has an Africentric orientation following the principles of Nguzo Saba. This is so because social Reconstructionism locates schools in a social and societal context; use schools as instruments or agencies of directed social change and reform, identifies society's current social, political, and educational problems. It reconstructs experience and culture, refashioning them to produce human growth and development. This theory according to Gutek (1997) is not based on abstract, speculative, philosophical, or metaphysical ontological notions, but on a pragmatic reality. For these reasons, social reconstructionism is the handmaid of Africentric redemptive pedagogy.

Multiculturalism and social reconstructionism are deeply concerned with oppression and social structural inequality based on race, social class, gender and disability. Social reconstructionism addresses serious social concerns that are prevalent in a pluralistic democratic society with the view of promoting social and cultural unity in diversity. It does not participate in social cosmetology – superficial cohesive integration. The social reconstructionist sees decisions that are made in education as being affected by and bound up with social, political and economic structures that frame and define the society. It is well known that schools reflect the normative values of the society. DeMarrais and LeCompt (1999) have shown that both "critical theorists and reproduction theorist agree that the purpose of schooling is to preserve the culture of the dominant class" (p. 32). Given that the schools are oriented toward and reflect values of the dominant class social reconstructionist philosophy must over turn this orientation in favor of the marginalized class so as to create a grass root, working class Africentric hegemony. Sleet & Grant (1994) describes the invaluable benefits of this approach to society:

> [T]he approach prepares future citizens to reconstruct society so that it better serves the interests of all groups of people and especially those who are of color, poor, female, gay and/or disabled. This approach is visionary. Although grounded very much in everyday world experience, it is not trapped by this world (p. 210).

In other words, social reconstructionism is concerned with the everyday matters that impact upon the lives of ordinary men and women and seeks to empower them by inspiring them to transform the world and not to conform to it. It seeks to transform the world without becoming a part of it – it has a catalytic impact upon social institutions.

Educational authorities have spent much time, effort, and money to decipher why students succeed or fail in school, especially children of racial, ethnic, linguistic, or social class background that are dissimilar to that of the dominant Eurocentric ethnic groups. The problem seems to be due to the prevailing monoculture which excludes and victimizes cultures which are not Eurocentric. That is to say, the curriculum does not tell the story of African ancestry and its achievement in art, music, science. Social reconstructionism has an archrival in conservatism which seeks to derail the progress that has been made by this type of education. Social reconstructionism poses a serious challenge to conservative hegemony because it threatens to explode all the myths that conservatism uses to buttress its position of power and dominance.

The philosophy of the Africentric Nguzo Saba and social reconstructionism are especially relevant to neo-conservative societies as a remedy for the disadvantaged position of Black folks "persistent poverty" (Fanon, 1963). The lot of the poor in the Caribbean must be improved economically and socially if the countries are to continue along a sustainable path of development in all aspects of social and economic endeavors. The impact of big media, plutocratic corporatism which fosters acculturation and a consumerist mentality must be attenuated through persistent educational efforts to raise criticalities in adult education from an Africentric approach. This justifies the incorporation of a redemptive philosophy into the post-secondary curriculum for the purpose of creating a greater participatory democracy which can only be cultivated in a social milieu where people are not lacking competence for critical analysis of their society.

Reconstructionism offers a thorough analysis of the role played by ideology and indoctrination in education and how education is used by the dominant powerful social and political forces to maintain their control over the major institutions in the society. Reconstructionist theorists are fully cognizant of the fact that schools have limitations in that they are only one of the several powerful media of education, others include big media, big corporatism, family, religious groups, peer groups, and advocates of globalization. However, as Dewey (1938) suggested it is not whether the school shall or shall not influence the course of future social life, but in what direction they shall do so and how. The Africentric redemptive philosophy would work well with social reconstructionism for the recreation of a society in which blackness is not a taboo.

CRITICAL PEDAGOGY

Redemptive pedagogy is the progeny of critical pedagogy. It has an overarching holistic approach to educational transformation from the psycho-social to the religio-political. Education can be a good servant or a bad master. It depends on the purpose for educating people; whether to be critically aware of the system in which they live or whether it is for the purpose of domestication: fitting people into their places in the social system so as to ensure that they buttress the existing social and political order. I believe education without liberation is useless. Education should not enslave the minds of people but should take them to the heights of philosophical creativity. But, alas! Education seldom walks along this path. We speak valiantly of pluralism and democracy and the goodness and riches with which they have endowed humanity. These fine qualities of life have been achieved and sustained through a sound educational system. But upon a close examination, the educational practices belie our political proclamations because inequities abound in relation to race, gender, and class. The salient point is that education has been used for many years as a political tool for the oppression of the working class. It is from educational oppression that working class people must redeem themselves. McLaren (1995) puts it bluntly when he writes:

> I will not mince my words. We live at a precarious moment in history. Relations of subjection, suffering, dispossession, and contempt for human dignity and the sanctity of life

are at the center of social existence. Emotional dislocation,
moral sickness and individual helplessness remain
ubiquitous features of our time (p.1).

In other words, there is human suffering because people are subjected
to many indignities which should not be – humankind inhumanity to
one another especially to those who are without a voice. Although these
unpalatable things happen in a democratic state, yet the objective of
democratic order is the advancement of human flourishing, promotion
of human freedom, social justice and a tolerance for difference. However,
in the present scheme of things moral apathy, oppression, and despair
pervade the society. The challenge for education here is to provide the
intellectual discourse for critical examination of these adverse social
situations. Educators must have the intellectual rigor and competencies
in order to be able to address these specters of human degradation.

Educators have a moral duty to resist the role which the dominant
ideology, based on capitalism, has arranged for them, that is, to teach
with the view of maintaining the status quo and without seeking to
challenge human degradation and despair which is imposed on them
by the prevailing order of things: "The rich man in his castle / the
poor man at his gate / God (or capitalism) made them, high or lowly,
and ordered their estate" (Hymns Ancient and Modern, 573). Radical
educators are not satisfied to leave the poor man at his gate, but desire
to bring him into the castle to share in some of the good life. Africentric
philosophy challenges the rich man/woman who lives in the castle in
the interest of the economic enfranchisement of the poor man/woman
at the gate. This is the *grund norm* of redemptive pedagogy.

Radical scholars must refuse to accept the task capitalism assigns
them as intellectuals, educators, and social theorists: to serve the existing
ideological and institutional arrangements of the public schools, while
simultaneously discounting the values and abilities of minority groups.
In short, educators within the critical tradition regard mainstream
schooling as supporting the transmission and reproduction of what
Paulo Freire terms 'the culture of silence' (McLaren, 1995, p. 32).

The educator is expected to be a silent capitalist accomplice in the exploitation of the poor and marginalized so that capitalist investors can make big profits for them to store up in their barns. All the educator is required to do is to blunt his/her conscience by teaching the working class to gratefully accept the place which society has designated for them; that they should count their blessings and name them one by one.

Critical pedagogy in corroboration with an Africentric philosophy based on the principles of *Nguzo Saba*, seeks to obliterate the debilitating impact of a bureaucratic, conservative educational system on working class people by exposing the intricate relationship between school and society for domination, contrary to the conservative view that school is an apolitical, a neutral zone. Critical pedagogy seeks to empower educators and learners to provide them with the critical tools to challenge and interrogate school policies, teacher ideology, texts and the experiences of learners. The purpose of this critical probity is to ensure that students are not duped into thinking that the educational system is innocent, and to arm learners and educators with the power of interrogation, the courage to challenge what is, to ensure that the educational system is not hijacked or continues to be hijacked by conservative political ideology. As McLaren (1995) points out:

Critical pedagogy commits itself to forms of learning and action that are undertaken in solidarity with subordinated and marginalized groups. In addition to interrogating what is taken for granted or seemingly self-evident or inevitable regarding the relationship between schools and the social order, critical pedagogy is dedicated to self-empowerment and social transformation (p.32).

Critical pedagogy then, provides educators with the language of critique; the tools which they require to interrogate the assumptions and presumptions about the curriculum: for whom was it created, and for what purpose was it created, or whether it facilitates redemption of the poor or their marginalization. Having provided the language of critique, we must be careful not to let our critical position remain in stasis, so that we do not become choked by stagnation and fixation.

We must go further and create the language of possibility. What is the future of our striving? Where are we going? We must carve out and articulate a future vision because without a vision we are sure to perish. It must be a vision of self-empowerment and social transformation through tertiary education. This view of the purpose of education and teaching are contrary to the general traditional view as described by McLaren (1995):

> Teaching is thus reduced to 'transmitting' basic skills and information and sanctifying the canons of the dominant cultural tradition. The moral vision that grounds such a view encourages students to succeed in the world of existing social forms (p. 35).

Redemptive pedagogy operates on a vision of rescue and redemption of working class people and pushes obdurately obsequious educational training of conservative education. Redemptive pedagogy is a politico-cultural tool for the transformation of school and society. School is far more than the transmission of the basic skills for survival. It is the core of social, cultural and political developments. We are aware that the classroom is socially constructed, historically determined by power and privilege but through critical thinking and reflection of redemptive pedagogy, both the teacher and the learner become aware, fully cognizant that the voice of the curriculum is not the voice of the poor and marginalized, but that it is the voice of the dominant Eurocentric culture whose objective is to maintain and sustain its own position of power and privilege in the society. An education that is redemptive would make us cognizant of the insidious operation of the hidden curriculum. The voice of the curriculum which contradicts the values of the majority of the people, that aims at subverting difference by holding it up to public ridicule and contempt so that it would be shunned and avoided by so called right thinking men and women of social standing. This insidious voice must be stoutly rejected. We must seek to level the playing field so that all voices, the stories of Blacks, Whites, Syrians, Chinese, East Indians, Mixed, and others can be reflected in the curriculum. There are no cultural, political, or social underdogs, just a rainbow of people all of equal value in and to the universe. Obviously, if we are to respect all the voices and stories of the different ethnicities, then ethnocentrism must be shunned and avoided. In this arena redemptive education operates as the handmaid of critical pedagogy, completing and perfecting the work which it had so effective set in training. Redemptive education is the ultimate critical educational philosophy which arises from below.

The various ethnic groups in the Caribbean, North American, and English society must face squarely the protracted enslavement of Africans and African descendants through education. This state of affairs will become increasingly dangerous to the point of revolt by the youths when they come to realize how completely hemmed in they are from self-realization in the very institutions of higher learning which they hope will bring their expectations to fruition: the lack of suitable text books in African civilization, or other things African and the Black educators who view their life worlds through the eyes of the White professors who trained them. Black youths are caught between the devil and the deep blue sea: the neo-colonial bureaucrats who determine the content of their education and the Black educators who have become Anglo-saxophones defectors. It follows then that both the educator and the educand need to be redeemed from the alienation which was inculcated in them through their miseducation.

It is crucially important that all social institutions: the home, the school, the church must make a conscientious effort to redeem the minds of the people for a more sustainable existence. While the psychological scars of slavery and racism may have made indelible marks on our minds, we must jettison White ownership of our minds, our bodies, and our souls. We must reinstate our dignity as descendants of former African slaves and obliterate the self-hate and self-effacement which was breed into our bodies through Caucasoid inhumanity. Williams (1987) vividly describes the extent of Black self-hate of which we must be cognizant:

> Blacks at home in Africa and Blacks scattered over the
> world bore the names of their enslavers and oppressors, the
> ultimate in self-effacement that promoted self-hatred which
> made pride in the race difficult. That these psychological
> shackles still handicap not only the rebirth of the modern
> African states, but also Blacks everywhere, should be
> obvious to all (p. 57).

In other words, Black's ultimate effacement was due to the Whites
arrogating to themselves all onomastic rights. They determined what
name should be placed on each African slave in order to reconstruct his/
her identity from African, as she/he knew it, to subhuman by pinning
him/her with some mocking or ridiculous Eurocentric name. As
Alleyne (2002) indicates: "Given the important role that the word, and
name in particular plays in African world view, this control of personal
names was another masterful strategy for psychological control: for
control of identity, for control beyond simple control over life and
death" (p.90). Blacks must first reconstruct their African identity by
first loving themselves in order to change their self-effacement and defy
self-hate. These psychological shackles can only be removed from our
minds through our own determination to be free, really free. Blacks
must rescue and redeem themselves because the beneficiaries of the
status quo will not do it for them; and we must do so through critical
education and re-education of ourselves and our children

CONCLUSION

In conclusion, I have presented aspects of radical thoughts in educational
philosophy and critical theory with the view of reinterpreting the
theoretical concepts from a radical Africentric perspective that is
applicable to post-secondary education in the African Diaspora. I have
relied on the work of several outstanding scholars in critical theory
including Brookfield, Freire, Giroux, McLaren, Colin and Guy, and
Gutek. Heavy emphasis is placed on the importance of a critical

consciousness for meaningful adult education. I have argued for a radical reform of the post-secondary curriculum on the basis of an Africentric world view that focuses on the redemption of Black folks from the excesses of some of the most egregious social circumstances. I believe that no meaningful change for the liberation of adult education can be made unless it is done through the lenses of a re-interpretive critical redemptive theory together with an emphasis on a multicultural philosophy.

CHAPTER THREE

Law and Education: Redemption by Due Process

> Power is viewed as both a negative and positive force; its character is dialectical and its mode of operation is always more than simply repressive... it means that power is at the basis of all forms of behavior in which people resist, struggle, and fight for their image of a better world (Giroux in Freire, 1985, p.xix).

In this chapter I critically examine the Law as it relates to the progress of African Americans and other minorities for equal education. The Supreme Court decision in *Brown v. Board of Education of Topeka* (1954) and other pivotal cases which flowed from the *Browne's* decision and their significance to educational progress for minorities are examined here. I will commence with a critical examination of the current predicament of affirmative action, racial preference, and their inconsistencies with the Constitution of the United States of America. The No Child Left Behind Act 2001 is also examined and the impact of standardized test on minority children, the continued inequality in educational opportunities for African Americans and other minority groups. I critically examine the issue as to whether minority peoples have been duped by a legal false consciousness about the extent to which the law reduces social injustice and promote social change and equity in the educational system and whether it is illegal to consciously and voluntarily take any action for the purpose of ameliorating racial inequality in the educational system.

JIM CROW'S EDUCATION IN AMERICA'S PUBLIC SCHOOLS: THE INEQUITIES OF SEGREGATION

The American 1776 Declaration of Independence proclaims: "We hold these truths to be self-evident, that all men (*sic*) are created equal, that they are endowed by their Creator with certain unalienable Rights that among these are Life, Liberty and the pursuit of Happiness." The proclamation that "all men are created equal" strikes a discordant note because this proclamation was made during the period of the virulent African American chattel slavery. It would seem as though the American Legislature failed to appreciate and acknowledge that African American slaves were men and women whose Creator had endowed them with "certain unalienable rights" one of which is liberty. These words are like granite in the teeth of African Americans. And it is difficult to reflect on them without a sense of irony and deep disappointment. To soften the American conscience it was necessary to demonize the African so that he will appear to be less than human. Perhaps some kind of subhuman species created to be "drawers of water and hewers of wood".

The inhumane and subservient conditions of the African slaves seemed to have pricked the consciences of some religious personalities, or economically sensible potentate who persuaded the American Legislature to pass the Emancipation Proclamation in 1863 and so set the Africans free. But full freedom came on the pain of the American Civil War. The Emancipation Proclamation stopped short of abolishing slavery throughout the United States. Therefore, it was necessary for the American Legislature to go a step further. This came in 1865 with the passing of the Thirteenth Amendment to the American Constitution that neither slave nor involuntary servitude, except as a punishment for crime whereof the party shall have been duly convicted, shall exist within the United States, or any place subject to their jurisdiction and Congress shall have power to enforce this article by appropriate legislation.

However, it would seem that despite the powerful steps which had been taken by the American Legislature to cure the previous malady in the law which was created by the monumental monstrosity in the decision of the Supreme Court in *Dred Scott v. Sandford (1857)*) fell short of its target. In *Dred Scott v. Sandford (1857)*), it was adjudged that the descendants of Africans who were imported into the United States, and sold there as slaves, were not included nor were they intended to be included under the word 'citizen' in the constitution. Therefore, they could not claim any of the rights and privileges which that instrument provided for and secured to citizens of the United States. Furthermore, according to the decision, at that the time of the adoption of the constitution, African slaves were 'considered as a subordinate and inferior class of beings, who had been subjugated by the dominant race, and, whether emancipated or not, yet remained subject to their authority, and had no rights or privileges but such as those who held the power and the government might choose to grant them (per Justice Harlan in *Plessy v. Fergusson* citing the decision in *Dred Scott v. Sandford*, p. 11).

The injustice to African Americans, subjected as a result of the *Dred Scott v. Sandford (1857)*) decision necessitated the Legislature taking another step to secure their freedom and put it on a firm footing by entrenching it in the constitution through the passage of the Fourteenth Amendment to the American Constitution in 1866 that all persons born or naturalized in the United States, and subject to the jurisdiction thereof, are citizens of the United States and of the State wherein they reside. No State shall make or enforce any law which shall abridge the privileges or immunities of citizens of the United States; nor shall any State deprive any person of life, liberty, or property, without due process of law; or to deny to any person within its jurisdiction the equal protection of the laws.

Despite the fact that these high ideals were enshrined in the constitution, the pernicious racism aimed at African Americans persisted and grew even more ferocious through the blatant refusal of municipal legislatures to accept African Americans as their equals. The Federal Government passed the Civil Rights Act 1866 which sought to protect African American and to create racial equality:

> [A]ll ...citizens of the United States ... of every race and color ...shall have the same right ... to full and equal benefit of all laws and proceedings for the security of person and property ... and shall be subject to like punishment, pains, and penalties and to none other.

The language of this statue is very forceful and very clear as to the intention of the Federal Government but it still fell on deaf ears. So it became necessary again for the Federal Government to enact the Civil Rights Act of 1875, the language of which was just as forceful and clear as the previous Act by the same name:

> [A]ll persons within the jurisdiction of the United States shall be entitled to the full and equal enjoyment of the accommodation, advantages, facilities, and privileges of inns, public conveyances on land and water, theaters, and other places of public amusement; subject only to the conditions and limitations established by law, applicable alike to citizens of every race and color...

I would have thought that given the statues which were enacted since the 1863 Emancipation Proclamation, and the Thirteenth and Fourteenth Amendments, together with the clear legislative intention to protect the rights of the African American in the post slavery society, issues as to the legal position of Black citizens of the United States and their place in that society would have been settled. But alas, this was far from the case. Racism was (is) so deeply entrenched in the minds of the majority of White people that it became almost like second nature to them.

In spite of all the legislative efforts which were made to create an equitable and just society for people of all races, they have failed to cure evil monstrosity that had been entrenched in the psyche of White Americans over the centuries. White hatred of Africans died hard. In 1896 the Supreme Court of the United States turned back the hand of time when it established in *Plessy v. Ferguson* (1896) the notorious, virulent doctrine of "separate but equal". This decision is nothing short of the re-enslavement of the African Americans; at the very least it has again given judicial support to their inferior status and gave racism a new lease on life.

The Supreme Court effectively derailed the intention of the Legislature and the effect of the Thirteenth and Fourteenth Amendments, and the Civil Rights Acts. The Court was adamantly set against recognizing the rights of Black citizens to equal treatment under the law. The Court failed miserably to appreciate, deliberately or inadvertently that the issue which was raised was one of constitutionality and not one of reasonableness. What is reasonable and what is constitutional are two different animals. Justice Browne in *Plessy v. Fergusson* (1896) expressed the view that as a conflict with the fourteenth amendment is concerned, the case reduces itself to the question whether the statute of Louisiana is a reasonable regulation, and with respect to this there must necessarily be a large discretion on the part of the legislature. In determining the question of reasonableness, it is at liberty to act with reference to the established usages, customs, and traditions of the people, and with a view to the promotion of their comfort, and the preservation of the public peace and good order. Gauged by this standard, we cannot say that a law which authorizes or even requires the separation of the two races in public conveyances is unreasonable, or more obnoxious to the fourteenth amendments than the acts of Congress requiring separate schools for colored children in the District of Columbia, the unconstitutionality of which does not seem to have been questioned, or the corresponding acts of state legislatures.

The powerful dissenting judgment of Justice Harlan belies the efficacy which the majority judgment sought to give the Louisiana statute. The issue was not one of reasonableness but of constitutionality.

The issue was whether the Louisiana statute was inconsistent with and repugnant to the constitution. That was the live issue in this case which the majority side-stepped. The long established doctrine of the separation of powers holds that there are three branches of government, the legislative, the executive and the judiciary. The powers are forbidden by the doctrine from usurping the function of the one over the other. The function of the judiciary is to interpret the laws and in fulfilling it, must give effect to the intention of Congress. The Court in this crucial case failed to carry out its solemn duty. Justice Harlan averred that the thirteenth amendment does not permit the withholding or the deprivation of any right necessarily inhering in freedom. It not only struck down the institution of slavery as previously existing in the United States, but it prevents the imposition of any burden or disabilities that constitutes the badges of slavery or servitude. It decreed universal civil freedom in this country and the court has so adjudged. But, that amendment having been found inadequate to the protection of the rights of those who had been in slavery, it was followed by the Fourteenth amendment, which added greatly to the dignity and glory of the American citizenship, and to the security of personal liberty. It declared 'all persons born or naturalized in the United States, and subject to the jurisdiction thereof, are citizens of the United States and of the state wherein they reside,' and that 'no state shall make or enforce any law which shall abridge the privileges or immunities of citizens of the United States; nor shall any state deprive any person of life, liberty or property without due process of law, nor deny any person the equal protection of the law'.

It is obvious that the passing of the Thirteenth and Fourteenth Amendments had a common intention and purpose. That is, to protect a race that had been recently emancipated from slavery from the worst excesses of inhumane treatment and to secure for them all the civil rights which the White race enjoyed. The court in giving effect to the Louisiana statute under the thin disguise of pretending to recognize equal rights: "can have no other result but to make permanent peace impossible, and to maintain the conflict between the races to the detriment of all citizens" (per Justice Harlan, p.12). This is the salient point of Justice Harlan's dissenting judgment. Justice Harlan argued for and would have implemented the true intention of Congress in passing the Thirteenth and Fourteenth Amendments to provide special legal protection for African American citizens. It is my considered opinion that Justice Harlan was, and history has proved him to be right and has vindicated his conclusion on the matter that the "*State of Louisiana is inconsistent with the personal liberty of the citizens, white and black, in that state, and hostile to both the spirit and letter of the constitution of the United States*" (p. 13) (Emphasis added).

Again to protect the African Americans, given their recent emancipation, their disadvantaged social, economical, and political status in the society, Congress enacted the Freedmen's Bureau Acts 1865, which were subsequently affirmed through the enactment of the Civil Rights Act 1866 to address the problem of racism in the post Civil War period. The Fourteenth Amendment, the Freedmen's Bureau Acts and the Civil Rights Acts were all intended to promote the good of the ex-slaves in American Society. They were the deliberate efforts of Congress to promote race conscious policies to support those men and women who have been victims of the worst excesses of a previously inhumane society.

Interestingly, it was necessary to amend the Constitution because the then sitting President, Johnson, refused to ratify the Freedmen's Bureau Acts, and the Civil Rights Act. The President put the classical conservative argument that providing special provisions for former slaves while not providing the same for unfortunate whites was unfair. Curious enough, hardly anyone found African American enslavement to be unfair and inequitable during its heyday, but now in seeking to remedy the wrong that had been committed to them for some three hundred years, a keen sense of morality has suddenly mushroomed overnight that sees the legislation as inequitable and unfair. This is the same red herring that became, (as I discussed below) the stumbling block for the derailing of affirmative action.

Those who were against providing assistance for the downtrodden were laboring under the misconceived view that the very characteristic of skin color which made African Americans suitable for enslavement could not be used as a rationale for ameliorating their condition. In the twisted, conservative logic, assisting African Americans might unfairly injure White citizens, although they were economically far better off than African Americans. Color was still a factor in the continued discrimination against people of color.

THE WIND OF CHANGE IN AMERICA'S PUBLIC EDUCATION: THE VICTORIES OF LEGAL STRATAGEM

In the meanwhile, the law, the iniquitous "separate but equal" ruling established by *Plessy v. Ferguson* (1896) continued to ensure that African Americans' education remained mediocre or non-existent. African Americans became absolutely fed up with White racial discrimination. They had enough of this injustice to themselves and their children. They wanted change and they wanted it eighty years ago and they were prepared to fight all the way to effect change in their social standing in their society.

The Supreme Court decision *Plessy v. Ferguson* (1896) was subsequently enshrined in the constitutions of many states. The inequity of "separate but equal" became deeply entrenched in the laws, the customs, and the habits of the United States. The courts failed to see the conflict that was fermenting between the "separate but equal" doctrine and the Fourteenth Amendment due to the courts' oblique interpretation of the Constitution. The Legislature for its part condoned the courts' oblique interpretation of the Constitution which set at naught and rendered nugatory the will and intention of the Legislature. The Legislature had the power to settle the judges who went astray but refused, connived, and/or neglected to do so.

When the courts paid scant respect to and neutered the Emancipation Proclamation by continued adherence to the *Dred Scott v. Sandford*

(1857) decision, the then Legislature saw the need to put in place the Thirteenth Amendment to make it abundantly clear that slavery was over. However, despite the Thirteenth Amendment the courts fixation on the lack of respect for the constitutional rights of Black people continued apace. Hence, the passing of the Fourteenth Amendment to establish under the Constitution the citizenship, privileges and immunities of Black people in the United States. These legislative efforts to protect the rights of Black people seemed to have eluded both the courts and the municipal legislatures. For example, section 207 of the 1890 Mississippi Constitution provides: 'Separate schools shall be maintained for children of the white and colored races." African Americans came to realize that they will only get justice if the courts are forced to recognize their right to equal treatment under the law, and the injustice of previous judicial decisions. They therefore commenced their own litigation to this end. By this time several African American men (Thurgood Marshall, Charles Hamilton) had gained degrees in law and were practicing lawyers.

In *Missouri Ex Rel. Gaines v. Canada, Registrar of the University of Missouri* Et Al (1938), the Petitioner Lloyd Gaines, a Negro, was refused admission to the School of Law at the State University of Missouri. He asserted that this refusal constituted a violation by the State of his right to equal protection under the Fourteen Amendment of the Federal Constitution. He was refused admission upon the ground that it was "contrary to the constitution, laws and public policy of the State to admit a Negro as a student in the University of Missouri".

It was further stated in the above case that the State Constitution provides that separate free public schools shall be established for the education of children of African descent, and by statute separate high school facilities are supplied for colored students equal to those provided for white students. While there was no expressed constitutional provision requiring that the White and Negro races be separated for the purpose of higher education, the state court on a comprehensive review of the state statutes held that it was intended to separate the White and the Negro races for that purpose also.

The Supreme Court found that the State by providing an adequate law school for Whites at the State University and none for Negroes to be repugnant to the Federal Constitution. The Court rejected the alternative which was offered by the State for Negroes to attend the law schools which were provided for Negroes in adjoining States. It was incumbent upon the State, in the opinion of the Court, that Negroes should be able to find law schools of equal standing in Missouri to those provided for White students. As the state had failed to do so, it was discriminatory and unconstitutional.

I am amazed that the Supreme Court had interpreted the constitutional violation not in terms of the Negroes not being able to attend the same law school as White students but in terms of not providing a school of equal standing for Negroes. The inequity was in the State not allowing the Negroes to attend the same law school that was well equipped with materials and faculty for the White students. I can hear the echoes of the powerful dissenting judgment of Justice Harlan in *Plessy v. Ferguson* (1896): "In my opinion, the judgment this day rendered will, in time, prove to be quite as pernicious as the decision made by this tribunal in the *Dred Scott Case*" (p. 11). Furthermore, Justice Harlan demonstrated that an oblique interpretation of the constitution would render its provision nugatory and void.

In the case of *Sweat v. Painter* (1950), the facts were very similar to *Gaines v. Canada, Registrar General* (1938). In this case a Black man was refused admission to the University of Texas Law School on the grounds that substantially equivalent facilities that comply with the requirements of *Plessy v. Ferguson* (1896) were offered by law schools open only to Blacks. The Supreme Court reversed the decision of the lower court on the grounds that the separate school failed to measure up because of the quantitative differences in facilities and intangible factors such as its isolation from most of the future lawyers with whom the graduates would interact.

The Court noted that there were many differences in relation to the University of Texas Law School and the separate law school for Blacks. The Texas Law School had sixteen full-time and three part-time professors and the separate law school for Blacks had five full-time professors. The Texas Law School had eight hundred and fifty students and a law library of sixty-five thousand volumes. The separate law school for Blacks had twenty-three students and a library of sixteen thousand, five hundred volumes. The Court therefore held that the State of Texas had failed to provide "separate but equal" education because the Texas Law School, as shown above, was far superior to the one that was hastily set up in a down town basement for Blacks. The provisions made for Black students who were admitted to the University of Oklahoma because there was no alternative Black law school, were thus:

> [T]hat he sits in separate sections of, or in spaces adjacent to, the classroom, the library, the cafeteria." The Court held these restrictions were unconstitutional because they interfered with his ability to study, to engage in discussions, and exchange view with other students, and, in general, to learn his profession" (Anderson & Byrne, 2004, p. 17).

With each of the above decisions, the Court came closer and closer to giving full and direct interpretation to the Constitution of the United States. The decision in the *McLaurin v. Oklahoma State Regents* (1950) was the boldest of all. Here the Court appears to be shaking off the temerity which has plagued it since the decision in *Plessy v. Ferguson* (1896): "That was a significant turning point in the argument against segregation because it was the first time a court acknowledged that equality of education was based on more than merely the physical facilities" (Anderson & Byrne, 2004, p. 17).

The greatest turning point in Black injustice under segregation came in the Supreme Court decision in 1954 in *Brown v. The Board of Education of Topeka* (1954). This decision brought to an end the Jim Crow educational practices: inferior buildings, outmoded second hand texts, underpaid teachers, and a stigma of inferiority characterized by the day to day reality of Black education hithertofore. The decision in the *Brown Case* was a watershed in U. S. legal and civil rights' history because it over turned the iniquitous Jim Crow doctrine of "separate but equal" which was first mischievously articulated in *Plessy v. Ferguson* (1896). The Supreme Court ended African Americans' fifty-eight-year-long practice of legal racial separation in public schools and paved the way for the integration of America's Public School system (Anderson & Byrne, 2004).

The Court gave a unanimous verdict against racial segregation which changed the course of history in the favor of African Americans and other minority groups. The judgment was delivered by Chief Justice Warren in which he declared that in "the field of public education, the doctrine of 'separate but equal' has no place" (Anderson & Byrne, 2004, p. 7). The Court was fully seised of the harm which segregation had inflicted on African Americans for half of a century. The learned Chief Justice Warren averred the view that segregation of white and colored children in public schools has a detrimental effect upon the colored children. The impact is greater when it has the sanction of the law, for the policy of separating the races is usually interpreted as denoting the inferiority of the Negro group. A sense of inferiority affects the motivation of a child to learn. Segregation with the sanction of law, therefore, has a tendency to [retard] the educational and mental development of Negro children and to deprive them of some of the benefits they would receive in a racially integrated school system.

In the *Brown* decision, the Supreme Court made a definitive pronouncement against racial segregation which commenced the dismantling of the regime to pave the way for racial integration in the public schools of America. However, both of the decisions in Brown I and Brown II stopped short of setting in gear the mechanism to be followed in the commencement of integration: "those concerned with social justice criticized the Court for weakening the Brown II implementation decree by including the ambivalent phrase 'with all deliberate speed.' Unlike the *Brown* opinion, *Brown II* contained ambiguous phrasing, even though it was intended to instruct the states on how to dismantle segregation in public education"(Anderson & Byrne, 2004, p. 9).

The *Brown* decision was a reinstatement of the American

Constitution and its 1776 Independence Declaration and gave meaning to the Emancipation Proclamation of 1863. The decision was the inauguration of the African American dream of freedom and equality under the law. This seminal decision can be viewed as the inevitable fulfillment of an American promise of freedom, justice, and equality for all of its citizens. *Brown* was a hard-won milestone in the ongoing African American history of the grassroots struggle to make America live up to its ideals, a launching pad for the civil rights movement of the 1950s and 1960s and a text book example of judicial activism (Anderson & Byrne, 2004).

The impact of the *Brown* decision has brought considerable change and growth to America's public education system. African Americans and other minority peoples enjoy a freedom which was hitherto unknown in America. Such freedom was the preserve of the privilege white group. Today, schools are more diverse than they have ever been. Of the 54 million students enrolled in public and private elementary and secondary schools, 62 percent are white, and 38 percent are African American, Hispanic, Asian, or Native American. School population are more ethnically, linguistically, and economically diverse than ever (Anderson & Byrne, 2004).

However, while we celebrate the fiftieth anniversary of the *Brown* decision, the signs of the time do not appear to augur well for American minorities. Anderson and Byrne (2004) have pointed out that the majority of the children in America's public schools in its twenty-five largest cities are from African American and Hispanic families. As if by some irony of the gods the schools in these cities are almost as segregated today as they were prior to the decision in *Brown*. *Brown's* abolition of *de jure* segregation has spawned a *de facto* segregation. Residential segregation has succeeded in keeping most of the nation's largest school districts racially and economically segregated.

AFFIRMATIVE ACTION:
CHALLENGE AND DEMISE

The policy of affirmative action grew out of government and public concerns to remove from the American society the scourges of racism which had its origin in the enslavement of African people. The Emancipation Proclamation in 1863, the Thirteenth and Fourteenth Amendments and the Civil Rights Acts of 1866, 1868 and 1875 are brave efforts which were made by the American Legislature to bring equal rights to all of its citizens by righting historical wrongs that were committed against African people and their descendants in America.

The work of the American Federal Government had advanced the search for equality. The intention was to protect the civil rights of all citizens and to provide the means of legal recourse when those rights were violated by giving citizens the right to sue. The aim of Affirmative Action is to give teeth to the protections already existing in the laws.

After President Kennedy took up office in 1961 he issued Executive Order 10925 establishing the President's Committee on Equal Employment Opportunity. The terms of reference of the Committee were the removal of discrimination from American employment practices. This was followed in 1964 by the passage of the Civil Rights Act. The combination of these two measures was to dislodge racial discrimination.

The opponents of Affirmative Action question the logic of promulgating legislation that was specifically intended to benefit African Americans. They considered it to be unfair, and that legislation should apply to all citizens equally, and that America should be a "colorblind society." This argument overlooks past and present inequities in favor of a system that allows the continuation of those inequities. Some of the opponents of Affirmative Action express the view that special protection is not necessary anymore because racial discrimination is now a thing of the past: "nearly 40 years after the enactment of the great Civil Rights Act, formal segregation in America is viewed as a long-suffered historical perversion, now forbidden and rightly despised. Many cannot even remember it" (Cohen and Sterba, 2003, p. 15).

This is absolutely astounding and manifestly absurd. These learned gentlemen must be living on fool's paradise. The law rightly forbids *de jure* segregation, but it is doubtful whether it can touch *de facto* segregation and even if it can the extent is doubtful. While the decision in *Brown v. Board of Education* and affirmative action have opened the doors of public education to all races, there are still deep seated problems where college admissions are concerned because minority applicants are generally less qualified than white applicants and the places available are limited. If the strict rules of admission are followed very few African Americans would get a college education because they had receive inadequate elementary and secondary education, and this would result in their not being competitive on the job market. They would have to settle for the low income, menial jobs. This is not to say that African Americans are should not be in employed in this kind of work, but when they provide the bulk of employees it signifies that something is still inherently wrong in the social system. This is why affirmative action is vitally important to the education of African Americans to level the playing field.

I find it to be inconceivable that anyone would challenge the objectives of affirmative action at this time because there are still significant imbalances between the Whites and African Americans and other minority groups in the society. This is common knowledge. The patent fact is that many minority children cannot compete on an equal footing with White children because there is no equality in the opportunities that are available. The imbalances are due to racial segregation, economic factors, or both. Even the staunch opponents of affirmative action admit this to be the case:

> Notwithstanding all such efforts, the racial proportionality that had been a reasonable expectation in public school systems remained an unrealistic expectation in law schools and medical schools, in laboratories and newsrooms. For many reasons, but perhaps mainly because of earlier

educational deficiencies, the racial balance hoped for was
not soon to be achieved, even after discriminatory barriers
had been torn down (Cohen and Sterba, 2003, p.18).

Cohen and Sterba (2003) have argued a strong case against affirmative
action as being contrary to the constitution of the United States
because it gives preferential treatment to African Americans on the
basis of race. This means that racial preference would have come full
circle. However, I am convinced that if some preference is not given to
African Americans and other minority peoples, they will be severely
disadvantaged where higher education is concerned. This does not
mean that African American and Hispanic students are intellectually
inferior to White students. But the deficiencies which are operating
in the environment of the African American and Hispanic children
from k-12 make him/her less qualified for admission to undergraduate
studies.

I can appreciate the cogent arguments that are put forward by
the opponents of affirmative action. Racial preference may indeed be
unconstitutional because it violates the Fourteenth Amendment equal
protection under the law and also Title VI of the 1964 Civil Rights Act
which prohibits any program or activity that receives Federal financial
assistance from discriminating on the basis of race, color, or national
origin. This is very frightening because this line of reasoning will create
serious drawbacks for minority people. Affirmative action is now under
siege. There is an eminent threat of elimination of a program which was
set up to help alleviate the lasting effects of continual discrimination. I
am afraid that the abolition of affirmative action will destroy the efforts
to bring about equality of opportunity in undergraduate programs.
My fears are evident in the Supreme Court decision in University of
California v. Bakke (1978). This case was a major constitutional test for
affirmative action.

In order to create diversity in its student body, the University of
California Medical School had created a bisected program for admission.
It had set aside sixteen of its two hundred places for minorities, who

would be selected under a separate and special admissions policy. For these slots, standards for grade point averages and test scores would not be as stringent as for regular admissions.

Bakke was one of the many applicants for the one hundred and eighty-four slots. He was rejected twice by the University. He therefore filed a lawsuit claiming that the School's special admissions policy violated his rights under Title VI of the Civil Rights Act of 1964, which forbids any program receiving federal funds from practicing racial or ethnic preferences. He also claimed that he had been denied equal protection of the laws, as guaranteed by the Fourteenth Amendment.

In its defence the University claimed that the need to remedy prior discrimination has influenced the right to admissions base strictly upon merit, and that diversity in the med school student body enriches the learning experience and projects favorable role models for minorities.

The Supreme Court rejected the University's defence and found for Bakke. It held that any such numerically based program constituted a quota system. Unless the University itself had discriminated, and designed the admission program specifically to correct that discrimination, quotas were unacceptable violations of the equal protection clause in the Fourteenth Amendment. Similar results were reached in the case of Gratz *Et Al v. Bollinger Et A*l (2003). The Petitioner filed a class action alleging that the University of Michigan's use of racial preferences in undergraduate admission violated the Equal Protection Clause of the Fourteenth Amendment, Title VI of the Civil Rights Act of 1964. The Court found for the Petitioner.

The decisions in *Gratz* (2003) and *Bakke* (1978) have dealt a mortal wound to affirmative action from which it may not be able to recover. So we have come full circle. I am inclined to believe that this may be the beginning of the end for affirmative action: the demise of affirmative action. It follows inexorably, that any institution of higher learning which is being funded partially or wholly by the Federal Government may not be allowed to give any support to affirmative action because such preferences will be struck down as being inconsistent with and repugnant to the Fourteenth Amendment of the Constitution and Title

VI of the Civil Rights Act of 1964. Ironically, the very instruments which were intended to cure the maladies that impacted on African Americans and other minority groups are now being used against them. I do not think the Legislature had intended to create a two-edged sword, but in fact, it has done so.

Cohen (2003) has made out a strong case against affirmative action on the ground that racial preference is morally and legally wrong because:

> [W]hat is done in the name of "affirmative action" is not exempt from this law. The plain words of the statute can hardly be misunderstood. Employers, university administrators, and all others who discriminate among ethnic groups to give special favor to some *break the law* (Cohen and Sterba, p. 48).

Given the present state of the law, the question which now haunts my mind is whether African Americans and other minority groups will get a chance at higher education. Interestingly, even Carl Cohen is forced to acknowledge that some form of racial preference is permissible:

> The equal protection of laws does not forbid *every* racial classification. Blacks and others who have been clearly injured by unlawful discriminatory practices may come to the courts for remedy, and a just remedy may require that the race of those who were earlier injured be taken into account. To give victims what they are due, the courts may be obliged to use the racial categories by which victims were earlier deprived of what they were due (Cohen and Sterba, 2003, p. 74).

Sterba (Cohen and Sterba, 2003) in rebutting Cohen's misconstrual of the affirmative action has argued strongly in favor of it. Sterba also pointed out the misinterpretations of Cohen in the recent Supreme Court decisions in *Gratz Et Al v. Bollinger Et Al* (2003) and *Grutter v. Bollinger Et Al* (2003). Sterba has also shown that the *Bakke's* decision did not totally strike down racial preferences but instead made racial preference permissible by an institution which had previously practiced racism in its admission policies. Cohen's argument if followed to its logical conclusion would see a dramatic under representation of minorities in undergraduate programs:

> Sometimes Cohen writes as though any degree of racial preference in college or university admissions is unacceptable. Race, he says, cannot be the basis of preference, presumably not even when it serves the goal of diversity. But that would mean that he wants the University of Michigan minority enrolment to drop from 13.6 percent in the undergraduate college and 10 –12 percent in the law school to about 3 percent at each institution, as has been projected to happen if using race as a factor in admission is abandoned at the University of Michigan. This would reduce under-represented minorities to a token presence at the university, and it would virtually put an end to the university's attempt to provide the educational benefits of racial diversity on its campus (Cohen and Sterba, 2003, p. 342).

The argument as put by Sterba is worthy. There are serious deficiencies in the educational development of African American children from the K-12 which they may never be able to overcome. These deficiencies are documented in the findings of Kozol (1991). Kozol investigated the tragedy of America's Public Education System in the big cities and found that there is a marked distinction between the schools in the inner cities which are poverty stricken where the majority of the student body is made up of Blacks and Hispanic minorities. While the schools that are located in the suburbs are wealthy and the student body is predominantly White. The great disparity between the inner city and urban schools is alarming.

Public School No. 26 in District 10, according to Kozol (1991), is housed in a former roller skate rink next to a funeral home hidden within a crowded city block. "The principal, who is also a white woman, tells me that the school's "capacity" is 900 but that there are 1,300 children here. The size of classes for fifth and sixth grade children in

New York, she says, is 'capper' at 32, but she say class size in the school goes up to 34" (1991, p. 86). Kozol (1991) further states that:

> The text books are not enough for every child to have one so they have to share their books. The play ground is non-existent, "the library is a tiny, windowless and claustrophobic room. I count approximately 700 books. But it had no reference books... The school I am told has 26 computers for its 1300 children. There is one small gym and children get one period, and sometimes two, each year. Recess, however, is not possible because there is no playground.
>
> I return to see the kindergarten classes on the ground floor and feel stifled once again by lack of air and the low ceiling. Nearly 120 children and adults are doing what they can to make the best of things: 80 children in four kindergarten classes, 30 children in the sixth grade class, and about eight grown-ups are aides and teachers. The kindergarten ten children sitting on the worn rug, which is patched with tape (p. 87).

The other school which Kozol (1991) discussed is Public School No. 79, an elementary school in the same district. This school is also over crowded. It has a capacity for one thousand but presently has an enrolment of one thousand, five hundred and fifty. Kozol found that the learning environment is just as poor as the previous school. He opines that it is a very sad situation in which these very young children must receive their education. What is worse is that the Principal paints a very grim picture for the future if the children do not get an adequate education to lead healthy and productive lives: "we will be their victims later on. We'll pay the price someday – in violence, in economic costs. I despair of making an appeal in any terms but these. You cannot issue an appeal to conscience in New York today. The fair-play argument won't be accepted. So you speak of violence and hope that it will scare the city into action" (1991, p.89).

From the squalid conditions of the poor schools which are

predominantly made up of Blacks and Hispanics, Kozol (1991) describes the more affluent school and the wonderful opportunities that they are given. One of these schools is Public School No. 24. Here the number of students is eight hundred and twenty-five. This school has a greater mix of the races, but the classrooms are racially segregated. In one classroom there are all the White children and may be one or two Black or Asian children:

> The school is integrated in the strict sense that middle and upper-middle-class white children here do occupy a building that contains some Asian and Hispanic and Black children; but there is little integration in the classrooms since the vast majority of the Hispanic and Black children are assigned to "special" classes on the basis of evaluation that have classified them "EMR" – "educable mentally retarded" – or else, in the worst of cases, "TMR" – "trainable mentally retarded."

> The school therefore contains effectively two separate schools: one of about 130 children, most of whom are poor, Hispanic, Black assigned to one of the 12 special classes; the other 700 mainstream students, almost all of whom are White or Asian.

> There is a third track also – this one for the students who are labeled "talented" or "gifted." This is a termed a "pull out" program since the children who are so identified remain in mainstream classrooms but are taken out for certain periods each week to be provided with intensive and, in my opinion excellent instruction in some areas of reasoning and logic...(Kozol, 1991, pp. 93 – 94).

Kozol (1991) writes that, according to a study done by the State Commissioner of Education, "as many as three out of four blacks...fail to complete high school within the traditional four- year periods" (p. 112). The dropout rates that Kozol present are startling and distressing. The shocking and horrific unjust situation in minority education is due to three main factors: the disparity in property taxes, racism and the conflict between state and local control. The differences in property tax are due to the various values which are placed on property in the suburbs and those placed on property in the inner cities. The affluent district will bring in more taxes than the poor district and is therefore able to spend more on the education of each child. For example, a classroom in Chicago "receives approximately $90,000.00 less each year than would have been spent on them if they were pupils of a school such as New Trier High" (p. 54). Cool (1991) presents the shocking scenario of a school in the poor Chicago district where the students suffer from severe health problems, they are subject to dreadful amounts of sewage in their schools and in their backyards, contaminating the water and the soil.

Evidently students from these backgrounds can hardly be expected to compete for admission to undergraduate programs at the same level as that for the affluent children. In any case, many of them will not even complete high school. Those who do will need the assistance of affirmative action to give them a fighting chance to get a good education and to enjoy the good life. Like Kozol, I am aghast at the number of so many Black and Hispanic children who are suffering from "brain damage." Kozol's (1991) findings are corroborated by Beth Harry's (1992):

> In light of the current pattern of underachievement among minority students, educational implications of these figures are immense. Essentially, the American school system is faced with a choice between accepting that at least half of its students may continue to be at risk for school failure and dropout, or else making a firm commitment to examining and remedying this trend (p. 10).

The unfortunate thing is that school failure of minority people especially the poor is not due to lack of intellectual ability, but to environmental factors. The home culture of most poor children and that of the classroom do not correlate. Far from that, they frequently clash. Harry (1992) has pointed out that it is in the regular classroom that their difficulties first become evident. These experiences will include a number of aspects: the overall attitude of the school and classroom teachers toward students from culturally diverse backgrounds, in particular such children who are also poor; the language in which instruction is offered; and the cultural congruity and efficacy of instructional procedures and curriculum.

Students are also impacted on by the teachers' bias or prejudice whether it be class or race. If there is an incongruity between the home culture and classroom culture, the teacher must be able to bring balance to the situation, seek always to identify with her/his students. Harry (1992) has pointed out that this is not always the case. Teachers tend to give greater attention to Anglo-American children than they give to minority children. Children who receive a warm reception of their teacher are shown to do better. Students are more receptive to learning when they receive instruction in ways that are familiar to them. It is argued that the children from diverse cultures have different learning patterns according to what they are accustomed to. The learning style of Black working class students is "less linear and more factual, more imaginative, and less adult directed than that of their white counterparts" (Harry, 1992, quoting Heath, 1983; Houston, 1973). It behooves the teacher to ensure that students' culture and language are accepted in the classroom or their ability to express themselves effectively will be greatly impaired.

This situation is further compounded by the decline of African American teachers in the American educational systems. African American students have lost a positive role model in this way. As Anderson and Byrne (2004) said fifty years ago, even forty years ago, African American teachers taught almost exclusively African American students. Today many students, including African American students, as well as students in general, may matriculate through elementary and secondary schools – even college – and never be taught by an African American teacher, much less see one in their schools. This situation creates a significant *lacuna* in the cultural education of African Americans which needs to be resolved. Perhaps more African Americans should consider entering the teaching profession. The absence of African

Americans in the system is lamented by bell hooks. hooks, being a child of the desegregation process, thinks that Black students were better off when they were being taught by Black educators prior to desegregation. The profound importance of this cultural link between teacher and student cannot be over emphasize. This 'cultural vacuum' facilitates and enhances the processes of deculturisation and acculturation of African American students. Faculty diversity is just as important as diversity in the student body.

Linguistic Disadvantage: Can the Law make a Difference?

Language is usually a main element in an individual's cultural identity. Limitations on students' ability to use their mother tongue coupled with limited facility in speaking the dominant language, that is, English – can exclude students from education, political life and justice. The use of a dominant national language is a powerful means of "encouraging" minorities who have a different language to assimilate a dominant culture by having those are economically, socially and politically victimized sideline their mother language. Such assimilation is not freely chosen if the choice is between the students' mother tongue and their future successful participation in the social and political affairs of the new society in which they are now residing. This has been the fate of many migrants who move to the United States, especially Latino but also including Africans from the Continent. Many of them have had to abandon their ancestral language in the interest of social mobility.

The ability of many students to use their language in education and in dealings with the agencies of government are particularly limited. Lack of education in the students' mother tongue can either stall or retard development. The work of Harry (1992) lends support to this view. Children who are educated in their mother tongue in their early years (elementary) perform much better than those immediately immersed in English. It is therefore not difficult to see the grave linguistic problem for students whose main language is not English, but the classroom instruction is done in English. Hispanic children are doubly disadvantaged because they do not speak English well and it may be incomprehensible to them. The civil rights of students are violated when they come to school knowing little English, and are confronted by the "sink or swim" instruction. This is a violation of their right of "equal opportunity." This matter was contested in the case of *Lau v. Nichols*, 414 U.S. 563 (1974). This decision has made it clear that children's language difference must be taken into account and that they must be given an opportunity to learn English.

ENTERS NO CHILD LEFT BEHIND: COMPOUNDING MINORITY INEQUITIES

Into the milieu of the American educational system dynamics was thrust the Elementary and Secondary Education Act (ESEA) which has been nicknamed, "No child Left Behind" (NCLB) enacted by Congress under the Bush Administration with the intention that this piece of legislation will be the panacea for the ills in the educational system. It was anticipated that it would improve the quality of education for low-income and minority students. NCLB far from enhancing minority education, like the counter affirmative action argument (Cohen and Sterba, 2003), threatens to further undermine the gains which positive affirmative action has brought to minority people because the legislation has fundamental flaws built into it which will aggravate the poverty-stricken working class families in America. I concur with the view of Neil, et al (May, 2004, p. ES-1) that there are two false assumptions underpinning NCLB:

> *1. Boosting standardized test scores should be the primary goal of schools.* This assumption leads to one-size-fits-all teaching aimed primarily at test preparation, and it works against efforts to give all children a high-quality well rounded education.

2. Schools can best be improved by threatening educators with harsh sanctions, since poor teaching is the primary cause of unsatisfactory student performance. Threats may get teachers to focus narrowly on boosting test scores. They fail, however, to address the underlying problems of family poverty and inadequate school funding that are major reasons why many students start off far behind and never catch up.

The Act requires that by the 2005-06 school years, all states must develop and implement annual assessment in reading and mathematics in grades 3 to 8 and at least once in grades 10-12. By 2007-08, all states must also administer annual science assessment at least once in grades 3-5, grades 6-9, and grades 10-12. These assessments must be aligned with state academic content and achievement standards and involve multiple measures, including measures of higher-order thinking and understanding. (US Department of Education et al, 2002)

These requirements when taken at face value are quite benign, but they have far reaching ramifications, especially in circumstances where all schools are not funded at the same level as in the case of urban schools where poverty is a major factor in the lives of young students. The Federal Government must first ensure that schools have adequate funding before the system which is envisaged by the NCLB can be implemented. What is even more threatening is the fact that NCLB has not only put in place a system of assessment but it is coupled with a system of punishment for those schools which do not meet what it calls the "Adequate Yearly Progress" (AYP). The punishment provided is harsh and far reaching. Schools and districts which are identified as being "in need of improvement" (INOI), may lose their student body in that students must be given the option to transfer to another public school that has not been identified for improvement. If a school fails to make adequate yearly progress for a fourth year, the school district must take corrective actions that are designed to bring about meaningful change at the school. These corrective actions must include at least one of the following: replacing school staff, implementing a new curriculum (with appropriate professional development), decreasing management authority at the school level, appointing an outside expert to advise the school, extending the school day or year or reorganizing the school internally (US Department of Education et al, 2002).

The sanctions which are provided by the Act go as far as restructuring the schools which fail to meet the requirements of the AYP. Such a school could find itself under entirely new management which could be a private enterprise. This is frightening because private enterprises are driven by the profit motive. This will no doubt impact negatively on the education of poor African Americans. Furthermore, if a school fails to make adequate yearly progress for a fifth year, the school district must initiate plans to fundamentally restructure the school. This restructuring may include reopening the school as a charter school, replacing all or most of the school staff that are relevant to the failure to make adequate progress, or turning over the school operations either to the state or to a private company with a demonstrated record of effectiveness (US Department of Education et al, 2002).

Teachers who are dismissed as a result of not meeting adequate yearly progress will have difficulty finding fresh employment in the educational system. This may result in a shortage of teachers which will only further compound an already untenable situation. NCLB therefore, poses a serious danger for both students of low income back ground, minorities and teachers – endangered 'species'. As Neil et al (2004) said, what makes NCLB so dangerous is the way it links standardized testing with heavy sanctions through the rigid "adequate yearly progress" (AYP) formula. Thus, the weaknesses of standardized exams – their cultural biases and their failure to measure higher order thinking – are reinforced by strict penalties. The consequence of narrow exams and strong sanctions is intensive teaching to the test. This response undermines decent education as well as efforts to ensure genuine improvements in educational quality.

How will this system work for children who are described by Kozol (1991) as being forced to attend school in extremely awful conditions due to poverty, compounded by inadequate funding for the schools in their district and children who are also subjected to dreadful amounts of sewage in their schools and in their backyards, contaminating the water and the soil. This situation makes me recoil and shudder. It is absolutely incredulous that a country with such tremendous wealth would treat its young with such inhumanity. Neil et al (2004) further stated that the lack of adequate funding for schools and the well-being of children intensifies these problems for low-income and minority group students. Overcrowded classrooms make it more likely that teachers focus on little more than the content of mandatory tests. The convergence of testing, sanctions and inadequate funding means too many children will continue to get a second-class education. A false accounting system based on testing and punishing will never bring about success for all children. This goal will be out of reach as long as there is worsening poverty and inadequate funding, that denies too many students access to a rich and comprehensive curriculum to prepare them to be lifelong learners, active participants in our democracy and successful in further education and employment.

Clearly, the point that is being made here is that political administrators must embrace these ideals if the cultural circumstances of African American life world are to be transformed. African Americans are an integral part of the American society and unless fair measures are put in place to ameliorate their educational deficiencies they will always be the third world within.

CURRICULUM JETTISON

NCLB creates a conveyor belt type of education which can only produce persons for employment on conveyor belts. Because teachers are at risk of losing their livelihood, they will be forced to narrow the curriculum so that it focuses on the areas on which children will be tested. Instead of teaching students critical thinking skills and useful information, teachers are forced to "drill and kill" the desire of their students to learn sound information. Teachers will drill students in practice questions that simulate the test questions or to emphasize the specific topics that are most likely to appear on the test paper so as to ensure a high score both for the teacher and for the students – much like Pavlov's conditional learning mechanism. Students are also coached in skills to decipher multiple choice questions. However, this will leave students ignorant as to the broader subject on which they are being tested and they may not be able to transfer the skills learnt to non-testing situations.

A study focusing on high-stakes accountability in 24 schools in Southern states looked at the link between high-stakes accountability and professional development. The report by Barnett and Berry and their colleagues (2003) states that:

> [H]igh-stakes accountability systems were more likely to make teachers in low performing districts feel pressured to narrow the curriculum. We also found that the pressure has also resulted from teachers who are overworked and exhausted from trying to cover increasing amounts of content and then having to teach to the test (Neil et al, 2004, p. 49).

If NCLB adequate yearly progress has had a negative impact in the well-to-do suburban school districts, then it is not difficult to see that it will have a greater negative impact on poor states with large minority groups who will bear the brunt of this intensified state testing. The policy is discriminatory in effect. As Neil (2002) pellucidly points out: "It is not an error in policy that results in structural and institutional mechanism that discriminate against all of America's poor and many of America's minority students" (p. 46). NCLB appears to have the potential for *de facto* re-segregating America's public school system. The gains which were brought about by *Brown v. Board of Education* (1954) and Affirmative Action are seriously further threatened by NLCB. The future will tell the tale, but as the matter now stands, African Americans are still suffering from the debilitations of unfair educational practices and limited opportunity that is colored by the continued presence of White racism.

CONCLUSION

I have critically examined the many efforts which were taken by the American Legislature and the Civil Rights Movement to bring about social justice at first for ex-African American slaves and later expanding the legal protections for all persons under the American Constitution as demonstrated in the several Supreme Court decisions which I have discussed above. All of the legal challenges have one aim, that is, equality and justice for all persons. However, Cool (1991) and Harry (1992) have shown that the inequities of the educational system continue to impact upon minorities, including African Americans. The impact on social justice, which *Browne* should have had, has become diluted. It seems as though African Americans have been duped by a false consciousness about the degree to which law can reduce social injustice and promote social change. Affirmative action has been short circuited by the very same legal reasoning that created it in the first place. The moots have been silenced and apparently routed. Such silence is not accidental, but is often deliberately constructed for political purposes. I fear that NCLB will not help but aggravate and further displace African Americans. The critical examination of the law as I have sought to do in this discussion has left me with a sense of powerlessness: the inability to use the law to end injustice and advance important social values and interest that will give Black people their rightful place in the African Diaspora. If the law is unable to promote social equality and justice, then what can? However, I am also left with the feeling of determination and commitment to get at least one person to walk with me on this arduous journey in search for the redemption of Black people in the African Diaspora through the medium of an adequate and efficient education. Our ancestors were torn from their home land and brought to the Americas and Europe where they were enslaved and treated with unabashed inhumanity by White people. The profound effect of slavery and colonialism continues to haunt us, even the best educated among us. We must find a way, a philosophy which is redemptive for Black folks. Such a redemptive philosophy must inform the legal philosophy of due process in the cultural politics of equal educational opportunities for African people in the Diaspora.

CHAPTER FOUR

Student Diversity in Higher Education: A Government Compellable Interest

> The ugly reality of racism and social class bias, among other forms of discrimination, and the ways in which these are manifested, are a taboo subject to discuss because they challenge the ideal that advancement and achievement are based on merit, not on social class status or racial privilege (Nieto, 1999, pp.20-21).

In the previous Chapter my investigation was based on legislative and judicial efforts to cure the iniquitous doctrine of 'Separate but equal' in America's education system and other racial discrimination against African Americans. I am left with a keen sense of dissatisfaction bordering on despair with what appears to me to be the precarious position of the education of African American people, hence my prayer: "The night is dark and I am far from home, lead thou me on" because I desperately need to encourage myself. I believe the philosophy of critical redemptive pedagogy has the potential to shed some light on the path which Africans in the Diaspora must follow to improve their economical and political standing wherever they reside in the world that is dominated by Eurocentric culture. This chapter critically examines the importance of students' diversity in the educational system for a healthy social and political development in a pluralistic society. The examination in this chapter is against the background of the challenge and demise of Affirmative Action. I am seeking a way forward for African Americans out of this quagmire.

Some light is cast upon the situation by the decision of Justice Powell in *Regents of the University of California v. Bakke* (1978) in his fourth principle that the attainment of a diverse student body "is a constitutionally permissible goal for an institution of higher education"(311-312, 98 S. Ct. at 2759). In that regard, "ethnic diversity" can be "one element in a range of factors a university properly may consider in attaining the goal of a heterogeneous student body" (314, 98 S. Ct. at 2760-61). This fourth principle created a new type of affirmative action known as diversity (non-remedial) affirmative action. This is the main issue that I propose to critically examine in this discussion with the view to establishing that diversity in higher education is a governmental compellable interest. Ironically, the very judicial opinion that brought about the demise of affirmative action in its remedial form has created the new affirmative action in its non-remedial diversity form.

AFFIRMATIVE ACTION CHECKMATE

As discussed above, during the late 1950's and the thunderous years of the 1960's, African Americans legally challenged the Jim Crow doctrine of 'separate but equal' and legal victory was won in the decision of the Supreme Court in *Brown v. Board of Education of Topeka* (1954). As a result of the many years of substandard education, significant deficiencies were created in the education of African Americans. Remedial affirmative action was used to correct some of the deficiencies and to remove, to a certain extent, the racism which fostered inequality. The Civil Rights Act 1964, Title VI, was the Federal Government's instrument for the promotion of equal opportunity for all Americans as provided under the Fourteenth Amendment to the United States Constitution. Under the Civil Rights Act, admissions to institutions of higher education are required to be made on a non-discriminatory basis. However, certain racial and ethnic measures were permitted in making decisions for undergraduate admissions to remedy previous discrimination by way of affirmative action, that is, the basic requirement for entry into a government funded or partially funded tertiary institution was reduced for African American students. Affirmative action has made a significant difference in the educational opportunities for many African Americans and other minority groups by affording them the opportunity to get tertiary education. This was a radical change in America's tertiary institutions which were hitherto deeply racialized in favor of White students.

The type of affirmative action that grew out of the decision in the *Brown's* case and Title VI of the Civil Rights Act, 1964 was remedial in nature - to compensate for past racial discrimination. This was important so that African Americans and other minority peoples who were disadvantaged by the system would get a tertiary education. However, in recent times affirmative action has been legally challenged successfully because it is based on race preference which is contrary to Title VI of the 1964 Civil Rights Act and repugnant to the Fourteenth Amendment. Furthermore, there is a current misconception that racism in the United States is a thing of the past and remedial affirmative action has played its role and is now moribund and obsolete. Those who advocate this view are laboring under a misconception that this line of reasoning is valid and has some merit. I would reluctantly concur with them as it applies to remedial affirmative action. However, racism in America is neither moribund nor obsolete. But there is another type of affirmative action, that is, non-remedial diversity affirmative action which is the progeny of Justice Powell's opinion in *Regents of the University of California v. Bakke* (1978). Affirmative action measures will now predominantly take the form of diversity:

> There is another type of affirmative action, however, that is not grounded in the ideal of remedying discrimination, whether that discrimination is present or past. The goal of

> this type of affirmative action is diversity, which in turn
> is justified either in terms of its educational benefits or its
> ability to create a more effective work force in such areas as
> policing and community relations. The legal roots of this
> form of affirmative action in the United States are found
> in Bakke (1978). (Cohen & Sterba, 2003).

The most famous of the legal challenges to affirmative action came in the case of *Regents of the University of California v. Bakke* (1978) which, as mentioned above, focused on the issue of preferential treatment on the basis of race or ethnic origin for admissions into higher education. Here Allan Bakke challenged the Medical School of California at Davis for its racial preferences in reserving sixteen of the one hundred places in each class for the members of certain minority groups. Candidates for these spaces were considered separately from others and a different standard for entry was applied to them. Bakke contended that, as a white student, he had been unfairly excluded from competing for one of the sixteen places reserved for minorities, even though his test scores and other indices were stronger than some of those of students who were admitted under special admissions programs. This he successfully averred was inconsistent with and repugnant to the equal protection clause under the Fourteenth Amendment and a violation of the Title VI of the Civil Rights Act 1964.

The *Bakke* case sets the precedent on the legality of quotas or set-asides in admissions to higher education, and the use of race and/ or ethnicity as factors to be considered for admissions to colleges and universities which receive federal funding. In the leading opinion, Justice Powell made it clear that racial and ethnic preferences are inherently repugnant to the constitution and the Civil Rights Act of 1964. The clear intention of the Legislature in passing the Fourteenth Amendment and the 1964 Act was to destroy the institutionalized discrimination against African Americans, but the basic constitutional objective is equal protection for all Americans, whatever their race.

However, it is of paramount significance that Justice Powell's opinion, and the other Jutices apparently concurred, that conscious consideration of race or ethnicity in decision making is not intrinsically unconstitutional, but its use must be strictly circumscribed. The rationale for permitting this kind of consideration without running afoul of the Civil Rights Act and the Fourteenth Amendment is that the presence of minority students together with other racial groups contributes to diversity in education which is congruent with the heterogeneous society in which the students will live out their adult life.

It is interesting to note that at first and second instance, proceedings in the courts below, both of them had ruled in favor of Bakke, but Justice Powell ruled that contrary to the view of the courts below, it is not a black or white matter (no pun intended), there are some grey areas in between the two:

> In enjoining petitioner [the University of California] from ever considering the race of any applicant, the courts below failed to recognize that the state has a substantial interest that may legitimately be served by a properly devised admissions program involving the competitive consideration of race and ethnic origin.

Clearly Justice Powell sees racial and ethnic characteristics as serving an important purpose in terms of university admissions because diversity is a government compellable interest in these circumstances. Justice Powell's view is consistent with the long standing principles of educational freedom which universities enjoy as enunciated by Justice Frankfurter in *Sweezy v. New Hampshire* (1957):

> It is the business of the university to provide that atmosphere which is most conducive to speculation, experiment and creation. It is an atmosphere in which there prevail "the four essential freedoms" of a university – to determine for itself on academic grounds who may teach, what may be taught, how it shall be taught, and who may be admitted to study (p. 21).

In his opinion Justice Powell refers to the "robust exchange of ideas." His Honor espouses the view that it is important that students learn about the "mores", the customs, habits, and outlooks, of other students who are "as diverse as this Nation of many peoples." This mixture of peoples on the university campus enhances students' interaction. The occasional racial out breaks on campuses do not detract from nor devalue such invaluable experiences. It augurs well for the long-term benefit which the society as a whole can derive from diversity: "The Nation's future depends upon leaders trained" in this kind of academic environment and the positive values which are derived from living and learning with people who are different leaves indelible impressions on the minds of both young adults and adults. The learned Justice Powell therefore set down four salient principles which will govern decisions in relation to race-conscious decision making.

First, strict scrutiny will be applied to a "...classification based on race and ethnic background."(289, 98 S. Ct. at 2747)

Secondly, if the purpose of an educational institution "is to assure within its student body some specified percentage of a particular group merely because of its race or ethnic origin, such a preferential purpose must be rejected not as insubstantial but as racially invalid."(307, 98 S. Ct. at 2757)

Third, "the State certainly has a legislative and substantial interest in ameliorating, or eliminating where possible, the disabling effects of identified discrimination. However, that will not justify a racial classification "in the absence of judicial, legislative, or administrative findings of constitutional or statutory violations." And "isolated segments of our vast governmental structures are not competent to make those decisions, at least in the absence of legislative mandates and legislatively determined criteria. As a result, when the purpose of the classification is simply to help "certain groups ... perceived as victims of 'societal discrimination' [that] does not justify a classification that imposes disadvantages upon persons ... who bear no responsibility for whatever harm the beneficiaries of the special admissions program are thought to have suffered" (309-310, 98 S. Ct. at 2758).

Fourth, the attainment of a diverse student body "is a constitutionally permissible goal for an institution of higher education" (311-312, 98 S.

Ct. at 2759). In that regard, "ethnic diversity" can be "one element in a range of factors a university properly may consider in attaining the goal of a heterogeneous student body" (314, 98 S. Ct. at 2760-61).

It would therefore seem that remedial affirmative action has been checkmated, muted, or at least attenuated by the judgment in *Bakke's* case. In fact California and Washington have outlawed the use of affirmative action by public institutions of higher education and have forbidden: " the state to discriminate, or grant preferential treatment to, any individual or group on the basis of race, sex, color, ethnicity, or national origin in the operation of public employment, public education or public contracting" (Wash. Rev. Code s 49.60.400(1)).

However, my concern here is less with remedial affirmative action given the current interpretation of the law, but the wider issue of diversity (as a measure of non-remedial affirmative action) in the student body and its potential to add to the quality of students' life and learning. Justice Powell's fourth principle makes allowance for this. This is not to say that remedial affirmative action is no longer available, clearly this is provided for in Justice Powell's third principle but the argument against and/or obstacles for remedial affirmative action is that it can only be used for remedial purposes, to curb, or ameliorate where feasible the vestiges of racism. As the argument now runs, racism is a past transgression which has been obliterated.

I am inclined to believe that diversity can lessen the effects of prejudice and racism. It would be foolhardy to create homogenous campuses in a heterogeneous society. Any such policy would tantamount to courting disaster for future generations. It is therefore imperative that campuses of African Americans, Jews, Latinos, Native Americans, and other minorities be part and parcel of excellent educational institutions. This has value in and of itself in enhancing all of the experiences of the learning community. On the basis of this line of reasoning, it follows inexorably, that higher education must consciously endeavor to provide a genuine heterogeneous student body which reflects the rich diversity of the society of the United States.

I believe that sound human learning, and understanding, and

wisdom are created and fostered in the universities. It promotes intellectual energy and toughness that inculcate greater knowledge, tolerance, and mutual respect which are crucial to the maintenance of human society. It is not enough for the teacher and students to discuss in some abstract manner in their academic citadel, the mode of thoughts and culture of other peoples without having any contact with them. They need to know in practical terms that other people exist by having interpersonal connections with them, to face one another openly, face to face in the class room, in debates, in discourses, and on social occasions in the life of the campus. In associating with others who are different their ethnic origin will challenge White traditional presuppositions, prejudices and bigotry, and it would do the same for Blacks and other minority groups. It is social interaction at its best. It is learning to live with other people in spite of their differences. It forces soul searching exercises in the oppressor as well as the oppressed.

The Impact of Diversity on Higher Education

The importance of diversity in the student body in the promotion of greater understanding and appreciation for people who are ethnically and culturally different is crucial for the democratic institutions of the American society. A society that is heterogeneous does not stand to benefit much from a system of higher education that is homogeneous. Such an arrangement will only further exacerbate social inequities. It therefore follows inexorably that diversity is the primary basis for arguing the constitutionality of using race as one of the many factors in the determination of college admissions. My challenge here is to convincingly demonstrate, or at the very least demonstrate satisfactorily how diversity can impact on education. This is crucially important for two reasons: 1) it is legally important to show that diversity is not repugnant to nor inconsistent with the Fourteenth Amendment and the Title VI of the Civil Rights Act 1964 and that it has sound judicial backing; and 2) it has practical importance for sustainable coexistence in a pluralistic democratic, multicultural society. The objective for advancing an argument for diversity in the student body is to create educational equity.

My desire to promote the acceptance and appreciation of diversity as a significant element in an undergraduate and a graduate student body is not in contradistinction to that which the Greeks sought for in their own communities so many aeons ago. I am amazed that even now we are still seeking to establish its importance in a heterogeneous society. The multiplicity of cultures in the United States is a given reality; a reality which should not be feared but one that should be embraced. Saxonhouse (1992) describes how the pre-Socratic playwrights, Plato and Aristotle dealt with their fear of difference:

> A focus on equality before the laws and a citizenry of equals bound to the city by their uniformity rather than their individuality released from those the Athenian polity. To achieve the unity of the city, the traditional bonds to the family needed to be fractured and the individual released from those ties that bound him to the private rather than to the public (p. 94).

The individuality of the individual must be sacrificed for the unity of the city, the polity, to preserve the continued existence of the city. Plato's fear of difference is profoundly depicted, according to Saxonhouse (1992) in myths of autochthony that unify the city excluded that which is other, those not born of the land, or those not necessary for the beginning of the city (i.e., the foreigner and the human female). The unity engendered by this form of autochthony depends on the exclusion of difference based on the fear that foreigners would upset the comprehensive unity based on a common ancestry from those born from the earth. Aristotle, unlike Plato, embraced diversity as an integral part of the city in that he saw no need to send the women out of the city in order to have a whole; nor is it necessary to transform them into men. There is no need to deny the diversity of the human reality rather we can observe variety and yet, by accepting priority of form over matter, we can see the unity of that "above and that below", of the stream that always flows, of the regime that survives over generations. Aristotle tells us further that the questions that he raises make us recognize the inescapable diversity within the city that we often pretend is a unified entity. Aristotle's queries make us reconsider the language that claims that the polis acts, *peprachenai ten praxin*, when of course it is only parts of the city that can act. In so doing he makes us explore the way in which the regime unifies the diversity of the city – but never overcomes it (Saxonhouse, 1992).

Historically, America has sought to create homogeneity where there was none and in circumstances where it was practically impossible. The policy was that all differences were to be assimilated by the Anglosaxon culture so as to create a common identity for all Americans, the so-called 'melting pot'. But this was only a resurrection of the Platonic fear. The Aristotelian approach is far more consistent with the tenets of democracy which is congruent with and embodies pluralism. As a matter of fact Prentice and Miller (1999) expressed the view that this notion of a melting pot is a theory of democracy that is more akin to that of the pre-Socratics and Plato than to Aristotle's has prevailed in the United States. It is the Republican tradition, represented by Rousseau on through Jefferson in which democracy and citizenship are believed to require social homogeneity, simplicity, and citizenship and an overarching common identity rather than heterogeneity, complexity, and multiple identities. This was the theory of democracy by which the founding fathers of America were guided. But they were faced with a critical dilemma, that is, they wanted homogeneity so what were they to do with the obvious heterogeneity (Native Americans, slaves of African ancestry, and Europeans not of Anglosaxon descent) of the new nation's peoples? Their answer was an absolute denial of diversity, but yet they advocated a policy of assimilation – an attempt to mute all differences and cultural identities. That obviously did not work hence, the current debate.

In my search for the importance of diversity in the student body,

I will shun the fear of Plato and embrace the Aristotelian concept of the importance of diversity. Higher education can and does expose students to racial and ethnic diversity and this may be experienced in a number of ways. One such way is "structural diversity" which refers to the number of students from the various racial and ethnic backgrounds. Increasing the number of non-whites on the campus creates an opportunity for productive social interaction. Social interaction provides the opportunity for one on one, and group contacts among the members of the student body. This is particularly important for shaping the social dynamics in the students' post college life in the society. The greater the number the better it is for student learning experiences. Narrow structural diversity does not help significantly and may only amount to tokenism which does not change the views of students but may perpetuate them during college and after.

Embracing diversity brings with it the positive values of integration and human fellowship. However, it also has the potential to bring conflict: "The embracing of the multiple will mean conflict, disagreement about the good and the bad, the just and the unjust. It will mean conflict between owners, between families, and between lovers..." (Saxonhouse, 1992, p. 235) However, the positive effects far outweigh the negative effects on human relationship. Hurtado (1999) avers the view that research suggests that campuses that increase their racial and ethnic enrollments can significantly improve the college expectation of historically underrepresented groups. Moreover, attaining a diverse student body and hiring diverse faculty result in significantly more opportunities for all students to learn how to deal with others from different cultural backgrounds after college.

The social interaction among students is the social antidote for racism and prejudice which is still deeply rooted in many aspects of the American society and psyche. We are well aware that the racial conflicts on campuses are not isolated incidences but are reflections, or symptomatic of the society. Still the goals of a democratic pluralistic society that appreciates difference must be cultivated for the continued existence of the nation. With the judicial demise of remedial affirmative action, there is the risk of perpetuating inequities in the education of minorities, and creating homogenous campuses which can only widen and deepen the racial divide.

Guarasci and Cornwell (1997) have lamented that even more alarming, almost forty years after the landmark case of *Brown vs. Board of Education* (1954) Supreme Court decision, the overwhelming majority of African American children attend virtually segregated schools. For example, in Illinois, New York, Michigan, California, New Jersey and Maryland the percentage of black children virtually segregated schools ranges from 72 percent in Maryland up to 83 percent in Illinois. In New York, the most liberal state in many social policies, 81 percent of all African American children attend virtually segregated schools. Not surprisingly, 86 percent of all white suburban children attend virtually segregated schools. In 1990, New York City schools came close to resembling Mississippi schools in 1960 (p. 6). This progeny of Jim Crow education must be eliminated from the educational system or it will make the American society a nation of strangers from the same country because the students from these various schools when they enter the work place will be disconnected from each other as virtual strangers are. A conscious effort to create diversity in the student body is imperative to counter this development.

I would be remissed not to advocate student body structural diversity without advocating the same for college faculty. The commitment to faculty diversity cannot be any less intensive than that for the student body. Hurtado (1999) gives five reasons why this must be pursued: first, faculty of color is able to provide support that benefits students from their particular groups. Students of color are likely to seek out faculty "who are like them" and whom they believe will understand them and the experiences that they are going through as students, greatly reducing their feelings of loneliness, alienation, and isolation as students of color. Second, a diverse faculty and staff serve as important representatives of the commitment that the institution has to issues of diversity. Third, a more diverse faculty and staff serve to create a more comfortable environment for faculty and staff as well. The stresses, strains, and challenges experienced by students at predominantly white institutions are also experienced by members of the faculty and staff. Fourth, a diverse faculty and staff bring more voices and more diverse perspectives "to what is taught, how it is taught, and why it is important to learn, which are contributions that are vital to the institution. Fifth, a diverse faculty and staff reflect one measure of institutional success for an educational institution in a pluralistic society" (p. 57). These five points which Hurtado (1999) has put forward are crucially important if the purpose of diversity is to succeed. To do otherwise would belie and belittle the motive of the institution. Students are better led by example than by precepts. The faculty must practice what it preaches.

I am supported in this view by Guarasci and Cornwell (1997) who express the view that in multicentric education, the faculty are critical role models. For this reason the faculty cannot ask students to achieve what they themselves are incapable of achieving: to recognize the value of diversity and demonstrate the ability to negotiate differences successfully. Faculty cannot expect to separate and isolate themselves from the very thing which they advocate for the student body. If they do, then they are reneging on their obligation to teach students that learning liberates us from isolation and frees us to engage with the world and not just live in it. If the faculty fails to demonstrate that learning is about participation in the great conversation and about the ability to enlarge that discourse continually, they will fail the students immensely. They will be simply teaching their students that learning is only about institutional politics and not about the expansion of human ability to negotiate difference in a pluralistic democratic society.

Apart from formal composite diversity, *informal events intra-action* also plays an important role in breaking down the barriers of racism and prejudice and expands students learning experiences during their undergraduate years. Social intra-action diversity may occur in the classroom but the majority of them take place outside of the classroom through informal discussion, interaction in the halls of residence, campus events and social activities at fetes, and bars. The observations of culturally significant persons and events on the campuses will also facilitate diversity appreciate. Discussing the cultural and political struggle of the different groups on these occasions can facilitate meaningful social change. However, informal social interactions can also be structured and this is important for the purpose of discussing a wide range of social issues such as relations between White and Black people, gender issues among men, women and gays, religion, international events in Europe, Africa, and the Middle-East. Diversity in the formal and informal life on campus for both faculty and student body is imperative for the continued benefits of the democratic system to be enjoyed by all and sundry.

DIVERSITY, COGNITIVE DEVELOPMENT AND PERSONALITY

The students in undergraduate programs at colleges and universities are in their late adolescence/early adulthood. They are still impressionable and are accommodating and more likely to accept persons who are different. Interaction at this stage with persons from different cultural background will create invaluable positive learning experiences for them that will shape the future of the American society for the better. This line of reasoning is supported by Erikson (1950). His findings show that the adolescent mind is essentially of the *moratorium*, a psycho-social stage between childhood and adulthood, and between the morality learned by the child, and the ethics to be developed by the adult. It is an ideological mind – and, indeed, it is the ideological outlook of a society that speaks most clearly to the adolescent who is eager to be affirmed by his peers, and is ready to be confirmed by rituals, creeds, and programs which at the same time define what is evil, uncanny, and inimical. In searching for the social values which guide identity, one therefore confronts the problem of ideology and aristocracy, both in their widest possible sense.

At this transitional stage young persons are faced with new situations, especially those who grew up and attended school in a homogenous environment. They will have to construct a new understanding of people of different cultural background. Interaction with persons who have different perspectives will challenge their own assumptions about people whom they only know through literature or from a distance. Being confronted with new multiple perspectives, young adults and adults will be obliged to discuss and argue the salience of traditional attitudes and approaches. They will *a fortiori* be required to think and rethink their point of views on matters such as racism, prejudice, and cultural differences. They will be forced to become intimately and emotionally involved with the persons with whom they interact. These encounters are important for individual moral and spiritual development in a multicultural society. This is the posture that is consistent with the flourishing human beings in a pluralistic democracy. I concur with the opinion of Guarasci & Cornwell (1997) that:

> The face-to-face intergroup dialogues are a unique feature of the IGRCC program. They represent an opportunity for people from different backgrounds and cultural identities to learn about each other's histories and experiences, to challenge stereotypes and misinformation, and to address issues of intergroup and intragroup conflict and community building in constructive ways (pp. 142-143).

The pertinent point here is to inculcate in young students that diversity is not averse to unity; diversity when properly directed is not divisive but enriches a culture and a democracy. At any rate, given the growing cultural heterogeneity of the United States population with the significant increases in the Latino population, it is impossible to turn back the hand of time to the pre-Socratic-Platonic philosophy that diversity is to be avoided, as shown by Saxonhouse (1992).

The position which I am advocating here is that students' entry into the universities' undergraduate program is a convenient point for philosophical, political, and cultural intervention. This is the point which Erikson's (1950) theory of personality identity makes so profoundly. I have further support for this line of reasoning in the cognitive development theory of Jean Piaget. This theory examines the development of thinking patterns from birth to adulthood. For Piaget, learning is an active process which is related to the individuals' interaction with the environment. According to Huitt and Hammel (2003), Piaget described two processes used by the individual in his/her attempt to adapt: assimilation and accommodation. Both of these reflexes control behavior throughout life as the person increasingly adapts to the environment in a more complex manner. Assimilation is the process of using or transforming the environment so that it can be placed in preexisting cognitive structures. Accommodation is the process of changing cognitive structures in order to accept something from the environment. Both processes are used simultaneously and alternately throughout life.

Furthermore, Piaget discovered that students learn through experience by interacting with their environment. Conversely, the type of knowledge that the students acquire will depend on the type of exposure which he/she receives. The point that I wish to affirm here is that at this stage of development, the acquisition of new knowledge about people who are different is crucially important for the development of new mental constructs and structures through social interaction. Students must be given the opportunity to discuss their present beliefs and concepts about racism, prejudice, culture, democracy, and sexism. Small and large group discussions would facilitate this process.

Piaget proposes four major stages of cognitive development: the sensorimotor period, preoperational thought, concrete operations, and formal operations (in Huitt & Hummel, 2003). I am concerned with the last period because this is on point with the line of reasoning that I have taken here with regards to adolescent development. Accordingly, persons who reach the formal operation stage are capable of thinking logically and abstractly. They can also reason theoretically. Piaget considered this the ultimate stage of development, and stated that although the children will still have to revise their knowledge base, their way of thinking was as powerful as it would get (Silverthorn, 1999).

The theory of the pre-Socratic thinkers and Plato would not help to facilitate an appreciation for diversity in a pluralistic democracy. As a matter of fact, pluralism is alien to Socratic and Platonic way of thinking. The theories of Aristotle, Erikson, and Piaget speak to the possibility of diversity and pluralistic democracy working together for the creation of an equitable society. The circumstances that are conducive to its workability are diverse others and diverse perspectives, seen on an equal footing building a civic community together. I am persuaded that these conditions will create the frame of mind that students will need to be citizens and leaders in a democracy that is increasingly heterogeneous. Students will develop empathy for differences and commonalities between social groups and will strive to contain them in the crucible of the American dream if they are given positive direction.

DIVERSITY ON TRIAL AT THE BAR: COUNSELOR STATE YOUR CASE

I have mentioned above the opinion of Justice Lewis Powell in the *Bakke's case* and his support for diversity in the student body of colleges and universities that may be a government compellable interest in certain circumstances. However, it must be remembered that racial and ethnic distinctions of any sort are inherently suspect and thus call for the most exacting judicial examination. The judiciary has taken this position because the use of race to achieve diversity apparently undercuts the ultimate goals of the Fourteenth Amendment, that is, the end of racially motivated state action. However, Justice Powell's conception of race as a "plus" factor would allow race to be a potential factor in admission decision-making of colleges and universities.

Any admissions program which gives consideration to racial and/or ethnic factors must satisfy judicial strict scrutiny. Two tests are applicable: 1) Does the racial classification serve a compelling government interest, and 2) is it narrowly tailored to the achievement of that goal? This is the test for efficacious constitutional consistency with the equal protection clause of the Fourteenth Amendment as laid down by the Supreme Court in the opinion of Justice Powell in the *Bakke's* case. This principle was challenged in the case of *Cheryl J. Hopwood, et al v. The University of Texas* (1996). Here Blacks and Mexicans were given preferential treatment for admission to the University of Texas Law School on the basis of race. They were placed in lowered categories to allow the Law School to admit more of them. The same consideration was not given to white applicants. Cheryl Hopwood, Douglas Carvell, Kenneth Elliott, and David Rogers who were the plaintiffs, applied for admissions to the Law School in 1992 and were rejected, although they had better qualifications than some of the Blacks and Mexicans who were admitted. Here the plaintiffs sued primarily under the Equal Protection Clause of the Fourteen Amendment and they also claimed derivative statutory violations of 42 U.S.C. 1981 and 1983 and of Title VI of the Civil Rights Act of 1964, 42 U.S.C 2000d. The plaintiffs' central claim is that they were subjected to unconstitutional racial discrimination by the law school's evaluation of their admission applications. They sought injunctive and declaratory relief, compensatory, and punitive damages.

It is trite law that the Fourteenth Amendment, by its terms, guaranteed individual rights, that is, rights which the individual has over against the administrative bodies and/or agencies of the state and/or the federal government. It is equally certain that Title VI of the Civil Rights Act, 1964 is pellucid in its requirements that no agency which is funded by government can or that receives government contracts is permitted to practice racial preference. The universities and colleges of the United States that are government agencies or funded by government fall within the purview of this the legislation, and are accordingly forbidden to practice racial preference. Any argument to the contrary would rest on very shaky grounds indeed, save and except that such an argument could convincingly demonstrate that there are compelling remedial and non-remedial justifications for the practice of racial preference which would attenuate the effect of the legislation.

Generally, as the law now stands, racial preference is permissible for remedial purposes, that is, to cure the residual effect of racism which was previously practiced by the particular institutions which had given the preference. However, Justice Powell had provided in his separate opinion in the *Bakke* case the original impetus for recognizing diversity as a compelling state interest in higher education as non-remedial racial preference which is permissible in some situations. It was with this view in mind that the court below " approved of the non-remedial goal of having a diverse student body. The reasoning being that obtaining the educational benefits that flow from a racially and ethnically diverse student body remains a sufficiently compelling interest to support the use of racial classifications" (p. 7).

The plaintiffs averred that Supreme Court precedents do not support the view that diversity is a compelling governmental interest. In fact they argued that only the remedial use of race is a government compelling interest. Furthermore, the court below had misapplied Justice Powell's principles because the Law School program that is being challenged used race as a strong determinant rather than a mere "plus" factor and in any case, the preference is not narrowly tailored to achieve any compelling interest. The defendants countered the claimant's submissions by stating that Justice Powell's formulation is the law. The law is therefore binding on the courts and it must be followed in the context of higher education, barring some good and sufficient reason(s) that warrants the courts' departure from it.

The Court of Appeal for the Fifth Circuit roundly rejected the defendant's argument and found in favor of the plaintiffs. The Court held that any consideration of race or ethnicity by the law school for the purpose of achieving a diverse student body is not a compelling interest under the Fourteenth Amendment. Justice Powell's argument in *Bakke's Case* garnered only his own vote and has never represented the view of the majority of the Court in *Bakke's Case* or any other case. Moreover, subsequent Supreme Court decisions regarding education state that non-remedial state interest will never justify racial classifications. Finally, the classification of persons on the basis of race for the purpose of diversity frustrates, rather than facilitates, the goals of equal protection.

The learned Mr. Justice Smith further opined that Justice Powell's opinion in *Bakke* was not a binding precedent on the issue and that four Justices implicitly rejected Justice Powell's position. With the greatest respect for the opinion of the learned judge, I beg to differ. It would seem that the learned judge unwittingly misdirected himself on the position of the case and what it decided. It is clear that the decision went against racial preference but it cannot be stated categorically or absolutely that race consideration can never be a compelling interest. Justice Powell said it may be a "plus" factor in some situations; "a plan like the "Harvard plan" ... is constitutional under our approach..." The thrust of the decision was not against this position. Race may be considered providing that it is not race *per se*, that race is not the only factor or the overriding factor in making admission decisions.

The United States 11th Circuit Court in the case of *Johnson v. Board of Regents of the University of Georgia* (2001) held the view that Justice Powell's opinion had only persuasive value but was not binding on the issue before the Court and that the Supreme Court may eventually adopt Justice Powell's opinion as binding, but for present purposes it is not.. The position taken by the Courts of Appeal for Fifth and Eleventh Circuit Courts is that Justice Powell's opinion is *orbiter dicta* (things said by the way) and therefore is not part of the *ratio decidendi* (the principle on which the decision is based). Further on the Judge stated that in that discussion, Justice Powell endorsed the constitutionality of the Harvard Plan, a "flexible" admissions' program which treats race as one factor among many that may be considered in making admission decisions. But Justice Powell also determined that the University's rigid quota system was not narrowly tailored. A university's interest in diversity is compelling in the context of a university's admission program, in which ethnic diversity is only one element in a range of factors a university properly may consider in attaining the goal of a heterogeneous student body. The learned Judge, with respect, had apparently contradicted himself. Be that as it may, three salient points stand out here: 1) that Justice Powell's opinion may one day become binding law; 2) race consideration is not absolutely proscribed providing that it is one among many factors; 3) that race is compelling interest for remedial and non-remedial purposes providing that it can stand up to strict judicial scrutiny as being narrowly tailored to the situation.

The Court in *Gratz Et Al v. Bollinger Et Al* (2000) unlike the Courts in *Hopwood's case* and *Johnson's case* held that under the fourth principle in Justice Powell's opinion in *Bakke's case*, diversity constitutes a government compelling interest in relation to education for the purpose of making admission decisions. However, this decision was not followed in *Grutter v. Bollinger* Et Al (2001) which held that diversity was not a compelling government interest. It is also interesting to note that the two decisions were given in the same district court.

The case of *Smith Et Al v. The University of Washington Law School* (2000) is very instructive for the position which I have taken here and is on all fours with it. Here Katuria Smith was denied admission in 1994, but attended another law school and obtained her law degree. In 1997 Smith filed a civil suit against the Law School alleging illegal discrimination against Caucasians and others on the basis of their race, which resulted in their being denied admission. The District Court designated two questions of public interest for the Court of Appeal to determine: "(1) whether educational diversity is a compelling government interest that meets the requirement of 'strict scrutiny' for race conscious measures under the Fourteenth Amendment to the United States Constitution; and (2) whether race may be considered only for remedial purposes" (p. 6) The District Court denied Smith's application. The District Court found the *Bakke's case* was a proper precedent for its decision and was binding on it because race could be used as a factor in educational admission decisions, even where that was not done for remedial purposes. Smith appealed to the Court of Appeal for the Ninth Circuit. In the opinion of Justice Fernandez the District Court decision "faithfully followed Justice Powell's opinion in *Regents of the University of California v. Bakke* (1978).

Justice Fernandez further stated that Justice Powell's fourth principle which makes diversity a compelling interest was a matter that could be properly considered by the defendants. The fourth principle does not suffer from the same disability as the third principle which is only available for remedial purposes. Although from the judgment in *Bakke's Case* there may appear to be some uncertainty with some of the judges, their position on the fourth principle is not obfuscated by any vacillation in their otherwise pellucid position. The Judge stated that it appears that the Justices would simply give more weight to the race factor than would the fourth principle, but they, it seems clear, would not have eschewed the use of a plus factor in a program that also looked to other considerations. Indeed, they saw nothing unconstitutional about a diversity based program that at least purported to take all kinds of special characteristics and talents, including race, into account, and they opined that a program of that sort is certainly constitutional. In other words, they agreed with the fourth principle's conclusion that a program of that type was constitutional.

I am firmly of the view that any attempt, legislation apart, to belittle the Supreme Court decision in *Bakke* should be stoutly resisted. I am well aware that the weight of most of the decisions subsequent to *Bakke* appears to support non-racial, not-ethnic consideration contrary to the submissions which I have made herein. I am also painfully aware that since the decision in *Bakke's Case* the courts have a tendency to look upon race conscious decisions with disdain, but the courts have refrained and, if I may say so, without having to exert much effort, from deciding that *Bakke's Case* is bad law. This is good because I suspect that the Supreme Court will one day rule in favor of the decision of *Bakke's Case* decision and so put this aspect of the controversy to rest. I am therefore inclined to hold opinion with Justice Fernandez when he said it followed ineluctably that the Fourteenth Amendment permits universities admissions' programs which consider race for other than remedial purposes, such as educational diversity as a compelling governmental interest that meets the demands of strict scrutiny of race-conscious measures.

We must pay the greatest respect to the Fourteenth Amendment to the Constitution of the United States and give to it a proper and true construction, but it would be foolhardy to destroy affirmative action altogether. So long as there are deficiencies in the elementary and secondary education of minority peoples, there will be the need for affirmation as a remedy for them and so long as the society of the United States is a heterogeneous society there will be a need for diversity in the student body of colleges and universities. This proposition is supported by the findings of Cohen and Sterba (2003) when they expressed the view that the court will be aware of the impact of shutting down affirmative action programs in education resulting from Proposition 209 and various lower court decisions. In 1996, before Proposition 209 took effect in California, there were 89 Hispanic Americans, 43 African Americans, and 10 American Indians enrolled as first-year students at the top three University of California law schools. In 1997, these numbers fell to 59, 16, and 4, respectively. That year saw only one African American enrolled in the freshman law class at Berkeley, where there had been 20 enrolled in the first-year class the year before. At the University of Texas at Austin, whose admissions system was challenged in *Hopwood*, the percentage of African American law students entering dropped from 5.8 percent (29 students) in 1996 to 0.9 percent (6 students) in 1997. American Indian enrollment at the law school dropped from 1.2 percent (6 students) in 1996 to 0.2 percent (1 student) in 1997. Hispanic enrollment dropped from 9.2 percent (46 students) in 1996 to 6.7 percent (31 students) in 1997.

The above statistics which were produced by Cohen and Sterba (2003) clearly show that every time there is a ruling against affirmative action, there is a corresponding drop in the enrolment of students from minority peoples. This is an alarming concern which does not auger well for the future of minority peoples in education, nor for their social and economic standing in the society. There is ample evidence that minority peoples who have had the benefit of affirmative action programs live successful lives after their graduation. This proposition is also supported by the findings of Cohen and Sterba (2003) and they find it particularly disturbing that the criteria for admission that are being used once diversity affirmative action was declared illegal have the effect of significantly limiting minority enrollment.

Furthermore the criteria are so tenuously related to the sort of graduates these educational institutions ultimately hope to produce that, for example, LSAT scores at the University of Pennsylvania law school have only had a 14 percent correlation with students' first-year grades. Moreover, they do not correlate at all with conventional success in the profession, as measured in terms of income, self-reported satisfaction, and service contributions. Moreover, almost all Michigan Law School minority graduates who pass a bar exam go on to have careers that are successful by these conventional measures, something that would not have happened for many of them but for affirmative action.

The evidence presented by Cohen and Sterba (2003) is pellucid and irresistible that affirmative action whether remedial and/or related to diversity is crucially important for the continued well-being of African Americans and other minorities in particular and the American society in general. The inescapable fact is that affirmative action whether remedial or non-remedial is inextricably connected to minority education, social, and political advancement. The inexorable fact also is that we cannot continue to provide African Americans and other minority groups with a conveyor belt education. It will backfire on the society eventually. It would therefore serve the society well, to accept diversity in the student bodies of colleges and universities as a governmental compelling interest for continued prosperity in the future.

CONCLUSION

Affirmative action has served the purpose of assuaging some aspects of racism and the vestiges of racism that exist in American's public education system. It has neither remedied nor cured racism, but it has helped to ameliorate the impact of racism and discrimination in the education of African Americans and other minority peoples. With the passing of the Fourteenth Amendment to the Constitution of the United States, and the Civil Rights Act of 1964, and several other statutes, racism as a governmental practice or an institution has been legally jettisoned. However, both racism and *de facto* segregation still persist in America's education system where most African American children attend elementary and secondary schools that are predominantly Black while White Americans attend schools that are predominantly White (Gurasci & Cornwell, 1997). Consequently many inequities still prevail in the educational system. African Americans and other minority peoples still suffer from gaps and deficiencies in their education. In the circumstances, diversity must perforce be a governmental compellable interest as one of the factors which institutions in higher education should take into account at admissions. Failing this, the society may end up having most of its colleges and universities with a homogenous student population who may have difficulty functioning in America's heterogeneous society in their post college life. It is therefore imperative that we shun Plato's fear of diversity and embrace Aristotle's love of diversity (Saxonhouse, 1992). I believe that this is an area that should be unquestionably protected on which government and the judiciary should be extremely reticent to tread.

CHAPTER FIVE

Human Rights Education in a Multicultural Society

> A pedagogy of liberation is one that is necessarily partial and incomplete, one that has no final answers. It is always in the making, part of an ongoing struggle for critical understanding, emancipatory forms of solidarity, and the reconstitution of democratic public life (MacLaren, 1995, p.57).

In the previous chapter I have made out a case for diversity as a non-remedial affirmative action that is a government compellable interest to demonstrate the importance of providing Blacks, who have deficiencies in their education with a fighting chance to improve their social, economic, and political standing in the society. In this chapter I state a case for education as a human right that should be enshrined in the constitution because it is so fundamental to the enjoyment of the good life. Non-idiotic education is a lifelong pilgrimage to the good life upon which every child and every adult who is able to should embark. It is therefore crucially important that education be available for all persons from the primary to the tertiary level. Given that some persons are born in adverse economic and social circumstances it is incumbent upon all governments to ensure that education is available to all citizens so that every person is given an opportunity to actualize his/her potential. Education is the guardian of democracy and liberty, the instrumentality for liberation from every form of domination and oppression. Therefore education is a government compellable interest. It is in this regard then, that I discuss the importance of human rights education and its connection to social justice education. I believe that human rights and social justice complement each other and should be teamed together. While human rights education seeks to call all persons to treat the rights and the liberty of others with respect and dignity, social justice education challenges the ills in society – classism, sexism, heterosexism, racism – which denigrate the human rights and dignity of oppressed peoples. This is education for freedom – a critical redemptive pedagogy.

HUMAN RIGHTS AND SOCIAL JUSTICE

Following the end of the Second World War, the United Nations hurriedly put in place the Human Rights Declaration of 1948 with the view of protecting people from the atrocities that necessitated the war in the first place. The objective of the United Nations is to ensure that crimes against humanity - genocide, ethnocide – are eradicated. While I accept that the Human Rights Declaration has humanized the world to a certain extent, it still has not been able to control the worst excesses of humankind's propensity for abuse and cruelty to their weaker brothers and sisters. We have witnessed the genocides in Eastern Europe, Rwanda and recently in the Darfur Region. These tragic events are powerful reminders of the crucial importance of the protection of humans which must be kept under constant surveillance. I believe an education in human rights and social justice can go a long way in preventing human kind's worse excesses as well as the everyday oppression with which ordinary people are forced to live. Human rights challenge the moral consciences of men and women in the society on the ground that we are our brother's/sister's keeper and we are accountable to each other for the wrongs which we commit against the least of them. For Puntambekar (in Spring, 2000), the purpose of human rights was to free the spiritual side of humans. He argued, " the ordinary condition of man (sic) is not his ultimate being. He has in him a deeper self, call it soul or spirit. In each being dwells a light and inspiration which no power can extinguish, which is benign and tolerant, and which is the real man" (p.15).

The Human Rights Declaration would have been less than magnanimous if it had not enshrined in its proclamation the right to education. The position is stated in Article 26 of the Universal Declaration of Human Rights.

> Everyone has the right to education. Education shall be free, at least in the elementary and fundamental stages. Elementary education shall be compulsory. Technical and professional education shall be made generally available and higher education shall be equally accessible to all on the basis of merit.

The right to education is crucially important because it is through education that people will be made aware of their rights as citizens. And I dare say that the right to an education within a democratic state that promotes individual freedom as oppose to an authoritarian state, imposes a moral duty upon the state to provide a sound education for all of its peoples regardless of sex, race, origin. While I do not definitively eschew other political models, I believe that a liberal education is the crucible of a good democracy and that a good democracy has the greater potential for human flourishing.

The Article requires that primary and secondary education be 'free' to all children and that tertiary education be available to all on the basis of merit. Education shall be directed to the full development of the human personality and to the strengthening of respect for human rights and fundamental freedoms. It shall promote understanding, tolerance and friendship among all nations, racial or religious groups, and shall further the activities of the United Nations for the maintenance of peace. Parents have a prior right to choose the kind of education that shall be given to their children. The emphasis here is on the important role that education plays in promoting understanding, tolerance, and friendship among the various families of the world in spite of their inherent differences. Education can be a powerful liberating and uniting force which breaks down the barriers of ignorance for the advancement of humanity and our cultural and political development. I believe, as I have argued above, that Africans in the Diaspora who have suffered from the iniquitous systems of colonialism and slavery, and who continue to suffer from pernicious White racism are at a decided disadvantage educationally. This retardation in educational exposure has an exponential negative effect in the society manifested in low income, drug abuse, and Black cultural *nihilism*. It follows inexorably against this background that there is an imperative need for a critical redemptive education for the healing of Black communities. For these reasons education must be made a fundamental right that is most deeply entrenched in the constitution just as it is in the Human Rights Convention.

THE RIGHT TO EDUCATION: WHAT RIGHT?

The right to education then, falls within the purview of Human Rights. The existence of this right naturally imposes a duty on the state to provide the facilities for education, especially given that it is the only entity which can provide mass education to remedy the inequalities which exist within a democratic state. Spring (1999) is of the view that there are different classifications of human rights including claim rights, liberty rights, power rights and immunity rights. He sees human rights as claimed rights. By claim rights he means rights that impose duties on society and government to ensure that people have the ability to exercise those rights. In contrast, liberty rights provide the right to do something without the obligation of ensuring that a person can actually exercise that right.

The nicety of the averment apart, this is a very intricate distinction which Spring (1999) is making here and one that is very cogent. When this line of reasoning is applied to the fundamental rights of the constitution it becomes very potent. For instance, the fundament rights and freedom of conscience and religion as set out in the constitution do not place a moral duty on the government. The government is not required to put any structures in place to protect this right, but it will avoid passing laws that infringe that right. Therefore these rights may be construed as liberty rights, and may as such reduce the weight of their high importance. Spring (2000) elucidates the matter further where he explains that liberty rights only require that individuals and government do not interfere with the exercise of the liberty. For instance, the right to an education as a liberty right guarantees that individuals will not be interfered with as they pursue an education for themselves or their children. However, it does not guarantee that a person or child can actually receive an education. On the other hand, the right to an education, as a claim right places a duty on society and government to ensure that every person can exercise that right.

As a liberty right, the right to an education places no burden on society or government to ensure that all persons, regardless of their race, color or creed receive an education that is non-idiotic. It follows then that if citizens are taught that the right to an education is a claim right they will come to realize that they have a duty to ensure that it is enshrined as a fundamental constitutional right. So entrenched in the constitution it will be immune to the ordinary legislative process of Parliament/Congress. An entrenched right to a non-idiotic education will insulate education from both legislative and administrative interference. This is no doubt the line of reasoning that can be gleaned from Spring (2000).

It follows then, that since human rights proclaim that everyone has the right to education and that everyone should have free access to education, the burden is placed squarely on the shoulders of the government to provide that education by putting the necessary infrastructures in place. If the government does not then the people, the populace has the right to protest and to impeach it.

The principles which are enunciated in Article 26 are enshrined in the American constitution, and its general laws in relation to education. Both the Human Rights Convention and the Rights of the Child Convention place the burden of ensuring that education is available at all levels on the government (State Parties) and both may be reasonably construed as creating claim rights to education.

But then, I must posit the question which leaps to mind. That is, whether government is the best provider of education, or an education that is liberating. I must also ask whether the education provided should be apolitical and non-indoctrinating. I am inclined to believe that both questions should be answered in the affirmative, but that would be to fly in the face of history. History shows that this has not been the case because governments have from time immemorial used education as a means of indoctrinating its youths, to wring obedience out of its people. Government sponsored education is far from liberating. Traditional education does not protect human rights. The history of education reveals that government schools are primarily used for indoctrinating the younger generation into the religious beliefs and other social practices of the state to develop a sense of loyalty to the political group or nation.

Spring (2000) further shared the contention as put by Kandel and I am inclined to hold opinion with him (Kandel) that education has always been heavily skewed in the promotion of the values of the elites to the detriment of the poor. Further, education has often been used to promote Eurocentric values to the detriment of Africentric values. Kandel (in Spring, 2000) argues that the indoctrinating function of education was accompanied by unequal educational opportunities which contributed to the separation of social classes. Inequality of education, he contends, was reinforced by the lack of awareness by the poor of the possibilities of using education to advance in the social system. Kandel states: "One of the tragic results of the traditional organization of education into two systems – one for the masses and the other for a select group – is that, even when equality of educational opportunity is provided, certain social and economic classes feel that the opportunities are not intended for them" (p. 17).

It is the duty of the government to facilitate the education of its people in accordance with Article 28 of United Nations Convention on the Rights of the Child:

1. States Parties recognize the right of the child to education, and with a view to achieving this right progressively and on the basis of equal opportunity, they shall, in particular:

(a) Make primary education compulsory and available free to all;

(b) Encourage the development of different forms of secondary education, including general and vocational education, make them available and accessible to every child, and take appropriate measures such as the introduction of free education and offering financial assistance in case of need;

(c) Make higher education accessible to all on the basis of capacity by every appropriate means;

(d) Make educational and vocational information and guidance available and accessible to all children;

(e) Take measures to encourage regular attendance at schools and the reduction of drop-out rates.

2. States Parties shall take all appropriate measures to ensure that school discipline is administered in a manner consistent with the child's human dignity and in conformity with the present Convention.

3. States Parties shall promote and encourage international co-operation in matters relating to education, in particular with a view to contributing to the elimination of ignorance and illiteracy throughout the world and facilitating access to scientific and technical knowledge and modern teaching

methods. In this regard, particular account shall be taken
of the needs of developing countries.

On the basis of the foregoing, it is therefore imperative that education
be seen as a claim right because this creates "duties for individuals and
government. Claim rights require all people to protect human rights
in contrast to liberty rights which require only passive non-interference
in the liberty of others" (Spring 1999, p. 161). Providing that education
is seen as a claim right, the government will be compelled to provide
money, staff, materials and buildings for educational faculties to
function "in particular with a view to contributing to the elimination
of ignorance and illiteracy throughout the world and facilitating access
to scientific and technical knowledge and modern teaching methods. In
this regard, particular account shall be taken of the needs of developing
countries" (Rights of the Child, Article 28(3). This article is reiterated
here for its emphasis.

If the burden of providing adequate and proper education falls on
the shoulders of the government, then we are faced with the intrinsic
problem that education will be tailored to suit the wishes of the
government, that is, training students for obedience to the political
directorate. Traditionally, education is normally the yard stick that is
used to determine a person's place in society and one of its fundamental
objectives is to teach people to accept the places to which they have been
assigned. The censorship of literature and the manipulation of historical
instructions are justified as the means of creating social harmony. In
addition, the education of rulers is considered the key to assuring that
wisdom rules society. (Spring 1999) This traditional notion of the
role of education in society is contrary to the ideal education for the
child which is envisioned by the United Nation's Convention. Article
28 is supported by Article 29 as it seeks to establish and set forth the
education of the child as an individual with a personality and talents
that are to be developed for his/her good in particular and the state
in general. States Parties agree that the education of the child shall be
directed to:

a. The development of the child's personality, talents and mental and physical abilities to their fullest potential;

b. The development of respect for human rights and fundamental freedoms, and for the principles enshrined in the Charter of the United Nations;

c. The development of respect for the child's parents, his or her own cultural identity, language and values, for the national values of the country in which the child is living; the country from which he or she may originate, and for civilizations different from his or her own;

d. The preparation of the child for responsible life in a free society, in the spirit of understanding, peace, tolerance, equality of sexes, and friendship among all peoples, ethnic, national and religious groups and persons of indigenous origin;

e. The development of respect for the natural environment.

Evidently, the intention is that education should be focused on the development of the talents of the individual for the individual's own advancement as a social being, not for the ulterior objective of the political machinery. However, I am fully cognizant that this is easier said than done and this is why even greater effort must be made to protect the rights of citizens to a non-idiotic education. Political regimes frequently thrive on its ability (right) to control and manipulate those over whom they rule to achieve their (the regime's) own objectives. This of course, is frequently to the detriment of the particular talents and abilities of the individual. This is neither a constructive nor progressive use of political power, as it bears the mark of political arrogance and thuggery. These qualities progressive societies should shun.

EDUCATION, AND PHILOSOPHY
AND EDUCATION

The idea that a child is endowed with a right to education is alien to the Socratic tradition because this inculcates individualism which is facilitated by a democratic state. Individualism, according to Socrates, breeds irrational emotions, especially physical emotions such as sexual desires which are to be controlled or shunned, so that the person can live a life of the mind as dictated by rulers who are philosopher-kings. Western educational systems are underpinned by this Socratic or Platonic philosophy, hence the traditional structures of the schools. Education, according to Socrates, is for schooling in acceptable social behavior that each individual can take his/her right place in the society. If one is born to be an artisan, then he/she must be the best possible artisan. The same line of reasoning is applicable to all spheres of employment in life. This notion of education is very similar to the caste system that is found in traditional Hindu society. Peoples' position in the pecking social order is fixed for life – there is no social mobility, neither upward nor downward. This system is cast in iron so to speak. One can attempt to move out of it with grave social and physical peril.

Therefore, the educational system in *The Republic* is designed to control the individual by teaching myths and censored literature, by teaching history lessons made "useful" to goals of the state, and by teaching that the highest ideal is for individuals to suppress their physical desires in the service of the good. The myths, fables, and history lessons are directed at shaping the content of the mind and building the right ideals (Spring 1999). The Socratic philosophy that the role of the educational system is for the maintenance of the stability of the social class system, to fit people in their places, appears to be consistent with totalitarian leadership as evidenced in the former Soviet Union. The 1936 Soviet Constitution provided the right to free universal education to all citizens. However, individual liberties, particularly liberty of conscience, publication, association, and ultimately, the formation of political parties were not necessary rights in the Soviet Union. These liberties were no longer necessary in a socialist state.

Evidently, the placing of such onerous restraints on fundamental rights and freedoms do not encourage the flourishing of human rights in any system. The democratic system seems to be predisposed to the actualization of human rights for all individuals. Of course, this is not to say that there are no drawbacks in the democratic system. The fundamental rights and freedoms which are very similar to human rights are enshrined in most if not all democratic constitutions which place them in a position of preeminence in a country's laws. These are heavily entrenched in the constitutions and cannot be amended through the ordinary legislative process. However, education in a democratic state when it is provided by the government seems to suffer from similar defects as in the totalitarian state. Most government schools are coercive institutions. Compulsory education laws require children to attend school, and governments mandate what will be taught to students. Students are coerced into learning particular behaviors, knowledge, and values through a system of reward and punishments that includes academic grades, grades for behavior, and the granting of credentials (Spring 1994).

The democratic society is obliged to respect the human rights of the students as set out in the Human Rights Convention and the Rights of the Child Convention because the country is a signatory to them and may have even enacted them in their domestic laws. Therefore, it must limit the coercive force of the school in terms of influencing the future of the students. In an authoritarian state the rulers determine the content of education because the state has arrogated to itself the right of being the only entity that knows what is good for the citizens. According to Socrates, the ideal state is ruled by philosopher-kings who are selected because they are born with intellectual abilities that can be educated to know the good. This argument gives important power to the rulers. The state that advocates such claims that only the rulers have access to the truth provides a justification for totalitarianism (Spring 1994).

The goal of education therefore is to produce and to educate philosopher-kings to control the masses, to keep their wayward desires for the transient physical things in check. On the other hand, in the democratic states, the majority of the voters determine the content of education through the mandate which they have given to the ruling party in the general election. The democratic system makes allowance for private educational institutions however, the government may still have a measure of control in terms of accreditation and subsidy.

I do not subscribe to the notion that education should prepare citizens to fit into the social structure. I believe education should facilitate freedom of thought, freedom of expression and conscience. Education therefore, must create critical thinking faculties in citizens, place great premium on discussion and dissent. This can be better achieved in the democratic political structure. I am inclined to hold opinion with John Dewey that "...critical thinking is necessary for the survival of a democratic society and a democratic society is necessary for the exercise of this form of critical thinking" (Spring 1994, p. 20). The tautology of this statement is evident, but the point is clear that critical thinking and democracy go hand in hand. The corollary to this line of reasoning is that a critical redemptive pedagogy is crucial to the education of African people in the Diaspora to assist them in making sense of the world and their experiences as a people of oppression and their future connections among the peoples of the world. I concur with Spring's (1994) assessment of the form of critical thinking that Dewey argues is necessary for a democracy that involves an understanding of the social construction of knowledge and the ability to test and judge the value of new forms of knowledge. Consequently, history is at the heart of Dewey's instructional methodology. It is through the study of history that students learn how and why knowledge and institutions were created. This point is crucial to the principles of critical redemptive pedagogy because it seeks to make sense of Black history in the Caribbean, North America, and the Metropole. It further seeks to reinstate Black dignity and pride based on an Africentric philosophy.

THE HISTORICAL CONSTRUCTION OF GNOSIS

Gnosis is the epistemology that has been instituted by a historical or current regime as the ideal to which all persons in state should adhere. The regime touts its gnosis as being infinitely good and perpetual. The concept that gnosis is historically constructed is vitally important, together with the intellectual ability to do critical analysis of the history of gnosis. Through critical analysis it will come to light that gnosis is not sacrosanct; it has a historical origin. Gnosis is a dynamic, cultural phenomenon which is not the special preserve of any one historical group. Gnosis changes over time because it is not etched in stone. We can take as an example the dogmatic positions which have been taken by the Church for many years, such as the notion that the earth is the centre of the universe, abortion, contraception, the place of women in the Church, human sexuality. In each of these situations the Church has had to beat a retreat in the face of a progressive gnosis which brought into being new scientific knowledge that belies the Churches dogmatic teachings. As Spring (1994) said the citizens in Dewey's ideal democratic society understand both the social usefulness of their work and are able to relate theory to practice. They understand that knowledge and institutions are products of particular social conditions, needs, and they are willing to change when ideas and institutions become outmoded. The citizens in Dewey's ideal democracy cooperate in testing new ideas and institutions to determine their value to the progress of civilization (Spring 1994). These citizens have this disposition because they have been cultivated in the understanding of the temporality of things that are made by humans and the imperfection of most if not all human endeavors. I wish to take the point that gnosis is a social construct created in particular historical circumstances further by agreeing with Giroux (as referred in Spring, 1994) that another element to the social construct is dynamo (power). Dynamo is the compelling force to carry out one's will even where it is unwarranted and objected to by those who are affected by it. Giroux (as referred in Spring, 1994) used this line of reasoning to explain the historical development of slavery because the Europeans had the power to impose slavery on weaker human beings. Where ordinary people have no power, they cannot make any meaningful contribution to the democratic development of the state in which they live and have their being. Gnosis cultivates dynamo in the intellect of the citizens through non-idiotic educational processes because knowledge is power and power is knowledge. The two social constructs of gnosis and dynamo go hand in hand in the cultivation of a critical, vibrant, intellectually competent *persona*.

For Giroux (as referred in Spring, 1994) the primary task of education is to help students understand the social construction of knowledge in the framework of power. The method of achieving this goal is critical pedagogy. The final aim of the process is the empowerment of the student and ultimately the empowerment of all citizens. Empowerment for Giroux is the process whereby students acquire the means to critically appropriate knowledge existing outside of their immediate experience in order to broaden their understanding of themselves, the world, and the possibilities for transforming the taken-for-granted assumptions about the way we live. This is a most apt encapsulation of the meaning of empowerment. The empowerment which is advocated by Giroux seeks to eliminate social injustice and decrease the inequality in power that is prevalent in some societies in terms of wealth, social status, occupation, gender, and race. The irony is, although there is greater freedom in a democratic system, there is also a great propensity for injustice and inequality. Even in the best democracy with all of its potential for human flourishing it is co-mingled with some of the most notorious and egregious violations of social justice. This is the human negative factor. For these reasons, there must necessarily be a constant struggle for empower of ordinary people to eliminate the social scourges that endeavor to imprison us. It is on account of this rationale that I strongly believe that the school is a site of democratic struggle. The school is the crucible in which ordinary people are empowered through exposure to a discourse which promotes social justice and the elimination of inequality. This is a critical discourse in human rights. In school ordinary citizens participate in and adopt a discourse other than the one into which they were born. In this way the school prepares all citizens for participation in the democratic processes of the state. Ordinary citizens are prepared to participate in this democratic struggle within the school and in other public spheres of democratic associated living. In other words, critical discourses in human rights are integral to the maintenance of a democratic state and the means by which the school becomes a democratic public institution for the pursuit of the good life through gnosis.

A NON-IDIOTIC DEMOCRATIC MODEL

Amy Gutmann (as referred in Spring, 1994) has theorized a model of democracy that is non-repressive and non-discriminatory. Gutmann is concerned about the use that can be made of education for the purpose of oppression by the majority, special interest groups, and politicians. Democracy for her means the rule of the majority, but it is this very democracy which she fears because it has the potential and the propensity to snuff out the voice of the minority. This is a real fear because the majority has the power to over-raw the will of the minority through the making of unjust and oppressive laws. This kind of abuse of power must be avoided because it does not augur well for the development of a healthy democracy. Parker (2003) cites a situation in the State of Florida where laws are used to disenfranchise ex-convicts who incidentally happens to be black males. He finds that Florida is one of 11 states in the United States that disenfranchise all felons for life. Thomas Johnson, an ex-felon and an African American man, has sued to restore ex-convict voting rights (Goldhaber, 2000). Disenfranchised ex-felons are 5% of the voting age population of Florida, and when one considers the Black community alone, 24% of Florida's Black males cannot vote. Supporters of the disenfranchisement of felons invoke social contract theory to the effect that citizens who have entered into an agreement with one another must be prepared to abide by the terms of that agreement. This line of reasoning is a patent hoax. It is simply a hang-over from Jim Crow. In 1868 Florida's new postwar constitution gave Blacks the vote, but not felons – and this was at a time when felons were overwhelmingly Black. It is highly improbable that this is random as oppose to calculative abuse of legislative power.

If we take the social contract theory line of reasoning to its logical conclusion, then not only felons, but whoever is in breach of the agreement should be permanently ostracized and marginalized by the society, that is, they should lose the right to vote, or any other right for that matter. Therefore, "those holding absolute power, whether slaveholders to slaves, conquistadors to the vanquished, men to women … kings to their subjects" can victimize with impunity (p.16). What makes this kind of law making all the more terrifying is that they were not made in good faith; they were made primarily to victimize African Americans. Such laws are therefore unjust laws, not unlike those which Gandhi, King, Parks, and Mandela fought against.

Gutmann is concerned with prevention of this kind of abuse of power by a majority of the population. For Gutmann, two of the hallmarks of a democratic education are the protection of freedom of ideas and non-discrimination. Her goal is to determine what political structure is needed to protect these democratic ideals. Her search for this ideal political structure begins with a consideration of four possible political models of education which she refers to as "the family state", "the state of families", "the state of individuals", and the democratic state" (Spring 1994, p.16).

Gutmann does not agree with *the family state* because this is based on the model which is provided in Plato's Republic. She sees the basic goal of education in the family state is to unite all people and teach them to desire a common concept of the good life. The major flaw with this concept is that, the "good life", is a relative term which depends on one's education and culture, and to allow a selected group in the society, the philosopher-kings, to determine the meaning of the good life is to impose their views on the whole society. Each individual must determine for him/herself what the good life means to her/him.

The second model of education, *the state of families*, is unlike the first in that the philosopher–king is banished from the particular family groups. The individual family will determine what is the good life and the educational content that should be taught to their children. In this model the family has a greater say in the education of its children, it can pass on its family culture and religion to its children. Gutmann rejects the state of families because some families might have customs and practices which are undemocratic and would therefore limit the education of the children. However the Human Rights Convention and the Rights of the Child Convention support the view that children must be educated according to the wishes of the parents of the children.

Gutmann's third model, *the state of individuals*, holds that education prepares children to make free choices. There is no one definition of the good life and students must be educated to make their own determination as individuals on what they consider to be the good life. This concept is based on Stuart Mill's arguments put forward in *On Liberty*. In educating for individual choices, the system of education remains neutral. Gutmann takes issue with this notion because the educational system comes loaded with values. The very fact that it is the system that determines what is to be studied is a value judgment.

The fourth model which is advocated by Gutmann is *the democratic state*. The Business of education in this state is to prepare children to reproduce and maintain democratic values – the active participation in the sharing of power and the shaping of society. The democratic process will determine the educational system. Gutmann advocates the basic tenets of democratic education to be dependent on two principles: nonrepression and nondiscrimination. She argues that one of the basic principles of democracy is the capacity to deliberate among alternative concepts of the good life. Simply stated, a democratic educational system allows and enhances the ability of future citizens to consider alternative ways of personal and political life. In this context, the principle of non-repression means that a democratic educational system will not repress students' consideration of different concepts of the good life. A democratic education must preserve freedom of thought (Spring 1994). This is why the framers of the Caribbean and

American constitutions have enshrined in them the fundamental right of freedom of expression and conscience. This fundamental right is deeply entrenched in these constitutions so that they cannot be altered through the ordinary legislative process.

The non-discrimination principle creates a mechanism of control because freedom of thought, although stated categorically in the constitution, is in fact not absolute and is therefore qualified because there are different ethnic and racial groups in any democratic society and the rights of each, whether religious or cultural must be respected. A democratic system cannot coexist with absolute freedom of religion or conscience, or any other absolute freedom for that matter, because that can be interpreted to mean the right to prosecute and persecute religious beliefs that are contrary to any citizen's or group of citizens' system of belief. Gutmann argues that educators have the authority to teach children racial, ethnic, and religious tolerance because these virtues constitute the kind of character necessary to create a society committed to conscious social production. In other words, allowing consideration of alternative concepts of the good life does not mean that education remains neutral. Rather, it is based on certain values that are to be transmitted by the schools. This is why a democratic education should not only avoid discrimination but should also teach values that reduce discrimination in the rest of society (Spring 1994). These goals can be achieved through critical redemptive pedagogy because of its non-idiotic philosophical underpinnings.

THE RIGHT TO EDUCATION SUMMONS THE COMMUNITY: ONE FOR ALL AND ALL FOR ONE

The posture which is created in students of critical redemptive pedagogy is crucial to the survival of freedom and democracy. In a very real sense we are our brothers' and sisters' keepers. We are the gatekeepers of the city of freedom and human rights. This is why it is incumbent upon each one of us, and I would push it further and claim that it is our moral duty, to stand against injustice and oppression whenever they raise their ugly heads in our society. We are the guardians of our human rights, our right to and education that is non-idiotic. Through the methodology of critical redemptive pedagogy all of us can obtain a voice. We can understand how the social construction of gnosis determines what we believe, and we can challenge the source and the veracity of those beliefs. Critical thought forces us to confront racism, sexism, classism and other social oppression within our society; the assumptions of everyday living. The possible outcome of such critical dialogue would be a better understanding of the origin of gnosis as a regime that was put in place by those who possess power for the oppression of those who are seen as the *Other* and the preservation of the power of those who are in charge.

The only thing that is necessary for the gnosis of the regime to continue *ad infinitum* is the continued docility of good men and women. Through critical redemptive pedagogy men and women can redeem themselves from the powers of oppression and clothe themselves with the instruments of justice and righteousness. In our transformed minds we become new men and women who must take up the mantle of redemption. We cannot sit passively by while injustices are committed or democratic institutions are made to collapse, in the hope that others will step in. That is the posture according to Parker (2003) of the free rider. But the free rider's passivity catches up with him eventually and destroys him when no one is left to look out for him and he cannot any longer get a free ride.

This point is compellingly illustrated by the Protestant Pastor Martin Niemroller as recounted by Parker (2003), when asked how the Nazis accomplished what they did. He said first by taking over Germany, then wreaking havoc on other states and engineering the Holocaust. Niemroller said it happened this way: "First they came for the Communists, but I was not a Communist so I did not speak out. Then they came for the socialists and the Trade Unionists, but I was neither, so I did not speak out. Then they came for the Jews, but I was not a Jew so I did not speak out. And when they came for me, there was no one left to speak out for me" (p. 54). Parker (2003) eloquently describes this kind of attitude as "idiotic". This word he uses with its etymological meaning:

> "Idiotic" in its origin is not what it means to us today – stupid or mentally deficient. This recent meaning is entirely and deservedly out of usage by educators, but the original meaning needs to be reclaimed. It is an ancient Greek term that shares with "idiom" and "idiosyncratic" the root *idios*, which means private, separate, self-centred – selfish. This conception of idiocy achieves its force when we contrasted it with *polites* (political) or *public* (p.2).

With the use of this definition Parker (2003) sets forth an argument for the great importance of communal endeavor to ensure that injustice and inequality are dealt with by the entire community because all is affected by the conduct of one or some. We must speak out against social injustice and inequality whether or not it affects us or our family. In any case, soon or later "they will come for us". He further demonstrates that there must be unity in diversity, "the interdependence of the *pluribus* and *unum*, diversity and liberty, and multicultural education and citizenship education" (p.2). The salient point that I wish to make here is that human rights must include a right to education, and education must include multiculturalism, and social justice education – an education that is not idiotic. Spring (1994) refers to this as planting a wheel in the head, but even Spring (1994) admits that there are some "wheels in the head" that are necessary. Everyone of us has a fundamental moral duty to protect and maintain the human rights of one another and our human rights include a right to a non-idiotic education that advances freedom in the world and economic security for all persons.

Parker (2003) contrasts the "pluribus", the public life, citizenship with the "unum", the private and self-centered life which is sterile, bereft of human connectedness. To illustrate "the non-idiotic life – the citizen's life" (p.8), he cites the civil disobedience demonstration of

Mohandas Gandhi and Martin Luther King Jr. as two examples *par excellence*. These two men were concerned for the public good, to end racism and injustice in their particular circumstances. If they were idiotic, concerned only with their own family, what Parker (2003) calls "amoral familism", they would not have taken the risk to challenge the status quo. Similarly, Rosa Park refused to sit in the back of the bus because a Negro is just as much a human being as any Caucasian. Parker (2003) cited a quotation from King's Birmingham Letter:

> Injustice anywhere is a threat to justice everywhere. We are caught in an inescapable network of mutuality, tied in a single garment of destiny. Whatever affects one directly, affects all indirectly. Never again can we afford to live with the narrow, provincial "outside agitator" idea. Anyone who lives inside the United States cannot be considered an outsider anywhere within its bounds (p.8).

Parker's (2003) opinion is corroborated by that of Spring (1994) that every citizen is morally obliged to stand and fight against unjust laws which promote injustice and inequality. He states that all the members of society have an obligation to ensure that everyone is treated equally before the law and that everyone has the right to life, liberty, and security of person. Everyone would be called on to fight discrimination based on race, color, sex, language, religion, political or other opinion, national or social origin, property, and birth and other status.

I hold opinion with Parker (2003) that everyone must ensure that the human rights of the others are protected against incursion by unscrupulous persons and institutions. Democracy goes a long way in protecting the fundamental rights of citizens as enshrined in the constitution. However, democracy alone is not enough. Citizens must be prepared to speak out in their own favor and in favor of those who do not have any voice, who can only groan under the burden of discrimination and marginalization. Democracy is important, but it does not guarantee protection of human rights. Without a civic political culture that commits all people to exercising a moral duty to protect civil rights, democracy can quickly slip into a form of government that strips people of their rights. The U. S. government claimed to be democratic or to be a republic while it committed genocide and ethnocide against Native Americans in the 19th century. If all U. S. citizens had been committed to protecting human rights, including the rights of indigenous peoples, this might not have occurred. However, the majority of U. S. citizens did nothing to stop the genocide and ethnocide committed by their government. Therefore, key to a democratic system that protects human rights is a civic political culture based on the moral commitment of all citizens to defend the rights of all (Spring 2000).

THE IMPORTANCE OF SOCIAL JUSTICE EDUCATION

As I advocate herein, I believe education is important to all citizens. It is absolutely essential to those who must go on to face continued obstacles of racism, classism, and sexism, to those who have been distanced and disenfranchised from the mainstream culture, and to those who have suffered lifetimes of oppression and marginalization (Adair in Parker 2003). I believe that all people can experience the good life through human rights education and education for social justice which seeks to right the evils of racism, sexism and classism which have a debilitating impact on minority and indigenous peoples. The right to education in human rights and social justice is crucially important for the redemption of oppressed peoples. They must be the architects of their own liberation and they can only do so if they become fully aware – conscientized – of the harm which the conservative educational system insidiously inflicts on them and their children. Belle (in Adams, Belle & Griffith, 1997) sees the goal of social justice education as full and equal participation of all groups in a society that is mutually shaped to meet their needs. Social justice includes a vision of society in which the distribution of resources is equitable and all members are physically and psychologically safe and secure. A society in which individuals have the right of self-determination (*kujichagulia*), that is, persons are able to develop their full capacities; and they are interdependent, meaning that they are capable of interacting democratically with others. Social justice involves social actors who have a sense of their own agency as well as a sense of social responsibility towards and with others and the society as a whole.

Advocates of social justice education have an uphill struggle in raising the consciousness of people who are marginalized by society for the purpose of exploiting their labor, and other resources over a long protracted period of time. Persons may have accepted and internalized their oppression as justifiable and legitimate. It is not inconceivable that oppressed people sometimes put up stout resistance to change because they have accepted and internalized their oppression. Such person would have adopted an obsequious state of mind which abdicates their freedom and encourages them to collude in their own subordination and enslavement. Operating under this slavocratic mentality they set upon members of their own group who seek to bring them up higher and so discredit their abilities and intentions. But the slavocratic mind will hastily endorse the credentials of those who wish to perpetuate their oppression. This is a hard irony and one which cannot be accepted, but extremely difficult to dislodge (Adams, Belle & Griffith, 1997).

The presence of this obsequious attitude of subordinate groups reinforces the point that conscientization for redemption must take place on two fronts, that of the oppressor and the oppressed. Critical redemptive pedagogy must therefore seek not only to redeem the oppressed but also the oppressor who is the perpetrator of the social oppression. Another hard irony is that the oppressor may not even be aware that he is oppressing his fellow humans because he was born into a position of privilege and comfort. Perhaps the persons who are more in need of an education in human rights and social justice are those persons who wheel power in the society. While it is imperative that we seek the education of the poor and the oppressed, we cannot afford to leave the members of the dominant group without education because this can make them all the more destructive. One could argue that those who *most* need democratic enlightenment, especially a highly develop sense of justice, are those who occupy the board rooms, legislatures, court rooms, and faculty positions at prestigious universities. We are led back again, then, to the conclusion that all learners, if they are to walk the democratic path with diverse others, require a high quality of non-idiotic education for freedom, justice, and equality. This applies equally to the powerless and the powerful.

The creation of a human rights' education is a prerequisite to the enjoyment of the good life facilitated through social justice education. An education rights' manifesto would therefore combine all the requirements for a good quality of life and a non-idiotic education which is promoted by *multicultural koinonia*. The salient features of that manifesto would contain *inter alia*:

1. All students are entitled to an education in universal human rights.

2. All students are entitled to an education that redeems them from racism, sexism, and heterosexism.

3. All students are entitled to an education in multicultural ethics.

4. All students are entitled to an education in cultural centeredness and multiculturalism.

5. All students are entitled to an education in pedagogical implications for gender and racial equity.

6. All students are entitled to:

    a. freedom of speech and expression;

    b. freedom of access to sound information and instruction;

    c. freedom from indoctrination;

    d. freedom from teacher abuse;

    e. freedom of self-actualization;

    f. freedom from substandard education;

    g. freedom from idiotic education.

I believe these the principles on which education for the good life must be based. I believe these principles can promote and enhance a global culture and economy that is beneficial to all. A good quality education in human rights which includes education rights, underpinned by the philosophy of critical redemptive pedagogy is imperative for good human relationships. Critical redemptive pedagogy must examine issues of racism, sexism, heterosexism, classism, to name few of the social ills that must be challenged with the view to obliterate them. Adams et al (1997) provide a number of comprehensive curricula for the teaching of these issues which can be used as precedents for the creation of curricula that are suitable to the particular environment in which social justice is being taught. The sagacity of a human rights education can only be overlooked at the peril of *cultural nihilism*.

CONCLUSION

Humanity continues to battle with injustice and oppression which, ironically is created by our fellow human kind. I believe education can bring great alleviation from social disaffection, but it is not a panacea for all the social ills that exist in the society. However, history has shown that positive social change can be brought about through education whether gradual or magnitudinal. The success or failure of non-idiotic education depends to a large extent on a critical redemptive pedagogy that is efficacious. Learners usually take the lead for social change from their teachers, even when these changes are contrary to the expectation of their families. I believe that students should be made aware of their right to an adequate, non-idiotic education, the protection of these rights under the Human Rights Convention and the Convention on the Rights of the Child. These must be incorporated into the national constitutions of each country. The crucial importance of critical redemptive pedagogy for the flowering and flourishing of human rights and social justice education cannot be overemphasized.

CHAPTER SIX

Education and Feminism: The Politics of Gender and Personhood

> Until black men can face the reality that sexism empowers
> them despite the impact of racism in their lives, it will be
> difficult to engage in meaningful dialogue about gender
> (hooks , 1990, p.75)

The issues of gender and sexuality were crucially important topics in traditional Western society just as much as they are today. Gender was used to determine what a citizen position is in the society under the sublime system of patriarchy which relegated women to the bottom of the social ladder in all spheres of life. This state of affairs was sustained for many centuries and it has impacted most heavily in a negative way on women. The oppression of women is a great concern for me because I view all forms of discrimination and bigotry as forms of social evil which any progressive man would wish to eradicate. In this chapter I critically examine the issue as to whether we can continue to use gender as the yardstick to determine how educational resources and political power should be distributed in the family and the society. I canvass the view that feminist concerns are part and parcel of the trend for positive social change which can only be obtained through a better understanding of the issues that are of concern to women. In juxtaposition with the need for a better understanding of women's issues, I believe there is also a dire need for a better understanding of gender issues generally, especially in the light of the availability of gender reassignment operations and recent psycho-medical developments. In my pursuit I do not seek to elevate one sex or one life style above the other, but rather to acknowledge the struggle of women for liberation from patriarchy and to lend my support to it.

The pertinent question is whether our educational constructs should be broadened to include other persons who do not fall into the traditional category. I also canvass the view that feminism has made significant advancement within the last forty-five to fifty years and this advancement for women's empowerment must be continued. A non-idiotic education underpinned by critical redemptive pedagogy would further advance the cause and liberation of women and other persons who are victims of gender oppression.

GENDER AS SOCIAL CONSTRUCTION

I have formed the opinion that gender is a social construct which was originally designed to glorify men and to subjugate and victimize women so that their male counterpart be installed in the social and political orbit as their overlords. Men's understanding of life and human nature have been so informed by the politics of patriarchy, sexism and heterosexism that these social constructs have caused men to grow up with very lopsided views that have been etched themselves very deeply into their psyche. In matters related to gender, human sexuality, and family life men are expected to be the leaders and women the followers. It is therefore of crucial importance that these nagging gender issues be visited and revisited by both men and women until we find a sensible, pragmatic, and unbiased (as far as that is possible) resolutions. This, of course, would mean that men will have to jettison their lopsided upbringing, the myths and bigotry of our traditional idiotic education.

Feminism has unmasked patriarchy and so exposed and belied its misconceptions about women. Given that patriarchy was wrong in this regard, is it possible that it is wrong with regards to other gender issues? We must now unlearn our bigotry and sexism through critical redemptive pedagogy that is informed by an Africentric philosophy for the reinstatement of harmonious relations between women, men, and those who do not fall in either category. Education must be a radicalising agent as well as the healing balm for the parties. Men, like women, must be the agents of their liberation from their own patriarchal predisposition.

I am inclined to believe that the traditional categorising of the sexes as being male and female is a social construct of patriarchy and sexism specifically designed for the marginalization of women and so prevent them from sharing in the political powers. I am further inclined to believe that the patriarchal casting of persons in these pre-made moulds is responsible for the many years of oppression which women have undergone and to a certain extent continue to undergo. Political power and property rights were unequally distributed between men and women simply on the basis of sex and some rationale was fabricated to make it palatable. The pertinent question is whether we can afford to continue to identify gender in terms of this classification given the cruel oppression to which some persons are subjected. Several legal challenges have been mounted against this myopic, parochial definition of gender in view of persons undergoing sex change operations and in view of the feminist struggle for women's liberation from patriarchal oppression.

Another pertinent question then, is whether we should allow our minds to come under the siege of sexism. Sexism can no longer be used as the yard stick for the determination of a man's or woman's dessert. We also must contend with and make a determination either affirmatively or negatively on the position of persons who have undergone a sex change operation for the purpose of being converted into an oppositional sex whether male to female or female to male, and how society should treat such persons. Should she be subjected to the same oppression given that she did not begin her life as a woman? To state the question bluntly, can a man or a woman change his/her sex artificially to that of a woman/ man in the eyes of the society and the law and how should the 'new' person be treated? Another question can be also posited: Should sexual identity be a factor in employment, education, or religious pursuits? These considerations should be treated with serious deliberation before we tender an answer. The response which is given by gullible, soft-minded religiousity is hardly an answer. Feminism has exploded many of the patriarchal myths and has demonstrated that women can achieve high levels of competency in any field of endeavour.

WOMEN'S LEADERSHIP ROLE HI-JACKED BY PATRIARCHY

In Western society, the unequal political power of women is rooted in the liberal political tradition of the seventeenth and eighteenth centuries. The denial of equal political power to women can be found in the educational and political writings of two prominent members of the liberal tradition – John Locke (1632-1704) and Jean-Jacques Rousseau (1712-1778). Besides making important intellectual contributions to classical liberalism, Locke and Rousseau wrote influential books on pedagogy that shaped the educational traditions of the Western world (Spring 1999, p. 107). Western liberal philosophy is still entrenched in the academy. The tradition was transplanted into the Caribbean and forms an integral part of the educational systems in the region. This has contributed to the social and political inequality of women in the Caribbean. That apart, African women in the Caribbean like their male counterparts are descendants of former African slaves. In the slave society women were treated as vehicles for procreation. Christianity as inherited from our former colonial masters has also contributed significantly to the oppression of women in the Diaspora.

Were women always an oppressed group in society without any political leadership role? This question can be answered in the negative or the affirmative depending on which epoch of history one wishes to examine. However, when taken generally, there was a time when women had positive political roles in their society, but this has been hi-jacked by patriarchal systems. Women of antiquity were successful political leaders but this has been discounted in most recorded history or glossed over as being insignificant. Even in the ultra conservative rustic Judaism, the woman Deborah became a Judge in Israel (a judge at this time was the tribal leader). "At that time Deborah, a prophetess, wife of Lappidoth, was judging Israel. She used to sit under the palm of Deborah between Ramah and Bethel in the hill country of Ephraim; and the Israelites came up to her for judgment" (Judges 4:4-5). Deborah delivered to Barak the military instructions which she received directly from Yahweh concerning the confrontation with the army of Jabin. This story evidences that women played a constructive role in previous times in organizing human society. But for patriarchal oppression women would have been able to play a constructive role in political leadership, as well as carrying out all of the other social responsibilities which women normally do. Budge (in Welch, 1992) draws on the positive portrayal of women in Egyptian mythology to illustrate the role of women in antiquity:

> Women were involved with organizing the innermost concerns of humankind's destiny. In the legend of Osiris, who died and returned to eternal life, it was Isis who searched and found the body parts of her husband Osiris so that life could be sustained. From this effort she helped spread the ideas of life, suffering, death, resurrection, eternal life, supporting rituals (p. 26).

This Egyptian mythology portrays the high importance of women in early Egyptian society and its conception of the world and life. As society evolved the role and function of women in it became more and more restricted, eventually relegating women to the duties of housekeeping and the caring of children. Women gradually lost their position as hunters and gatherers thus making the man more prominent and to assign to women an inferior position. It is to be noted this was not based on merit or ability.

Africa provides some powerful examples of women's leadership in their societies as civil leaders, warrior women, and queens. Welch (1992) argues that African American women may be inspired by the leadership qualities of Queen Hatshepsut who ruled Egypt 1500 years before the birth of Christ. She organized the first trade expedition to the land of Punt. In 960 B.C. Queen Makeda (Queen of Sheba) ruled Ethiopia and planned an arduous journey to Jerusalem to learn the wisdom of Solomon. She built the capital city and named it Debra Makeda after herself. In 69 B.C. Cleopatra and her brother, Ptolemy XIII, ruled Egypt together during trouble times. Queen Nzingha of Ndongo/Kongo successfully resisted the Portuguese occupation with a fierce army of women warriors from 1623 to 1663. She also organized the Moni-Kongo groups, national and international, to oppose European domination of Africa.

This evidence illustrates that women played a very significant role in African society both in the military and in the civil society. It would seem therefore that the notion of women being the weaker sex, inferior to men is a myth that was fabricated by patriarchy at some later time for the oppression, marginalization, and subjugation of women. There is a corollary between racism and the oppression of women. The enslavement of Africans was for the main purpose of providing labour for a white, male dominated society; white women although they did not wear the shackles of slavery were just slaves of another class. Welch (1992) gives some more examples of the leadership role of women in earlier times when women were free:

> Other African women organized resistance to the slave trade and the colonial system were Madame Tinubu of Nigeria; Nandi, mother of Chaka, the Zulu warrior; the female army led by the Dahomian King Bowelle; and the brave Yaa Asantewa, Queen Mother of the Ashanti people of Ghana, who led the war against the British in 1805. The

Yaa Asantewa war was the last major one led by a woman
in African (per Diop in Welch 1992, p. 27).

The above evidence shows that the role of women in early times so as
to provide ample evidence that women were not always marginalized in
some societies but that it was foisted upon women by patriarchy. Welch
(1992) has aptly explained that this historical message demonstrates
that women provided leadership and managed the affairs of states and
institutions. Although some African women were forced to leave their
country, they did not forget all of their cultural knowledge. It was that
social, political, and economic foundation upon which they structured
their understanding for a new beginning under different circumstances
in new lands – the Caribbean and North America.

The cruelties of slavery did not daunt the spirit of African women
who were uprooted from their native country and brought to North
America and the Caribbean to work on the plantations. Women were
determined that their children will not remain in slavery and as soon
as the opportunity presented itself they made a move for freedom for
themselves and their children. African women did not fail to pass on
the message of freedom to their children; that the circumstances of
their lives were not natural and that they were simply imposed on them
by the will of White patriarchy. Life under the plantation system was
grinding and brutal, the master possessed formidable powers which he
could unleash at his whim upon the slave. Welch (1992) recounts the
daring operations of a well known American female slave:

> One of the more daring leadership acts and messages
> relative to the freedom goals was made by Harriet Tubman,
> who was born a slave in 1823. Not only did she escape
> from a Maryland plantation to Philadelphia, but in spite
> of the $40,000 bounty issued for her head, she returned to
> the South several times to help her family and some three
> hundred slaves escape to the North via the underground
> Railroad (p. 28).

African women were the ones who dared to commit subtle breaches of the slave laws, for example taking on the challenge of learning to read. The defiance of African women inculcated in their children a hope that freedom will come one day:

> This was a signal of hope because the majority of African women were severely exploited as child bearers and home and field workers for three centuries without pay. Many others were convinced to exist as concubines and were given empty promises. Yet in spite of such difficulties many women were able to assert themselves toward the goal of education with the help of interested whites and freemen who were more concerned with their advancement (Welch, 1992, p. 28).

Interestingly, in Africa the cradle of creation "...in the lake region of central Africa, the source of the Nile" (Welch 1992, p. 26), the society was matriarchal. Leakey (in Wellch, 1992) describes the ancient position of African women:

> In Africa the first organized human group was matriarchal. Everyone was considered a descendant of the mother, in that the identification of the father was known only to her (Jackson in Welch 1992, p. 26). Furthermore, woman was pivotal to the organization of the family for survival. In the early human economy the first tools were made for women; they gathered four-fifths of the food supply, including plants, eggs, ants, and honey. Men hunted meat, providing one-fifth of the food supply. The sharing of the two operations foster cooperation for a developing human existence (pp.26 -27).

Through the cooperation of women and men society was created. This is borne out by scientific evidence, that by putting their efforts together women and men and their children were able to survive the adversities of prehistoric life:

> Anthropological and archaeological evidence now confirms that it is humankind's ability to cooperate with one another, not dominate one another, that led to civilization. What allowed societies to advance and enabled a sense of community and self did not spring from nasty, brutish, argumentative displays of male bravado. It blossomed from cooperation, communication, and the ritual celebrations of life (Leakey & Lewin in Welch 1992, p. 116).

Therefore, the notion that women are weaker or inferior to men is neither inherent nor innate. It is a social construct which was created by patriarchy for the oppression of women and to deprive them of their leadership roles in their societies. This was a calculated subjugation of women as a group. Hence, the stereotyping of women and other minority groups to justify the domination which is exerted by patriarchy: "Whites develop negative stereotypes to justify the exploitation of and discrimination against minorities. Negative stereotypes about African Americans are the most common and resilient" (Welch 1992, p.15). As Welch (1992) argues, one of the critical elements is to understand the white male agenda and the resulting stereotypes that adversely impact on women and people from various racial groups. The impact of the white male system is so subtly intertwined in academe that it is difficult to discern. It is important that all women understand how the male system causes conflicts and has an adverse effect on male relationships with women as they pursue positions of authority in the academy as well as in the society in general.

   This male patriarchal system is the root of sexism and racism. This system is portrayed or presented as the system par excellence and any other social arrangement is bound to be contrary to nature. The system which was devised by male patriarchy for the oppression of women is not unlike the one which was designed for the enslavement and exploitation of Africans. I find it curiously interesting that white women were as much subjugated to this system of oppression as black women, although white women would sooner support the system because they see it as being an integral part of their own quest for power and survival. However, while white women have one strike against them, their gender; black women have two strikes against them, their gender and their race. This has made the oppression and marginalization of black women all the more difficult to counteract:

> The first tenet of the White Male System is the belief that the male system is the right and only way of life. All other perceptions are viewed as incorrect, stupid, invalid, incompetent, or crazy. Accordingly, men in the male dominated institutions tend to discount, disparage, destroy, or minimize other perceptions. The system consistently and methodically denies or questions the perceptions and experiences of women and minority groups (Welch 1992, p. 14).

Life in the post-modern world has exploded the myth of male superiority through women's quest for liberation. The sceptre of male dominance has been gradually eroded and continues along that path.

PHILOSOPHICAL MISCONCEPTION OF WOMEN

In Western patriarchal systems women were relegated to playing second fiddle to men. This is evident in the liberal tradition of the seventeenth and eighteenth centuries. Philosophers such as John Lock and Jean-Jacques Rousseau, both men in their education philosophy refused to recognise women as having equal political power with men. Women were expected to take their place in the home and expressed their citizenship through their husband. Therefore it was proper that women should be educated to play a subservient role to their husbands. Locke was labouring under the misconception that once women understand that the man is the king of the home this would protect the property of men from falling into the hands of women. This is why laws were put in place to ensure that women could not own property or entered into contracts. Locke was also labouring under the misconception that people are born with minds that are blank slates that can be moulded through the *modus operandi* of reward and punishment. As Spring (1994) points out: "The family model of government clearly places women in a subservient role to men. In this model, which Locke used in his discussion of education, the ruler of the family is the father (p. 108).

Locke locates the fountain of authority both in the society and in the family in the man. The woman was free to pursue matters that fall outside the purview of the common interest of husband and wife and this carried the caveat that they must not violate the laws of God or the government. This would of course leave the woman with mercifully little independence in activity or though:

> The idea of the father as ruler of the family is carried over into Locke's educational proposals. Locke informs parents that one of the first things they should do is "Be sure then to establish the authority of a father, as soon as he [the child] is capable of submission, and can understand in whose power he is". The power of the father over the child, according to Locke, should continue until the age of twenty-one. Locke argued that while children are born free and with reason, they still must remain subservient to their parents until they have the capacity to know the law. Until they are able to know and to reason about the laws of the state, the father functions as "a temporary government (Spring 1994, p. 111).

Although Locke's patriarchal liberal ideology advocated individual freedom, this did not include women, perhaps because in his view women were not quite individuals, perhaps as non-entities or just extensions of her husband. "John Locke contended that the individual, born with a God-given gift of reason, was the possessor of fundamental, natural rights, including those of life, liberty, private property, and the pursuit of happiness" (Cohee & Kemp 1998, p. 124). The pertinent question which comes to mind and begs for an answer is whether women are included in this divine endowment? And a second question that follows close behind the previous one is, what is the moral basis which is provided by Locke for treating women as an entity of less significance than men? The resounding answer is that Locke does not provide any proper or sufficient evidence to justify his relegating women to a second class status:

> The reigning justification for the exclusion of women from the domains of individual freedom promised by this early brand of liberalism was that women, by nature, were different. Deficient in reason, they were suited for life in the private sphere of domesticity, child-bearing, nurturance, emotionality, dependence, and obedience to the fathers and husbands who represented and defined the interests of the family (Cohee & Kemp 1998, p. 124).

This line of reasoning has provided no empirical basis for arriving at such conclusions. I am therefore driven to the inexorable conclusion that women were victimized on the superficial basis of their sexual difference followed by a creation of the myths of their inferior status as promulgated by patriarchy. There is a correlation in Locke's line of reasoning with the American Independence Declaration "that all men (sic) are created equally by their Creator", and this declaration was made in the teeth of a virulent system of slavery. I do not believe that the "all men" is a grammatical occasion when the masculine included the feminine. The architects of the declaration were killing two birds with one stone: women and Negroes. Here too individuals (men) are proclaimed to have been endowed with the God-given gift of reason, the possessor of fundamental, natural rights, and the whole nine yards. I have tremendous difficulty trying to fathom how any right thinking person could dole out such tripe moral sentiments for other so-called right thinking persons to endorse. But they were endorsed by the society:

> The unequal power of women is reflected not only in the idea of the father as ruler of the family, but also in Locke's educational proposals. In the first place, his educational

plans are intended for the education of young boys, specifically for "a gentleman's son." Second, whenever there is a discussion of women in his educational writings – and this does not occur very frequently – it is clearly indicated that their education should be limited. (Spring 1994, p. 111).

It seems as though there was a deep seated hidden fear of women. Women do not fare any better in the educational proposal of Jean-Jacques Rousseau, although he acknowledged that all people are born free, including women. However, in his education of *Emile*, there is no fair distribution of power between men and women. His ideal education for women is portrayed by Sophie and it is inferior to that of Emile her male counterpart. Given that this good gentleman had neglected the upbringing of his own children, I wonder how much weight I should attach to his educational philosophy.

Rousseau wants Sophie's education to prepare her to accept the ideas and will of her husband he describes the intended results of Sophie's education as:

> Her mind is still vacant but has been trained to learn: it is well-tilled land only waiting for the grain. What a pleasing ignorance! Happy is the man destined to instruct her. She will be her husband's disciple, not his teacher. Far from wanting to impose her tastes on him, she will share his (Spring 1999, p. 120).

This is the absolute objectification of women as perceived by Rousseau. Rousseau like Locke believed that women should be educated for domination by men. Interestingly, Rousseau's educational arrangements for women was challenged and rejected by a woman of his time, Mary Wollstonecraft. Wollstonecraft felt that the view of women as portrayed by Rousseau was lopsided and that women had the capacity to be educated on equal footing with men:

> Responding to Rousseau, Mary Wollstonecraft argued that female reasoning is the same as that of men. Consequently,

she dismissed Rousseau's plan to educate women as
companions to men and have them gain citizenship through
their husbands. Wollstonecraft argued that women, like
men, should be educated to exercise their reason and should
have the same rights as men (Spring 1999, p. 126).

The position which was argued for women by Wollstonecraft is a worthy
line of reasoning. In fact the work of Wollstonecraft in that early period
demonstrated that the minds of women are not "vacant". Evidently,
Rousseau and Locke were labouring under a grave misconception. It is
clear that the main intention of patriarchy was to ensure that women
are properly harnessed to play the part which it has designed for them.
This is evident in the eighteenth century women's fashions: long flowing
dresses which impede movement and ensure that women walked with
a mincing gait, tightly drawn waist which I am sure impacted on their
respiration, umbrella, hat and all. I am amazed by women's fashion
which still put the zipper or the buttons at the back of the apparel. The
woman must get some assistance to button; there is no similar fashion
design for men. The educational philosophy of Locke and Rousseau
fashioned the patriarchal value of women in society; a regrettable
development and a social travesty in the affairs of men and women.

FEMINIST CRITICAL PEDAGOGY: EDUCATION THROUGH FEMINIST LENSES

Feminist pedagogy examines the content and the instructional
methodologies of education with the view to a critical examination of
them from a woman's point of view. Main stream academics tend to
see this exercise as a challenge to their established position instead of
complimenting it; calling it to re-examine its presuppositions about
women and women's learning. In any case feminist pedagogy is based
on a critical appraisal of what patriarchy considers to be education. It
is this patriarchal paradigm which feminist are prepared to interrogate
to expose its gender bias:

[T]he worthy content of education is defined by the interest of men, the suitably worthy recipients of educational effort are boys and men, and the primary exemplars and transmitters of advanced knowledge are expected to be men" (Gore 1993, citing Morgan, p.22). Given this view, feminist pedagogy informed by radical feminist thought may be particularly reluctant to cite male educators or educational researchers as authors on pedagogy (Gore 1993, p. 22).

The difficulty of feminist pedagogy, as I perceive it, is not so much the source on which it relies for authority, but the system of patriarchy itself. There are many male authors who support the cause of women against oppression. Although Gore (1993, pp. 33-43) made a blistering critique of the critical pedagogy of Giroux and McLaren, Gore (1993) was obliged to admit that Paulo Freire's critical pedagogy is exceptional. Furthermore, hooks (1994) declares that Paulo Freire's writings on critical pedagogy has had a tremendous impact on her life as a young woman and as a feminist intellectual:

> Unlike feminist thinkers who make a clear separation between the work of the feminist pedagogy and Freire's work and thought, for me these two experiences converge. Deeply committed to feminist pedagogy, I find that, much like weaving a tapestry, I have taken threads of Paulo's work and woven it into that version of feminist pedagogy I believe my work as writer and teacher embodies. Again, I want to assert that it was the intersection and the lived pedagogy of the many black teachers of my girlhood (many of them women) who see themselves as having a liberatory mission to educate us to effectively resist racism, white supremacy that has made a profound impact on my thinking about the art and practice of teaching (p. 45).

The real problem is the way in which patriarchy has compartmentalized the functions of the sexes. As I have pointed out above in the educational philosophy of Locke and Rousseau women fall short of intellectual rationality, the ability to think and philosophize which falls outside the purview of feminine cognition but men (the prized human species) have a monopoly on this special gift, or special faculty because they have been specially endowed with them. This perception of male intellectual monopoly and predominance has been perpetuated by patriarchy for centuries, hence the up-hill struggle of women for recognition in the academy, in employment, in religion. The irony is that this (mis) conception has only feet of clay.

The expectation which society has of women, as fabricated by patriarchy, is that they would be nurturers; this is the special gift with which they have been generously endowed and a dearth of which is found in men, as the argument goes. Authority is therefore vested in men and women to find their fulfillment in serving the purposes of men. In other words, women are expected to be men's 'sidekick'. This view of women was further entrenched in the social habits and practices of both Eastern and Western religions. The religio-philosophical rational basis has always been questionable.

Social constructs have created segregation between authority and nurturance and has so created an apparent tension between the two: authority being strictly masculine and nurturance being strictly feminine. This is a false dichotomy, a social rationality which has no legitimate basis, a farcical construct which was devised by men for the oppression of women. As I have shown above, women have been in positions of power and have been mothers and they have managed those roles well. The leadership of African women is an excellent paradigm. However, in Western society the patriarchal enterprise has devised the dichotomy of male things and female things, male functions and female functions which created unnecessary complications in social life to the detriment of women. It is then the task of feminism to penetrate the bulwark of patriarchal pedagogy which is embedded in the schools and universities through the articulation of feminist critical pedagogy and feminist scholarship, and feminist male allies to expose the injustices which women suffer as a result of being marginalized by the social and political systems:

In terms of the pedagogy argued for, the discourse of feminist pedagogy attends to aspects of content and aspects of classroom processes, with the emphasis on processes (especially Women's Studies writers). In terms of content, three main approaches (often used in conjunction) are evident: (1) presenting "new" texts, previously marginalized or overlooked within disciplinary knowledge; (2) engaging in "new readings" of old texts, (for example, Carol Gilligan's "readings" of Kohlberg' studies or moral development or feminist readings of Shakespeare); (3) drawing on the personal experiences of teacher and students as the basis of knowledge production (Gore 1993, p. 78-79).

Over the past four decades significant positive changes have taken place in the position of women through feminism and Women Studies classroom using oppositional politics and pedagogy to counter patriarchal marginalization of women. hooks (1994) has formed the view that the challenge to feminist teachers today is greater than it was previously. At any rate diversity has changed the dynamics of the feminist classroom and that has brought with it a challenge of a different hue which the feminist teacher must meet:

The feminist classroom and lecture hall that I am speaking in most often today is rarely all black. Though the political progressive clamor is for 'diversity,' there is little realistic understanding of the ways feminist scholars must change ways of seeing, talking, and thinking if we are to speak to the various audiences, the "different" subjects who may be present in one location. How many feminist scholars can respond effectively when faced with a racially and ethnically diverse audience who may not share similar class backgrounds, language, levels of understanding, communication skills, and concerns? As a black woman professor in the feminist classroom teaching Women's Studies classes, these issues surface daily for m. (p. 112).

The concerns that are raised by hooks (1994) show that feminist teachers cannot afford to take a linear approach to the subject matter of their discourse, the exposure of patriarchal oppression of women, because academic issues have become very complex and they beckon the attention of feminists scholars if feminist pedagogy is to maintain the position which it has gained in the academy, and the respect and recognition which it has secured for women generally:

> But if the claims of feminist pedagogy are taken seriously, it teaches that the classroom is ripe with complicated dynamics that undermines the hypothetical marketplace. Thus, there is a schism between the goals of feminist pedagogy and the marketplace approach to free expression in the classroom is, at times, a perpetuation of the inequities and injustices that feminist pedagogy attempts to overcome. The question becomes, then, how do feminist teachers negotiate this schism when they deal with harmful expression, such as hate speech (Cohee & Kemp 1998, p.107).

Feminism has fought with patriarchy and has won much ground from it. I have no doubt that it will be able to deal with current challenges just as effectively as it has done previously. Feminist Philosophy is crucial for educational and political activism for Black women in the African Diaspora. It is for Black women in particular that critical redemptive pedagogy has the greatest significance. Black women must be critical of their redemption from the shackles of patriarchy. The need for redemption is not only applicable to women of intellectual abilities, but also for women of ordinary means. In other words, while intellectual women are able to redeem themselves from patriarchy, ordinary women must be enabled to wage the same battle for redemption from patriarchy.

FEMINISM AND MALE FEMINISTS

The equal treatment of women for which Wollstonecraft contended came two centuries later, obviously she did not share in this new awakening for women but she planted a little seed at a time when it was a serious social risk to her, so that today's women can enjoy a better life. In the last century three very important human events took place. These are the abolition of slavery followed by the outlawing of *de jure* segregation, and the significant improvement in the oppressed social and educational standing of women in general and Black women in the African Diaspora in particular. The social, educational, and political advancement of women go to the credit of the Women's Liberation Movement. Patai and Koertge (2003) see the central aims of feminism (or the Women's Liberation Movement, as it used to be called) as exemplary: to end discrimination against women, to protect women from sexual assault and economic exploitation, to transform traditional attitudes about gender roles, to help women gain the confidence and skills they need to pursue their life projects, to make our society truly one of equal opportunity, and to discover what sort of society men and women, working together as equals, might construct. These goals they see as noble and urgent goals (p.207).

These are the laudable goals which feminism has set for itself to effect the liberation of women from the vices of patriarchy to enable women to live a more fulfilled life. This is not an insurmountable task, especially when we consider that the gender differences which pass as natural are in fact social constructs which were created by patriarchal society for the subjugation of women. Women have successfully challenged patriarchal social construction of them and their place within their society and they have demonstrated that both sexes can co-exist in an equal society that is far more productive than the lopsided patriarchal society. As Patai and Koertge (2003) state the changes in the status of women are undoubtedly among the most important social development of the twentieth century. Each demand for equality has been contested; each step has made a vivid impression on the women who lived through it; each advance has become part of the birthright of the next generation. Despite the apparent lull in, and to some extent, even reversal of some of women's gains during the 1950's, the contemporary feminist movement in the United States, now in its fourth decade, has carried the redefinition of women and their roles steadily forward.

Women's contention for equality did not come easily, and I can see why this should have been so. The stout resistance which was mounted by some aspects of patriarchy: the academy, religious, political, and judicial institutions for example, to keep women 'in their place', is unwarranted and unjustifiable. If I did not know better I would have thought that women were making all kinds of inordinate demands on men or on their society when they sought to change their social standing. But perhaps I should not be so surprised because the fight for African American emancipation was met with the same kind of cruel and bigoted resistance when all that the slaves were pleading for is the white plantocracy's recognition of their common humanity. The plea of women is not unlike that of the slaves. That men did/do not appreciate this message is astounding. Feminism had to show that the traditional education with its male oriented focus and misogyny has failed to satisfy even the very standard which it has set for itself. The big challenge for feminism was aptly put by Gore (1993) when she says:

> If indeed patriarchal pedagogy is built into our schools
> and universities, a question emerges as to whether feminist
> pedagogy, as articulated, *can* exist within those institutions.
> Is it possible to relocate/revise/reclaim authority when this
> would require us all, teachers and students alike, to unlearn
> years of "patriarchal pedagogy? (p. 83)

This was indeed a formidable task, at least so it appeared, but the answer to Gore's (1993) question must be given in the affirmative. But women were not alone in the struggle for equal treatment; they had a forerunner in the civil rights movement which no doubt gave impetus to the feminist call for equal rights and justice. Indeed Patai & Koertge (2003) recounts the objective and achievements of the movement for women's liberation:

> In important ways, both intellectual and practical, this
> movement's agenda was shaped by the work of feminist
> scholars in the academy. The result of their efforts has
> been an enormous flowering of Women's Studies programs,

feminist scholarship, and women's culture, as well as an increase public awareness of job discrimination, domestic abuse, sexual assaults, and other impediments placed on women in the public and private spheres. Complementing all this attention, albeit on a more modest scale, have been political and economic gains for at least some women (p. 1).

Women's Studies are now firmly planted in the academy which provides a forum for women to discuss women's issues. The aim of Women's Studies then must be the liberation of women from the social structures which oppress women. However, this overthrowing of the traditional patriarchal guards should not be done in isolation to men who are progressive because women's liberation is to produce equal opportunity for both sexes. The principle or objective of women's liberation can never be the emasculation of men so as to pacify them, even though Locke and Rousseau must be turning in their graves. Be that as it may, Patai & Koertge (2003) have argued that things in Women's Studies have gone awry. They have lauded the achievement of women over the past forty years, but they seem to be dismayed by the in-flight in Women's Studies and the indoctrination of young women. They further argue that female scholars in Women's Studies have made two fundamental blunders which are academic separation and an over emphasis on activism albeit that these are important features of the movement for liberation.

Both authors argue that separatism in Women's Studies is readily and graphically illustrated by the widespread exclusion of male authors from course Syllabi, assigned reading lists, and citations in scholarly papers. In particular cases, there can, of course, be practical reasons for mentioning only female sources, and probably scholars in every field tend to over cite close colleagues and allies. But a systematic refusal to read or respond to male authors harms feminist scholarship in many ways. These moves they claim "are debilitating to the cause of feminism, and they may lure female students into the – obvious false – belief that all intellectual work produced by males is irrelevant to, or in conflict with, feminist projects" (p. 6).

This position has inevitably led to the alienation of some men from things feminine because women have made their program into a gender forum instead of a search for truth and cooperation. I find this approach to lack maturation because so long as we are on this planet, it is imperative that we, women and men, work together for our continued co-existence and posterity. We do not require a university education to be so informed. Following emancipation and *de jure* segregation, African American women would be foolhardy to think that they should inculcate the same lessons of virulent racism, bigotry, and segregation (that is reverse racism) in their own children. Redemptive pedagogy seeks to redeem and to teach redemption for those who are oppressed and down trodden by the social structures in their society. Redemption is for both the oppressed and the oppressor. It is interesting to note that when Nelson Mandela became President in the new South Africa, he sought to reconcile Whites and Blacks for the common good of the country.

Mahatma Ghandi taught that if we practice "an eye for an eye" the whole world would soon be blind. If men are perceived as the enemy with whom women must not contaminate themselves, but with whom they should combat then how do we work together to produce workable solutions to the myriad problems that are plaguing our planet? The world's problems cannot be solved by one sex only. As a matter of fact, I am inclined to believe that we have been down this road already and dance this jig already. I recall that during the Greco-Roman period there was a prevailing view that if a man wants to be a scholar he must shun the company of women or he will be stupid, a fool; we cannot afford to reproduce and replicate the errors of the past. Women should not conjure up the social situation where the sexes live in a separate but equal society. As Patai & Koertge (2003) put it:

> In addition, feminists often claim that the morality and
> value systems of oppressed groups are inherently superior to
> those of the oppressors, whose long history of exploitative
> behaviour has demonstrated their moral bankruptcy.
> Last but not least, it is assumed that the only way for an

oppressed group to remedy its unsatisfactory situation is by single-mindedly pursuing the needs of its own members (p. 51).

Patai & Koertge (2003) chronicled the story of the rejection of a young man, Allan Hunter, who was a member of the Women's Studies class. Many men, like Hunter, are put off by being rejected by women when they strongly desire to be a part of the feminist movement with the view of correcting the ills of patriarchy:

> Writing ten years later of his experience in a feminist theory class, Hunter ... says that his attempts to debate theoretical issues in this class invariably led to "constant question of 'Who asked you? Why should any of us give a damn if YOU don't like the direction that feminist theory is taking? It's our stuff, not your Stuff.'" He finally concluded that it is conceptually problematic for any male to be a full-scale committed participant in the political effort to transform patriarchy (p. 53).

It would therefore seem that feminism is a closed shop where men are concerned. It would also seem that Women's Studies are not only pursuing the intellectual elevation of women by making them aware of past and current oppression, but it seems to have become a system of indoctrination not unlike fundamental religiosity and all members of the clan are expected to condescend to it without any dissention. This is patriarchy in reverse. 'Too far east is west'. The transformation of our society for the betterment of all persons cannot be realized if we simply dish out more of the same under a different label. A rose of any color is still a rose. Can it be reasonably said that women today are still exposed to victimization and oppression by patriarchy? The answer to this seems to be in the affirmative. But the answer is not in the victimization of men, especially progressive men. The exclusion of men is evident in the type of topics which are scheduled for Introductory Women's Studies courses: rape, incest, physical abuse of women and children. These matters are of course, of crucial importance to women because of the physical and emotional trauma and indignity which they cause to women. But this is a lopsided view because there are women and children who have good, healthy relationships with men in the absence of all these negatives. Patai and Koertge (2003) have given the answer to the question which I have mooted here:

> Listening to what is taught in many Women's Studies courses and what is claimed by women's organizations, the answer would seem to be an incontrovertible YES. Never mind the massive evidence – statistical, judicial, and legislative, as well as anecdotal – of enormous and continuing improvement in women's status in the United States. Society has changed, but feminist activists seem determined either not to notice or not to admit it. Instead, hackneyed stereotypes are repeated as though they were startling insights (p. 229).

Clearly, the social, political, and economical positions of women have improved tremendously within the last four decades. However, women cannot rest on their laurels because there are still areas of serious oppression against women. Sexual harassment of female employees by male bosses and violence against women in the domestic setting as indicated above are two current examples. Women who find themselves in these degrading situations are forced to choose between keeping their conjugal relationship or their jobs (which they need to provide for their families) and their dignity. This is a moral and social outrage. Feminists must be prepared to partner with their male feminist activists to eliminate this scourge.

I have referred above to the experience of Allan Hunter in his efforts to make a connection with feminism and to share in the struggles of women and the rebuffs which he received. Women must be prepared to let men into their studies because all men are not set on the continued oppression of women. I have found the approach of bell hooks (1994) to be very empathetic with men whose views are like those of Allan Hunter. Feminist politics and pedagogy cannot exclude men and others. In other words diversity has a vital role to play in this struggle against feminine oppression, as it has in all cases of oppression. The fact is many men are unaware that their relationship with women is informed by sexism. It is therefore incumbent upon enlightened women to share their feelings with men who are willing to listen and these men can inform other men who will not listen to women. Hence there is the need for a critical redemptive pedagogy for the liberation of both females and males. Bearing in mind that both the oppressor and the oppressed need to be redeemed from their situationality of oppression. Many men act in accordance with the way in which they were socialized. Chauvinist men would be more inclined to listen to other men rather than women. Critical redemptive pedagogy would produce similar results that are reported by hooks (1994):

> In recent years, I have been teaching large numbers of black male students, many of whom are not aware of the ways sexism informs how they speak and interact in a group setting. They face challenges to behavior patterns they may have never before thought important to question. Towards the end of one of the semester, Mark, a black male student in my "Reading Fiction" English class, share that while we focused on African American literature, his deepest sense of 'awakening" came from learning about gender, about feminist standpoint (p. 114).

Critical redemptive pedagogy brings to student's awareness an awaking that removes the scales from their eyes through its methodology of critically analyzing gender and feminist views. The aim is to bring the students to the point where they recognize the need for redemption their patriarchal social construction. I am inclined to believe that feminists concerns would be given a better hearing by redeemed black men because they know what it means to be oppressed because of their color. Perhaps if they are made to see the similarity between sexism and racism, this might help in their conversion to the feminist cause. However, I do not believe that men, especially those who do not seek to perpetuate patriarchal oppression, should be made to internalize an awful sense of guilt. This is even more important for those who have always respected women. I go back to hooks (1994) for another encounter with her experience with another male student:

> Brett, a close partner of one of the women, was taking another class with me. Since he was named by black women in the group as one of the black males who was concerned about gender issues, I talked with him specifically about feminism. He responded by calling attention to the reasons it is difficulty for black men to deal with sexism, the primary one being that they are accustomed to thinking of themselves in terms of racism, being exploited and oppressed. Speaking of his efforts to develop feminist awareness, he stressed limitations: "I've tried to understand but then I'm a man. Sometimes I don't understand and it hurts, 'cause I think I'm the epitome of everything that's oppressed (p. 116).

Patriarchy is so rooted in the psyche of many men that it will take considerable work to dislodge it and reorient men away from the prejudices of sexism. We must also bear in mind that black men have their own issues of racial oppression to deal with in their everyday living. Be that as it may, I believe that the concerns of black men and feminism would make a good marriage especially if black men are made aware that while they have one strike against them (being black), black women have two strikes against them (being women and black at the same time) which perhaps make their struggle all the more difficult. hooks (1994) has expressed the view that some inroads are being made especially with young black men:

> Since it is difficult for many black men to give voice to the ways they are hurt and wounded by racism, it is also understandable that it is difficult for them to "own up to" sexism, to be accountable. More and more, individual black men – particular young black men – are facing the challenge of daring to critique gender, be informed, and willingly resist and oppose sexism. On college campuses, black male students are increasingly compelled by black female peers to think about sexism. Recently, I gave a talk

where Pat, a young black man, was wearing a button that
read "Sexism is a male disease: Let's solve it ourselves." Pat
was into rap and he gave me a tape of rap that opposed
rape (p. 116).

I am further intrigued by a story which is reported by hooks (1994, p.
72) of the transforming impact her work has had on men in prison.
Well, I never! Through their study of feminism these incarcerated men
are able to critically reflect on the way in which patriarchy has shaped
their lives and coming to that point of realization they saw the need to
reform their outlook on women. There is something to think about.

FEMINISM TRIUMPHANT

So what is the position of women today: Are they still living under a
regime of oppression? Patai & Koertge (2003) seem to think that by
and large women have been liberated, despite the presence of vestiges of
marginalization and oppression. They pose the question whether women
are in fact still oppressed by patriarchy in today's modern societies. They
aver there has been enormous and continuing improvement in the
status of women in the United States.

Given the proliferation of Women's Studies in the universities, it
would seem that feminism has achieved much of the goals which it
had originally set out to achieve. Patai & Koertge (2003) expressed the
view that "It is high time that progressive women and men stopped
waxing sentimental about both the plight and the latent virtues of the
oppressed and start exercising a little tough-minded common sense in
proposing realistic, workable reform" (p. 209). This seems to be a hard
position to take because sometimes the more things change the more
they remain the same. Certainly, there are those who will argue that
African slavery ended many years ago, a pet claim for those on the
political right, because it lulls Black people into a national amnesia.
This state of sleep walking makes Black labor easy to exploit while
keeping them on the periphery of social and political advancement. I

believe the same thing can happen in relation to women's liberation. Therefore sharp care must be exercised in this particular situation. The women sentinels must neither rest on their laurels nor fall asleep. The same instructions hold true for men who are feminist activists.

Feminism has done a tremendous job in uncovering the ills which were created and fostered by patriarchy and put forward its claim for equality with men in a very forceful way. This quest to right the centuries of wrongs perpetuated by masculinity seems to have been met with little resistance, when compared to the resistance with which the liberation of African slaves in the Caribbean and North America was met. It seems though once patriarchy was found out it was willing to "own up" to its guilt and to make amends for past injustices. The conversion of patriarchy seems to be genuine, for unlike the case of *de jure* segregation which has given way to *de facto* segregation, it cannot be convincingly argued that there is a similar development in relation to feminism. This view is supported by Patai & Koertge (2003):

> Contrary to feminists who insist, absurdly, that modern-day universities have remained essentially patriarchal institutions, the stories in this book convey quite a different scene: an entire society on the move, which meant that feminist academics could often count on the active collaboration of well-placed male allies who stimulated the institutional receptivity to feminist ideas.(p. 241).

Some feminists still maintain a militant posture as though nothing significant has happened within the last four decades and still holding the fort and sounding the rally cry to take up arms.

Further support for this opinion can be found in Gore (1993) when she says that while the academy is seen to constrain feminist pedagogy, it also plays a role in structuring and supporting the discourse and practice of feminist pedagogy. She cites Magda Lewis (1989) in support of this opinion where (Lewis) acknowledges that educational institutions are contradictorily both the site where reactionary and repressive ideologies are entrenched *and* the site where progressive, transformative possibilities are born. The transformative possibilities of Women's Studies are cited as a typical example. The rapid ascendancy of Women's Studies must have been facilitated by a willingness or at the very least complicity of the beleaguered patriarchy because it did not rise to its own defence or in the interest of 'self-preservation' sought to combat the claims of feminism:

> Where was the much-maligned patriarchy while this unprecedented expansion and reconfiguration of the academy was occurring? Why was the patriarchy not defending its bastions? How can one explain the ready help and willingness to change on the part of male administrators and colleagues described by one after another of the contributors to this volume? The remarkable fact is that feminists succeeded spectacularly. Within the first decade (1970-1980), approximately 350 Women's Studies programs – that is, about half of the currently existing ones – were set in place (Patai & Koertge 2003, p. 241).

The impression that is formed here is that feminist concerns were welcomed in the academy with open arms. Of course, it would be a gross misrepresentation of my mind if I were to say that there was not an iota of resistance. I am sure that there was some measure of resistance however meager because people who are entrenched in special positions are usually afraid of change, especially reactionary persons, but those who are progressive will see the good in new and innovative ideas, in the need to rid academia of prejudice and oppression. It would seem that the reception of feminism was far better than that which was received by anti-segregation proponents to which there was a firm wall of resistance:

> There is no history in this book of concerted male resistance, no evidence of a generalized institutional rejection of efforts of feminist faculty, students, and staff. On the contrary, what all this suggests is a society prepared for change and indeed embracing it, bolstered by legislation endorsed by

the "patriarchal government" in Washington D. C. (Patai & Koertge 2003, p. 241).

I suspect this positive acceptance of so profound a change, an alteration of liberal Western political and educational philosophy was due to the fact that its advocates were White women. I wonder what would have been the response if they were Black women, like the Black men who advocated for the abolition of segregation. Would they have been given the time of day? I doubt it would have been any easier. I believe it would have been just as much an uphill struggle as was the struggle against pernicious segregation. Be that as it may, the frontier of patriarchy has been deeply penetrated and rolled back. I am persuaded that feminism triumphant will continue to break down the barriers of oppression, marginalization, racism, sexism, and cultural hegemony to create a politics of equality. I would like to chronicle and reiterate here the noble goals of feminism as given by Patai & Koertge (2003, p. 207):

1. to end discrimination against women,

2. to protect women from sexual assault and economic exploitation,

3. to transform traditional attitudes about gender roles,

4. to help women gain the confidence and skills they need to pursue their life projects,

5. to make our society truly one of equal opportunity, and to discover what sort of society men and women, working together as equals, might construct.

CONCLUSION

It is clear that both men and women must work together to create an equal society in which both sexes can co-exist. Feminism has rolled back patriarchy and has gained significant improvement in the social and political standing of women. Critical redemptive pedagogy has a crucial role to play in the education of both male and female. It is the catalyst in the process of educational transformation which will bring about an exponential effect in all aspects of associated living in a democratic society. But it is pre-requisite for feminist and male feminist activist students to be conscientized through the principles of redemptive pedagogy. These men in prison that are referred to above by hooks (1994) have been redeemed from their patriarchal social construction were therefore able to critically examine their own social construction and were persuaded that they needed to change. Critical redemptive pedagogy deconstructs the life world of the student as created by his/her social construction and lead the student to reconstruct a new life world without racism, bigotry, and sexism. Both men and women must work together for the creation of the new life world of equality.

CHAPTER SEVEN

Marketing Public Education: The Pied Pipers Resurrection

> Learning itself – the learning of a skill, or the enjoying of a book, and even having an idea – is now defined increasingly not as a process or preoccupation that holds satisfaction of its own but in proprietary terms, as if it were the acquisition of an object or stock-option or the purchase of a piece of land (Kozol, 2005, p.96).

The media, Reagan, and Bush administrations have painted a grim picture of failures in America's public education systems, and they have diagnosed the problem to be poor quality teaching so No Child Left Behind was enacted to combat the decline in public education. This piece of legislation was backed up by calls for the privatization of education to bring about greater efficiency in students' achievement. Many have recommended school choice in the forms of voucher and charter schools. The issue which I critically examine here is whether there is any genuine crisis in the public education system in the first place, and secondly whether the market metaphor which is being advocated for school choice can improve public education, or whether it will simply compound and exacerbate what is mooted to be a crisis. The impact of school choice on African Americans and other poor minority people is also examined. The current methodology of education and the new advocacy of school choice are weighed in terms of their advantage and disadvantage. And the disadvantage is in favor of African American and other minorities. This is another step in the further educational disenfranchisement of the poor in America. The idea of school privatization has not come to the Caribbean as yet, but given that we have this mocking bird propensity whereby we ape whatever is done in the American system, education and otherwise, I suspect it is just a matter of time before our Eurocentric political directorates and educational administration jump on the band wagon and dance to the jig of the Pied Piper while he leads us and our children into uncritical intellectual zombification.

MULTICULTURALISM AND THE DEMISE OF THE MELTING-POT BIGOTRY

The debate over the effectiveness of the United States public education has been brought to the fore under the presidency of Ronald Reagan and the two Bush Presidents. The cut and thrust of the debate appears to be mounted against the continuation of the common public school system as it presently exists in the United States of America. The debate to dismantle the public educational system is being pushed aggressively by various politico-social blocks and/or interest groups from the Right, such as religious fundamentalists, nationalists, and political conservatives. The paradigmatic model of this debate is the laws and ideology of the market place. Added to the market place paradigm is the anti-progressive movement of the ultra-traditional cultural outlook which is threatened by the achievements of multiculturalism in education.

The market place ideology has been promoting the importance of individual choice in terms of schooling over against the need for communitarian values. Competition is seen as being of greater importance than the need for corporate learning among students.

Competition is touted as the most effective method to stimulate and measure students' educational progress. However, competition can be and is dangerous because it has a blind spot which precludes any concern for equity through the promotion of what is perceived to be academic excellence. Competition does not take into account the needs of those who are slow or less capable. They are usually the children of the poor and disadvantaged. They are the ones who are frequently left behind, and who consequently develop serious deficiencies in their educational development. It is not surprising then, that so many of the children of the poor become social outcasts who live a life of rebellion against the society. The concepts of market paradigm are: privatization, competition, standardized testing, and individualism. The pretext that is used for the need to privatize schooling is the upliftment of the educational standard in the United States of America which has fallen below acceptable levels. But the modus operandi of privatization has always been to the exclusion of those who are least able to purchase the goods and services provided by privatism. This was anticipated by Rawls (1971) and this is why in his theory of justice he advocates the difference principle to place the responsibility upon the members of the society who are better able to provide reasonable social opportunities for those who are least able so that there can be a reasonably level playing field.

However, I believe the real reason for this aggressive onslaught on the educational system is to counteract the recent emergence of a new cultural movement in the schools which is now demanding that schooling takes seriously the meaning and purpose of living in a multicultural and pluralistic democratic society in the United States of America. The multicultural movement in education has and continues to gain significant grounds through the works of many educators. Multiculturalism promotes unity and equality in diverse and demands that this be reflected in education.

The broadside against the advancement of multiculturalism is seen in the Right's demand and promotion of standardized testing, a negative attitude to multiculturalism through the attempt to resuscitate the defunct notion of the 'melting pot' and what it means to be American, the so-called "common culture", and the efforts to center curricular development around the notion of this common culture, but in effect it is the promotion of Eurocentric values to the detriment of all others. The implications of the notion of a common culture are to counteract any attempt by African Americans and other minority people to seek to promote their own cultural identity through educational reform. The idea is that if minority peoples are able to establish their own cultural identity this would significantly diminish the control which the Eurocentric ideology has on the society. This line of reasoning is supported by Henig (1994):

> The power of the melting-pot image has lessened over time. In small part, this probably is due to changes in the nature of the immigrants themselves. Then, more than now, immigrants brought with them elements of a common heritage. The Irish might hate the Italians, and Protestants might hate Catholics, but potent as these antagonisms were, they were balanced by shared presumptions associated with a Western, predominantly European background. Sharper differences separate the new American immigrants – Asian and Arabic, Buddhist and Islamic, Afghani and Ethiopian – from one another and from the dominant norm (p. 8).

As Henig (1994) further noted even more than the ethnocentric notions of Americanism, is the fact that the melting-pot notion has lost its appeal and legitimacy:

> More significant, though, the power of the melting-pot vision has lessened because the ideas behind it have lost legitimacy. In an earlier and perhaps naïve era, education reformers such as Horace Man could base a call for common schooling on an unabashed confidence in the transcendent universality of American ideals. The ethnocentric imperialism with which such calls were imbued would not go unnoticed today (p.8).

The cut and thrust of the debate have revealed the importance of school as places of political and religious contestation for cultural identification. More than that, the contestation that is going on in education throws up and either belie or challenge the democratic notion that America is an open, democratic society which treats all people equally and where all people are free. In other words, America's democratic values and ideals are being put to the test to prove their veracity that the country really cares about all of its peoples.

The idea that schools are neutral, passive sites in the society for the transmission of knowledge and culture is an exploded myth. It is frequently becoming evident that schools are sites of critical and transformative activities which are impacting profoundly, or, at the very least have the potential of so impacting on the lives of both teachers and learners in particular and the society as a whole. This has serious ramifications for the agenda of the New Right which is seeking to etch its moral and religious values into the school's curriculum. Hence, their retreat behind the market model for the operation of schools to create private educational enclaves for slavocratic indoctrination of Blacks and other minorities. The efforts of the New Right must be stoutly resisted in the interest of Black children's cultural identity and in the interest of the society as a whole in order to preserve its democratic ideals. The market metaphor emphasizes the need to create minds for the market – this is a nice way of describing the markets requirements for mindless workers - drones. Progressive educator should not be intimidated by the movement of the Right and so retreat into the culture of silence because that would pave the way for conservatives' domination of education reform to the detriment of the poor and disadvantaged:

> It is this urge to retreat that ultimately accounts for much of the popular appeal of both the broad privatization movement and the specific segment of the education-reform movement that draws on market models for inspiration. Although the market metaphor reinforces the impression that privatization is directly deduced from economic theory, interwoven with this cognitive element

is a more visceral, cultural impulse for privatization as a
retreat from responsibility to a broader collectivity (Henig,
1994, p. 9).

Critical, liberal educators must be in the vanguard to protect the
curriculum from right wing fundamentalism and to meet the challenges
of the cultural and educational transformation of schooling for the
purpose of creating meaning for the reality in which their students
live. The living fact is that the American society is not homogenous and
never was but there are those elements which would like to keep the
homogenous myth alive to serve their own vested self-interest. America
is a heterogeneous society and the culture of the one group cannot be
allowed to be the dominant model for all to the detriment of many. Can
the market paradigm fulfill what America needs to unite its peoples?
Henig (1994) expresses the opinion that faced with disparate groups
– each with its own notions of what ideas and values are important to
preserve and which to discard, and all protected from direct challenges
by the widely accepted philosophy of "to each its own" – it is tempting
to beat a retreat from the idea of collective purpose, and to settle more
comfortably into bite-size communities of like-minded folks or to draw
the wagons around in even smaller circles of family or individuals.

Progressive educators must exercise due diligence with the rhetoric
that surrounds educational reform for it is a wolf in sheep clothing
seeking to devour the unsuspecting and uncritical persons. The
packaging of the rhetoric is wrapped in the terms of raising educational
standards and making and accountable. I concur with Cool (2005)
who states:

> And much of the rhetoric or "rigor" and "high standards"
> that we hear so frequently, no matter how egalitarian in
> spirit it may sound to some, is fatally belied by practices
> which vulgarize the intellects of children and take from
> their education far too many of the opportunities for
> cultural and critical reflectivenss without which citizens
> become receptacles for other people's ideologies and ways

of looking at the world but lack the independent spirit to create their own (p. 98).

In this way the market model denudes the intellects of the students through its commodification of education to meet the demands of the job market. Through this methodology the poor and disadvantaged become trapped in a cycle of low paying jobs creating wealth for others through the manipulation and control of their labor but never for themselves. This is naked idiotic education which must be countered by critical redemptive pedagogy for the uplift of the poor and oppressed.

THE MEANING OF SCHOOL CHOICE

Prudence must be exercised when seeking to understanding the meaning of choice and the history behind choice as an alternative school system. Much of the talk on choice has been up to this point more rhetoric than the reality of the situations in America's public school system:

> Much of the debate over educational choice is couched in rhetorical flourishes that simply do not face the reality of education in our inner cities. Supporters of choice are quick to praise competition. Make schools compete with each other and the schools from which all families can choose will be better. But where else has competition worked in our inner-city neighborhood? Has it worked in housing? In grocery stores? In health care? In retail? (Witte, 2000, p.5)

School choice is a call for greater involvement of parents and children in making a determination as to where children of a particular family will be educated. The idea of choice indicates that children will no longer be obliged to attend the schools in their neighborhood, nor will they have to change residence to go to a school of their choice. This of course may mean that the government will have to privatize the public schools.

> In the education area the impetus to privatize finds
> expression most directly in the call for increasing
> educational choice. Educational choice involves expanding
> the freedom of families to send their children to schools
> other than the public schools in their assigned attendance
> zones. Choice plans can be based on vouchers, tuition
> tax credits, or administrative procedures. They may allow
> parents virtually unconstrained freedom to select the
> school of their choice (Henig, 1994, p. 4).

In these circumstances of parental choice of school for their families,
schools will be forced to compete to hold and keep a place in the
market; schools will be required to pander to the ebb and flow of
the market place if they wish to stay alive. It is believed that this will
make schools more responsive and effective, and cater to the overall
improvement of the educational system.

Brighouse (2002) has identified four types of school choice being
operated in the United States of America: private voucher programs in
Milwaukee, San Antonio, Indianapolis, and New York: secondly, the
magnet schools – inter-district transfer programs which allow students
from the inner-city schools to choose schools in suburban districts: the
third form is the Charter Schools, and the fourth is the public/private
school in Milwaukee and Cleveland:

> The proponents of school choice argue that it gives the
> parents a greater role in deciding where their children attend
> school. School choice will relinquish the traditional model
> of neighborhood schooling. In neighborhood schooling,
> children are allocated to schools solely on the basis of where
> they live – every child from any given neighborhood will
> attend the same school (Brighouse, 2002, p. 23).

However, in reality there is a measure of choice in this model because
the rich can change their residence so as to get their children into the
particular school which they desire. But the poor will be forced by their
economic circumstances to school their children in the neighborhood.
This in fact, happened in many of the urban areas leaving the children

of the poor Blacks and other minorities in the poorly serviced inner-city schools:

> Those who favor choice always stress freedom, often positing
> freedom as an expression of equal opportunity. The most
> powerful of these arguments points to the simultaneous
> inability of the public education system to produce
> anything approaching equal outcomes, while at the same
> time restricting the choices of those families who suffer the
> most. Those families, in inner-city school systems, cannot
> buy private education, and they lack the resources and are
> the wrong color to move to higher performing suburban
> districts. Thus, the argument goes, they are trapped in
> school systems that are not serving their needs and within
> which their children are failing (Witte, 2000, p. 18).

This is an attractive argument and easy to buy, but it belies the reality of the situation. Those who are not in favor of choice fear that the system will turn upon the persons who the advocates of choice claim will get a better deal. As a matter of fact it seems that the children of the poor in the inner-city school will still or will be further prohibited from capitalizing on the education that is available in the suburban school systems. Witte (2003) makes the pertinent point that:

> They argue that voucher systems will accelerate the already
> significant differences between those who attend public
> and private schools. They believe that at best voucher
> systems will cream off the best students remaining in the
> public schools, and at worst will also subsidized those
> elite students already attending private schools. The result
> will be more inequitable distribution of resources and an
> increasing achievement differential between schools and
> socio-economic groups (p. 18).

The pertinent question is whether voucher and charter schools provide a better educational system than the traditional public education system in terms of student's achievement. I am inclined to hold opinion with Witte (2000) that school choice will work to the disadvantage of the poor, especially African Americans. It will perpetuate the present *de facto* segregation in inner-city and suburban education.

FEAR TROUBLING THE WATERS

The clamor for school choice stems from the perception that America's public school system is failing miserably for a number of reasons and the remedy or the 'fix' for the failure is the privatization of America's public school system. I am inclined to hold opinion with Henig (1994) that there has been a misdiagnosis of the problems within America's public school system.

> While there is much that is wrong with American education today, claims of broad gauge failures have been overstated, and the link between school performance and the array of economic and social problems that are the real source of citizens distress is more tenuous than education reformers proclaim. More importantly, the market-oriented proposal favored by the "restructurers" are unlikely to work as projected and are more likely than not to make things considerably worse (p. 5).

What is of even greater concern to me is that the advocates of school choice who are pushing full steam ahead for the privatization of public school, seem not to have given any consideration to a contingency plan for an exit should privatization turns out to be a failure. Chubb & Moe (1990) sees the problem of the public school system as being caused by its over bureaucratization and the politics of school administration. They advocate the solution as an immediate removal of the bureaucracy that is debilitating the school system. Chubb & Moe (1190) offers an easy solution to the problem:

> Our solution to this problem is to look beyond the public school system and seek out alternative institutional arrangements to which it can be compared. This is why we find the private sector so useful. It helps us to compare

institutions – and thus, in the process, understand the public schools (p. 27).

To use corporatism as the yard stick for measuring what will be successful in education is not a comparison of apples with apples. Corporatism is driven by the profit motive. I do not believe that school should be driven by that motive. Children's advancement cannot be compared with turnovers in stocks and bonds. They further argue that the institutional setting of the private sector in terms of its control is quite unlike the public sector management which follows the democratic process and so hampers the process of getting things done in an expeditious manner.

> All schools in the private sector, however, have two important institutional features in common: society does not control them directly through democratic politics, and society does control them – indirectly - through the market place. This is what makes the private sector distinctively different from the public sector as an institutional setting for schools (p. 27).

This line of reasoning is, *prima facie,* logical and cogent. While the private sector is propelled by competition and competition, theoretically, should produce good quality product, we are also well aware that the bottom line for private sector operation is the profit motive. When businesses fail to make a profit the owners simply fold them up and move on to other economically feasible areas. School cannot and should not be handled in this manner. Furthermore, competition breeds individualism which destroys communitarianism.

Chubb & Moe (1990) see the decentralization of authority in the market place as its redeeming feature because the management of the school can move with the ebb and flow of the market place creating a product which the market desires. This feature is totally lacking in the public school system, hence its failures.

Effective authority within market settings, then, is radically decentralized. In private sector education, the people who run each school decide what they will teach, how they will teach it, who will do the teaching, how much to charge for their services, and virtually everything else about how education will be organized and supplied. Students and parents assess the offerings, reputations, and costs of the various schools and make their own choices about which to attend. No one makes decisions for society. All participants make decisions for themselves (p. 29).

The conclusion reached by Chubb & Moe (1990), and the position they have taken in tendering what they considered to be the solution to America's public school crisis have been rejected by Henig (1994):

Chubb and Moe turned to markets and choice to save education after reaching the bleak conclusion that efforts to reform schools through normal political channels were destined to fail. Theirs is something more than mere frustration with the slow pace, uneven responsiveness, and bureaucratic inefficiency of government. They charged that most fundamental causes of the problem "are in fact the very institutions of direct democratic control" In a heterogeneous and pluralistic society like ours, they argue, the will of the majority necessarily becomes express through hierarchical regimes and bureaucratic modes of implementation (p. 9).

However, the position of Chubb & Moe is supported by educational theorist who *prima facie* makes their argument appear convincing to the public. For example:

Paul Hill, Lawrence Pierce, and James Guthrie argue that conventional public schools are too heavily bureaucratized, rule bound, and interest-group dominated to consistently operate effectively. They believe that the operation of schools by political bodies distracts schools from their basic educational mission, interposing educationally irrelevant concerns about compliance, standardization,

and employment (Gill, Timpane, Ross & Brewer, 2001, p. 70).

The position of Chubb & Moe (1990), is tantamount to a vote of no confidence in the democratic administration of the public school system because it prohibits educators from creating the kind of programs and curricula that would make public schools work more effectively. The autonomy of the principals and the teachers would foster a team spirit of professional camaraderie and solidarity in producing as oppose to reproducing, effective education. I am not convinced that the market metaphor will provide the effective education which they have envisioned.

> Drawing on a market analogy, Chubb and Moe portrays an inherent tension between majoritarian principles and the private held interest of families as education consumers. Unfortunately, in their eyes, democratic institutions and ideals give parents no favored status. The sovereignty of the family can be won only by trimming the sovereignty of the majority (Henig, 1994, 10).

I believe that those who are clamoring for education 'restructure' have either naively or deliberately misinterpreted the poor performance of some schools and have blown it out of proportion by labeling educational failures as reaching 'crisis' proportion. This is unfortunate because it has put the general society in a state of panic over the future of its children.

> By defining poor school performance as a "crisis" they have helped to propel it higher on the nation's agenda and justified their claim that only radical change will suffice. By selectively retelling the history of education policy, they have reinforced prejudice about governmental ineptitude, benign markets, and intimate communities. By portraying empirical analyses as if they decisively establish the workability and effectiveness of experiments in choice, they have created the mistaken impression

that fundamentally restructuring education is a low risk
enterprise with predictable results (Henig, 1994, p.11).

The way in which choice is marketed through the use of the market
metaphor is very seductive because it gives the impression of painless
restructuring – a panacea. However, anything that claims to be a
panacea should be treated with suspicion. It is inconceivable that
fundamental restructuring to an education system as enormous as the
United States of America can be painless, without any fall outs. Its
seduction is further seen in its portrayal of choice as an educational
alternative as the best development in the educational system. The word
'choice' is pregnant with connotations and I fear that this pregnancy
may result in an educational miscarriage or it may be still born.

Choice offers two alternatives to the public school system. These
are vouchers and charter schools. These have been touted by choice
proponents as the alternatives that will make schooling in America more
effective. The emphasis is on competition for survival. The empirical
evidence was investigated by Gill, Timpane, et al (2001) and they have
not found any significant differences in the educational achievement
between the children in the public education system and those in the
private systems – vouchers and charter schools:

> Results from the program consisting of a few hundred
> students attending seven sectarian voucher schools are of
> minimal relevance to predicting the results from a program
> enrolling 9,500 students at 103 voucher schools, most
> of which are sectarian. As we show below, the literature
> on public and private schooling suggest that, compared
> with other private schools, Catholic schools may have a
> unique advantage for low-income minority children. In
> sum, the findings from the early years of the Milwaukee
> voucher program tell little about the effectiveness of
> voucher and charter programs generally. Rouse's results
> are methodologically solid, but they speak only to the
> effectiveness of a handful of nonsectarian private schools
> in Milwaukee in the early 1990s (p. 84).

The proposition that the choice alternatives of voucher and charter schools will improve the learning of students is not supported by the empirical evidence as illustrated by Gill, Timpane, et al (2001). Furthermore, I am inclined to hold opinion with Berliner & Biddle (1995) that they smell a rat in the proclamation of the manufactured educational crisis. The so-called crisis in their view is just another political red herring which has been dragged across the media frontiers of America and has spawned a great panic in parents and teachers.

> Some readers may be reluctant because they don't want to acknowledge that they have bought into fraudulent ideas, that they were victimized by a massive "con game." To appreciate their plight one must come to understand that the Manufactured Crisis was not merely an accidental set of events or a product of impersonal social forces. It also involved a serious campaign by identifiable persons to sell Americans the false idea that their public schools were failing and that because of this failure the nation was at peril – this campaign involved a great deal of effort, chicanery, playing on people's worries, pandering to prejudices, and misreporting and misrepresenting evidence (Berliner & Biddle, 1995, p. 9).

It seems pretty harsh to accuse public officials of misrepresenting the evidence, but nonetheless this is the position taken by Berliner & Biddle (1995). To determine the justification of this accusation, they have critically examined the evidence which the public officials have put forward as demonstrating that America's public schools are failing. One of such piece of evidence is the scholastic aptitude test (SAT), the aggregate scores. Berliner & Biddle (1995) accept that between 1963 and 1975 SAT scores fell and this decline has been used as evidence of the falling standards in the public school system. But they contend that this evidence has been misconstrued to bolster "the myth of achievement decline is not only false – it is a hysterical fraud" (p. 14):

> This decline has been cited as evidence that our schools were failing by many people – such as William Bennett –

who were ignorant or wanted to rubbish public education.
These doomsayers argue that such a "huge" decline in SAT
scores – ranging from 60 to 90 points, depending on the
years used to compute the figure – was sure proof that the
nation was in trouble. And to this day the press continues
to report annual figures for aggregate national SAT scores
(sometimes citing shifts of one or two points in those
scores) as if they were a report card that can tell Americans
something about the effectiveness of their schools (pp. 15-
16).

I am inclined to concur with Berliner & Biddle (1995) that it is misleading
to rely on simple shifts in SAT scores to make the pronouncement that
America's schools are failing. Furthermore, aggregate SAT scores seem
to be a shaky ground on which to make such a profound judgment.
Berliner & Biddle (1995) rely on three weaknesses of The SAT scores to
support their case. First, the SAT is taken by high school seniors who
wish to be admitted to colleges and universities.

[A]nd for some years has required those students to answer
138 multiple choice questions, 78 concerned with verbal
materials, 60 focused on mathematics. (It has not examined
student's knowledge of history, the sciences, the arts, the
humanities, foreign languages, social sciences, or other
important subjects that high schools also teach.) Although
new questions are developed for the SAT each year, those
questions have been carefully checked so that each new
edition of the SAT has been presumed to be equivalent to
the first "standardized" of the test ... (p. 16).

Apart from the frightening limitations of the SAT, greater apprehension
and distrust are engendered by the fact that students are supposed to
prove their knowledge on the basis of answering 138 multiple choice
questions within a few hours after spending some twelve years in school.
It is obvious that such tests can only cover a narrow range of students
learning. The second point which Berliner and Biddle (1995) make is
that the use of aggregate SAT scores is unreliable in terms of measuring
students' achievement.

Since students had to answer 138 questions in all, this means that the "terrible" decline in SAT scores was in reality a drop of perhaps 5 percent in the number of questions answered correctly. Put this way, the decline in aggregate SAT scores that began about 1963 seems a good deal less "massive." Moreover, the drop that did occur in aggregate SAT scores ceased in the mid 1970s, and there has been no evidence of a decline since then. Recent annual shifts in aggregate national scores have been minute, often amounting to only one or two scale points, which probably means that the students of America have answered, or failed to answer, one or two tenths of an additional SAT question (p. 17).

The third drawback of the SAT is that it is a test that is taken voluntarily by High School seniors who wish to continue their education in a college or university. Every high school senior will not take the test, therefore it would be misleading to use the results for those who took the test to make the assumption that America's public schools are in trouble. This is lying with statistics for the purpose of perpetrating a public hoax for ideological gains. "SAT scores were never intended to be aggregated for evaluating the achievements of teachers, schools, school districts, or states, and such scores have no validity when used for such evaluations" (Berliner & Biddle, 1995, p. 17). There is obviously a greater force or cause at work here to undermine the public education system for ideological or economic gain. If this suspicion has any merit, it is very frightening. Witte (2000) has also formed the opinion that there is more in the 'mortar than on the pestle':

Voucher programs also provide the best assault on a very significant constitutional limitation. There is evidence that educational vouchers and the evolution of voucher policy were part of a large strategy to affect much broader issues circumscribed by current First Amendment precedents. The ultimate goal of some very powerful advocates may not be to "break these chains," as McGroary rhetorically stated, but rather to break the wall between church and state in the United States (p. 191).

It is to be noticed that the strategy that is being used by the advocates of choice is not the aggressive kind of politics, but a more gentle persuasion to beguile the public into believing that the level of parental and students involvement which is offered by choice is the ultimate exercise of their democratic will. Witte (2000) sees it as a soft, subtle political persuasion:

> The politics of educational vouchers are not the bully politics of employers controlling jobs and making commensurate demands on the community (Lindblom, 1977). Nor are they the politics of the wealthy crudely buying political access through election donations. Rather, vouchers exemplify a subtle politics that uses a social problem to gain advantages for people well beyond the parameters of that problem; and proponents do so by understanding and successfully manipulating the incremental and pluralist nature of our system. Thus in some ways it is a much more impervious form of power. It occurs slowly, continuously taking advantage of inattention and inability of opposing groups to maintain constant counter pressure (p. 191).

In other words, the very principles of democracy are being used to defeat the system of public education – free choice. The soft under belly of democracy is being gently, consistently, and persuasive eroded. Notice the argument that Chubb & Moe (1990) have mounted to launch their assault on public education – excessive democracy in the public school and that an authoritarian system would remove the bureaucratic bungling in education.

TESTING THE LEGALITY OF CHOICE AS AN EDUCATIONAL ALTERNATIVE

The alternative to public schooling is private. The private school system is run by two entities: one religious the other secular. If students are to be educated at private schools using United States tax dollars in the form of vouchers, this may create a problem for religious schools as this may be in breach of the First Amendment none-entanglement clause. That is, the Constitution proscribes any entanglement between state and religion:

> Congress shall make no law respecting an establishment of religion, or prohibiting the free exercise thereof; or abridging the freedom of speech, or of the press, or the right of the people to peaceably assemble, or to petition the Government for redress.

When Congress enacted the First Amendment to the American Constitution it seemed to have been fully cognizant of the potentiality of a religious explosion in the society which may lead to witch hunting and all the negative fall outs that come with religious bigotry. We may not come to know exactly what they had in mind, but the courts have interpreted it literally to mean that the state should not become entangled with any religious institution neither denouncing them nor supporting them.

> The Court, however, determined that the amendment means more than that the federal and state governments are not to set up official religions or punish individuals for their personal religious beliefs. "Any excessive entanglements" between the government and religions must be avoided. Any public policy with "the purpose or primary effect of aiding or inhibiting religious education" is considered to be unconstitutional (Henig, 1994, p. 69).

The First Amendment therefore, creates a bulwark against entanglement with religion on two plains. The first is that the public dollars cannot be used to support any religious establishment, school or any other form. The second is that the State since it cannot support also cannot regulate religious institutions because that would mean the Government becoming engrossed in the operations and management of such institutions and this is repugnant to the Constitution. Given that Government's involvement with religion is repugnant to the

Constitution that would further mean that they are not eligible for Government funding.

The legal position on the issue was enunciated by the Court in *Lemon v. Krutzman* (1971). Pennsylvania had adopted a statutory program that provided financial support for nonpublic elementary and secondary schools by reimbursement of the cost of teacher's salaries, textbooks, and instructional materials in specified secular subjects. Rhode Island had adopted a statute under which the State pays directly to teachers in nonpublic elementary schools a supplement of 15% of their annual salary. Under each statute, state aid has been given to church-related educational institutions. Both statutes were held to be repugnant to the constitution.

> That decision set up a tripartite test as to when government actions affecting religious practice are constitutional. The tests were (1) the action must promote a secular legislative purpose; (2) its primary effect must neither advance nor inhibit religion; and (3) there must be no excessive entanglement between the state and religion (Witte, 2000, p. 21).

The decision in *Lemon* was followed in *Committee for Public Education v. Nyquist*. Here New York (1973) had developed low income tuition reimbursement and tax credit programs, the Court held that both the grants and the tax credit violated the establishment clause of the First Amendment. Justice Powell noted that:

> If the grants are offered as an incentive to parents to send their children to sectarian schools by making unrestricted cash payments to them, the Establishment Clause is violated whether or not the actual dollars given eventually find their way into the sectarian institutions. Whether the grant is labeled a reimbursement, a reward, or a subsidy, its substantive impact is still the same (Levin, 2001, p.49).

However, if public money is provided for secular purposes this would not be inconsistent or repugnant to the establishment clause. This is exemplified in the decision of *Mueller v. Allen* (1983).

The above-mentioned judicial decisions are clear with regards to the position of the establishment clause. However, the water seems to have become a little murky in recent decisions. In *Zorbrest v. Catalina Foothills School District* (1993), the Court expressed the view that the use of public funds to pay an interpreter in a Catholic school because the service being rendered was non-religious was not inconsistent with the establishment clause. Similar results were reached in the case of *Agostini v. Felton* (1997). Under Title 1 of the Elementary and Secondary Education Act of 1965 provided that full education be given to every child regardless of economic background. Public funds were used to provide remedial education, guidance, and job counseling to eligible students on a neutral basis to low income children in sectarian schools. The Court found that this did not violate the First Amendment. It would seem then, that laws which give benefits to sectarian schools indirectly or obliquely may be constitutionally sound. "Thus the Court recognizes a distinction between direct governmental aid to parochial schools (unconstitutional), and aid to families to reimburse certain costs associated with attending parochial schools (may be constitutional) (Henig, 1994, p.69).

Given the jurisprudence that has been cultivated in the recent case law, it would seem that the Courts are leaning in favor of public funding for private schools which have a secular program providing the funding is not being used to promote religious objectives. This type of funding seems to be acceptable. Witte (2000) avers the view that the voucher system may be the ultimate test of the First Amendment. However, I am inclined to believe that short of amending the First Amendment, no constitutionally sensible court could ratify the payment of tax payers' money to any religious institutions directly. However, it may be possible to do so if the moneys are paid to the parents who will in turn pay it to the school: *Agostini v. Felton* (1997). Should the state go ahead and put in place a full voucher scheme which includes sectarian schools, it will be obliged to put all of the other administrative structures in place for supervising the spending of the funds and making the institutions accountable. In short, the state would be required to regulate such institutions. But this would no doubt lead to state entanglement in religious affairs in the manner forbidden by the constitution.

> Since Mueller, the Supreme Court has issued four decisions base on the Mueller precedent that suggest the Court is prepared to uphold a voucher system wherein the voucher goes to the parent and not to the school, the parent has a wide choice of public and private schools, there is no favoritism extended to sectarian private school (Levin, 2001, p.49).

Whether this approach would include religious schools will be determined *in futuro* but it seems to be constitutionally harmless providing that the Government moneys reach the coffers of the religious institution indirectly. There is not harm in Government using tax-payers moneys to support the education of students from low socio-economic backgrounds. This is an integral part of the programs that are normally found in welfare states. The difficulty which the court will have to surmount is the fact that private entities, unlike state entities, are not bound to follow the fundamental rights of the citizens as laid down in the Constitution because they are only justiciable in so far as they challenge the actions of public administration which are perceived to be *ultra vires*. Therefore religious schools can discriminate on the basis of sex, race, religion, and handicap. But under the Fourteenth Amendment, the state is obliged to give effect to the federal constitutional rights of the citizens. However, as Levin (2001) points out as political subdivisions of the state, public schools must recognize all the protections of the U.S. Constitution that federal courts have applied to public students and teachers. Subject to some limitations, these protections include the freedoms of speech, religion, association; the right to be free from state-supported religious indoctrination and the right to equal protection of the laws. These hard-won rights are not inconsequential in that they are beyond the power of government officials to circumscribe or ignore.

SCHOOL CHOICE: FEET OF CLAY

The advocates of school choice seek to persuade the public that the solution to the failures, according to them, is the privatization of the public school system. This would force schools to compete in the open market as commodity for their survival; failure to provide a product which the public wants will naturally lead to their demise. This is the position that is advocated by Chubb & Moe (1990). They see the problem with the educational system as being due to its high level of democratic, bureaucratic governance which prevent the system from working effectively, hence the importance of choice through market forces control. Educators and administrators are invited to relinquish democracy for an authoritarian system which is subjected to the whims and fancy of the owners, and one that bends to the will of the Almighty profit-mongering of competitive market pressures. The irony is that Chubb & Moe (1990) also admitted that there are serious imperfections in the market system. I think they are inviting us to jump from the frying pan into the fire. I must quote the whole paragraph to do justice to the enormity of the fire that we are asked to jump into:

> [W]e do not mean to imply that markets are somehow capable of perfectly satisfying parents and students. Obviously, they are not. Markets are inevitably subject to all sorts of real-world imperfections, just as democratic institutions are. Monopolizing, price-fixing, territorial agreements, and other restrictive *practices by producers may limit the choices available to consumers.* Consumers may be too poorly informed to make choices that are truly in their best interest. Transportation costs may eliminate many options. *The unequal distribution of income in society may bias certain markets in favor of the rich and against the poor.* To the extent that these and other imperfections are serious, *markets are less likely to generate the diversity,*

quality, and levels of services that consumers want, and prices are likely to be higher than they otherwise would be (Chubb & Moe, 1990, p.34) (Emphasis added).

Given this clear admission of the potential harm which a shift to the marketplace can do to education, there is no reason for us to entertain the propositions put forward by Chubb & Moe (1990). In fact, we should not hesitate to jettison their proposal. The proposition is simple: the market will be regulated by demand and supply. The consuming family will choose the type of school they want for their children and how much money they will spend on education. "The supply side picture is difficult to predict in all relevant parameters, but it seems obvious that elite schools would flourish – elite in the sense that schools would attempt to attract the highest income students with promise of the best education for them" (Witte, 2000, p.202). This kind of marketing would obviously create educational enclaves similar to what is obtained in manufacturing. Educational enclaves would not enhance the principles of multicultural education but may create a deepening of *de facto* segregation.

However, this is not to say that the market would not cater for the education of the middle class and working class children. The market would because there would be a huge market, but the quality would not be the same as that for the elite. The quality of the goods in a Ninety-nine cents store is not the same as the quality of goods in the better well established stores.

> But relative economies of scale and cost controls would be put in place. As with the current differences between wealthy districts and public and private schools, poorer schools would have larger class sizes, lower teacher salaries, and fewer resources to accommodate the lower price for services. Thus just as the market stratifies consumption patterns by income for hundreds of other products, it will also stratify the purchase of education (Witte, 2001, p.202).

It is difficult to see how vouchers would promote equality of educational opportunity. Rich parents will be able to subsidize their children in terms of educational supplies and transportation if the school of choice is far from the place of residence. Poor children may very well still have to stay in the neighborhood schools because the better quality schools may be outside of their district. Furthermore, the wealthy have the wherewithal to ensure that good quality schools will be far removed from the reach of the poor. Brighouse (2000) points out that children should not have significantly better access to education simply because they have wealthier parents, or live in wealthier communities, than others. Jonathan Cool (as cited in Brighouse, 2000) has documented the 'savage inequalities' within the US public school system, whereby twice as much per pupil is spent on schooling in wealthy suburban school districts as in poorer inner-city districts.(p.112).

> Widespread poverty, inadequate job prospects, and lack of social services all contribute to the loss of dignity in many families in the country and, therefore, to loss of hope among children. This is especially so for the most vulnerable of our citizens, those who must endure the additional burdens of prejudice. Given these facts, "school improvement' often really requires improvement in the overall quality of life of the members of the community. Unfortunately, many federal and state politicians seem disinterested in this message. They ignore it at our collective peril (Berliner & Biddle, 1995, p. 288).

Burliner & Biddle's (1995) dim view of school choice is an apt, realistic appraisal of how things are especially in the African American community. The school choice scheme can only work mischief for the life of the poor, to bamboozle them into thinking that these changes will benefit them. The benefit will be a reinstatement of the shackles of slavery for people of African descent. I fully endorse the eight principles for "A Vision of School Reform" as put out by the editors of Rethinking Schools, (2000):

1. Public Schools are responsible to the community, not to the marketplace.

2. Schools must be actively multicultural and anti-racist, promoting social justice for all.

3. The curriculum must be geared toward learning for life and the needs of a multicultural democracy.

4. All schools and all children must receive adequate resources.

5. Reform must center on the classroom and the needs of children.

6. Good teachers are essential to good schools.

7. Reform must involve collaboration among educators, parents, and the community.

8. We must revitalize our urban communities, not just our schools.

I would add another requirement to this list,

9. We are all collectively responsible for the provision of good environment and good schools for all of our children.

CONCLUSION

Clearly, America's public school system faces many problems which are in urgent need of redress. However, the solutions to these problems are not a 'one fix' as advocated by the proponents of school choice. The fact is many of the problems in the public educational system are the results of unwise social planning, prejudice, and racism. It is obvious that children who live in poverty will arrive at the schools' doors with less intellectual capital than the children from the well to do families. The children with the less intellectual capital are the children of African Americans and other minority peoples. With the expansion in education which followed the victories of affirmative action since the decision in *Brown v. Board of Education,* the landscape of education in America has been changed significantly. The expansion in education required increased financing for the school and if this is not forthcoming, the quality of education will be impacted negatively. Added to this is the growing migrant population in America from third world countries many of them speaking a language other than English.

School choice in the form of vouchers and charter schools will only serve to exacerbate the current problems in the public education system especially for poor Black children. I do not believe school choice provides the panacea as its proponents are advocating. I believe the acceptance of multicultural education, and the improvement in the social conditions of the poor, constructive portrayal of the achievement of Black leaders, greater financial support for schools especially those in the inner-cities would go a long way in solving the problems in the public educational system. The educational approach which I believe that is best suited in this melee is critical redemptive pedagogy for the conscious awakening of African Americans, other minorities and the majority White population. Hope for a better and brighter tomorrow can only be achieved through an education that is non-idiotic.

CHAPTER EIGHT

Education and the Politics of the Mass Media

> A critical theory of media education offers a pedagogy of empowerment, resistance, invention and hope. The building bridges between critical pedagogy and media studies represents a first step in this project (Sholle & Denski, 1994, p.148).

Mass media communication is one of the major current hype in the American society and many of the countries in the Caribbean. The mass media are very powerful political tools and those who control them can sell their message easily to the entire world. Liberals seem to be cognizant of this, but the neoconservatives appear to be even more aware of the political value of the mass media and they have been using their big corporate dollars to buy up the media. Neoconservatives are fully aware that the educational system and the media system are two social instruments which have powerful influences on the lives of citizens for the shaping of their political views, morality, and ideology. They have spared no effort in gaining or seeking to gain control of education and the media for the purpose of propagating their cultural and political goals for the society's consumption. Progressive educators must use every effort to counter this trend with a non-idiotic education which is underpinned by critical redemptive pedagogy

Hence, the concerted effort to disintegrate the public education system through the erosion of democratic control and to put in its place autocratic control by private owners who can skew the curriculum to tell their cultural and political stories for the purpose of maintaining and buttressing Eurocentric hegemony. If these goals are achieved the private owners will be able to create elite schools for the rich and well-to-do and substandard school plants and schooling for the poor and Blacks. Substandard education will disable the poor and Blacks in terms of their ability to compete successfully in a free market oriented society. Their lives will therefore be relegated to the performance of menial tasks, not unlike the work of African slaves. Similarly, if neoconservatives are able to control all or the bulk of the mass media then they, being private owners, can determine what will be published, what will amount to news – of course much of the media is already in private ownership. Control of the two institutions – the school and the media - will provide the means through which they can suppress popular culture and the efforts of multiculturalism. The fact is that private corporate controllers of the media can use it to reproduce neoconservative cultural hegemony and the maintenance of the already dominant classes and the concentration of wealth and power in the hands of those who are culturally and ideologically aligned with them.

Given that journalism is one of the bulwarks of free, democratic, pluralistic societies I believe that the education of journalists should take a critical redemptive pedagogic approach along the line advocated by Sholle & Denski (1994) in order to produce journalists who are critically aware of their cultural and political situation – men and women who would fearlessly defend the principles of a radical democracy. I believe that this is the proper posture that any journalist who is worth his/her salt must take because their work plays a pivotal role in keeping democracy and freedom of speech alive. This would no doubt place a huge onus on them because many of them will be employed by some media corporation that will expect them to buy into and sell the politics of their employer. It would obviously take men and women of good charactertude to do the right thing in the interest of the general good and well-being of the society. This is why I believe a critical transformational journalism education is crucially important for the continued preservation of fundamental right of freedom of speech and a democratic society.

THE MEDIA AND DEMOCRACY

In a democratic society the media play a vital role in the protection of the fundamental rights of the citizens and in maintaining the checks and balances among those who sway power in the society, be it the executive, the legislative, or the judiciary. The media are vitally important to ensure the liberty of the citizenry and that there is fair treatment of all regardless of race, creed, origin or any of the other categories that human beings are so fond of using to designate one another's status and consequentially their social treatment in terms of preference, denial, or degradation. We are well aware of the use of the media in totalitarian states – to bolster and maintain the regime. Interestingly, if the political powers in the democratic states have their way with the citizenry they will do the very same thing as their totalitarian counterpart. Totalitarianism can take many guises even in the form of a democratic regime. The plight of Haiti is well known to the world. Today big media is being controlled by big corporations with big bucks to maintain their strangle hold on the media and use it to promulgate their chosen political ideology on the rest of the society. This strangle hold of corporatism seems to have brought about the demise or the near demise of the free press. Unless the press is rescued from corporatism the free press will become a thing of the past. In fact, McChesney (2004) reminisce that the vision of the free press which the first generation of the American republic envisioned is diametrically opposed to the current meaning that is given to the free press today – letting the media owners do whatever they want to maximize their profits. He pointed out that in the early days the Government heavily subsidized the free press in order to promote diversity in media reporting. I am inclined to believe that some such arrangement should be pursued today for the same noble purpose.

All democracies are based on the principle that the populace is well informed and therefore can make rational choices whether in a general election or generally. Of course, the principle begs the question as to whether this actually happens in reality. However, it is one of the pillars on which a democratic society is based, that is, informed consent and the media have a significant role in ensuring that the populace is well informed on the issues that are crucial to the society and to good governance: "virtually all theories of self-government are premised on having an informed citizenry, and the creation such an informed citizenry is the media's province" (McChesney, 2004, p.17).

The conservative right has argued that the media falls with the purview of the free marketplace and is available for whosoever will buy it. Perhaps this is the heart of the problem. We must not forget the fundamental role of the media in a democratic society and it cannot be left to be charmed and carved up by the wolves of the free marketplace because this will be to the detriment of the citizenry and democracy. The conflict in this arena is essentially centered around the media as profit driven commercial entities on the one hand, and on the other, entities which are required to provide the basis for informed self-government. Media corporations get the bulk of their profits from corporate advertising; failure to toe the line of corporatism may result in loss of profits due to the discontinuation of business from these entities. I am inclined to hold opinion with McChesney (2004) that the United States has not satisfactorily addressed the problem of the media in the present generation. Consequently, the media have fallen into the hands of large profit driven media corporations who make policies behind closed doors to the exclusion of the general citizenry, " while the broad and vital interest of the population have been largely neglected" (p. 19). Ironically, despite the presence of the First Amendment "freedom of the press" clause in the Constitution of the United States which proclaims itself to be the supreme law, the media seem to have become one of the salient undemocratic institutions, due no doubt to the nature of their ownership and their emphasis on profit.

Indeed the problem of the media is political and the solution must be political as oppose to apolitical. But a political solution seems to be long in coming. In fact it would seem that there is no political will to override corporate commercialism where the press is concerned. This is especially so given that it is the very corporations that monopolize the media who shell out the big bucks during the election campaign and upon donees of the corporate largesse taking office, he/she must pay back what was given to him/her. Hence, the prostitution of the free press. The free market metaphor has ardently advocated the view that the market will take care of its own needs. I believe McChesney (2004) is right when he averred the view:

> The commercial interpretation of a free press has been in ascendancy for much of the past quarter century, if not longer. Proponents assert that this right is absolute, because the First Amendment says "no law." Therefore capitalists can do as they please in the realm of media and they need answer only to their bottom lines; the market will prove to be a superior regulator of the press (p. 31).

The line of reasoning that the market is a "superior regulator" is fallacious because what the market wants and needs depends on the level of education which the market has received and the media has a tremendous role to play in the education of the citizenry. There is a principle of natural justice that a man/woman cannot be a judge in his/her cause, but this principle seems not to be applicable to big media corporation whose emphasis is on the almighty dollar bill and the ideology that best serve their commercial cause. The rabid attitude of the big media owners is vividly captured by McChesney (2004):

If journalism is atrocious and the culture hyper-commercialized, if the public is uniformed or misinformed, if self-governance is a sham, the fault is not the press system but the moronic citizens who demand such fare and reward those who provide it. The government can't do a damned thing about it except indirectly, through improving education so that the next generation will not be composed of idiots. From this perspective, the connection between a free press and democracy, which inspired this nation's founding fathers, is dead (p. 31).

Ironically, those who advocate the commercialized, bottom line oriented press do not support any effort for educational expansion because this is inconsistent with their pernicious hold on the minds of a poorly educated citizenry. Furthermore, they must, *a fortiori*, join forces with those who wish to remove democratic control from school authorities and replace it with the free market. After all it is the same line of reasoning which is used by big media owners: let the free market be the sole regulator of the media correlates to let the free market control the demand and supply for education. The use of the market metaphor in the commercialization of the free press and public education may, *prima facie*, appear to be a reasonable argument, but when it is critically examined, it becomes pellucid that the aim is to reinforce the position of those who already hold power in the big media business, and to create an educated elite and relegate the populace which comprise the poor and minorities to a substandard education.

I am therefore inclined to hold opinion with Sholle & Denski (1994) that the aim of connecting education to industry enhances the goals of the New Right: educating the elite for leadership and training (as opposed to educating) the masses for menial tasks. In other words, this emphasis is seeking to turn back the hand of time. This direction in which the New Right wishes to take the society must be stoutly resisted because this will result in the demise of multiculturalism and the gains of the civil rights movement.

I dread the result of this New Right movement if they were to succeed. Therefore, those who are aware of what is happening must work inexorably and assiduously to counter the reproductive culture which is presently being foisted upon us by the neo-conservatives. The line of resistance must take the form of creative public media literacy and a critical redemptive pedagogy for the education of journalists.

The current process of media education appears to be geared towards the reproduction of the dominant culture for the perpetuation of its hegemonic powers in the society. I believe this is the salient point that is made by Sholle & Denski (1994). I further believe that a critical education for journalists is the key to the avoidance of reproducing cultural and political ideology of the dominant group in the society. The media, especially in film and television are in the invidious position to reproduce the dominant power relations among race, class, gender, and sexual orientation. They have the power to stereotype and stigmatize these relations. The media are the purveyors of social values and they must use their influence as responsible corporate citizens. Sholle & Denski (1994) informs that educators have a crucial role to play in the training of journalists:

> [U]niversity educators whose value-neutral and atheoretical pedagogy has trained a generation of media (re)production students and (value) maintenance engineers must be asked to examine the wider and unavoidable political dimensions of their efforts. As teachers of mass communication this suggests the potential impact of the project of critical pedagogy upon our professional, personal and political lives (p. 24).

The salient point which Sholle & Denski (1994) make above is that media educators must be critically aware of their role in the educating of those persons who will eventually produce or reproduce what we view and read. Therefore care must be taken that future media workers are exposed to a critical redemptive view of things as they are; they must be critically aware of how social identities are constructed for the benefit of the dominant culture and how this dominant culture discriminates and oppresses Black people. That it is still cultural oppression from which Black people need to redeem themselves through a critical redemptive education. In short, both media educators and students need to appreciate what it means to be interactively involved in a conversation with their audience, the people for whom they create the news, the movies, the dances, the portrayals. They must be careful how they depict the culture of minority peoples.

Many people have been turned off by the lopsided reporting of the news in the media; some media seem to be particularly connected to particular political parties or political personalities and so fail to produce news item that are worthy of public viewing. This situation might change in the near future, given the recent development in the new media as demonstrated by Gillmor (2004) in his assessment of the new media involvement in the last election. The internet seems to be opening new avenues for journalism that were not previously available and they are accessible to a wider range of the citizenry. This seems to have created a fresh interest in the politics of the country. Gillmor (2004) hails this as a good thing for America's culture:

> This evolution is also about reinforcing citizenship. The emerging form of bottom-up politics is bringing civic activity back into a culture that has long since given up on politics as anything but a hard-edge game for the wealthy and powerful. The technologies of news making are available to citizen and politician alike, and may well be the vehicle for saving something we could otherwise lose: a system in which the consent of the governed means more than the simple casting of votes (p. 88).

The point is that with the Internet being available to such a wide cross-section of the citizenry has made it possible to create a greater measure of inclusiveness for the grass root peoples – politics from the bottom up to the top. The Internet has the potential of creating a truly participatory democracy which goes further and deeper than the occasional electoral voting.

CRITICAL REDEMPTIVE LITERACY FOR MEDIA EDUCATION AND THE GOALS OF DEMOCRACY

Given that the vanguard of America's democracy is a free press, as provided by the founding fathers in the First Amendment and the framers of the fundamental rights, we cannot leave our destiny in the hands of rabid capitalists whose sole interest is in making a profit – corporate prostitution. We must therefore make critical redemptive pedagogy one of the bedrocks of media education. The media provide us with the practices which define what is worthy knowledge and how such knowledge is constructed. The media are by their very nature instrumentalities of propagation. It is therefore incumbent upon media educators to ensure that future media personnel are trained in critical reflection on the nature of the work in which they are involved, the ideological positions of the society, and the place of culture and politics in creating a radical democracy. This is vitally important because "critical pedagogy must link itself to the goals of a radical democracy, it must engage and critique the condition of knowledge production and it must provide a language of possibility for transforming those conditions" (Sholle & Denski (1994), p. 23).

The problem with the application of critical pedagogy is that students may be encountering this reflective kind of thinking and meta-questioning of what passes for knowledge for the first time at undergraduate level. The media educator may have the Herculean task of unearthing, or 'de-educating', so to speak, all that was inculcated into the students' knowledge during their primary and secondary schooling. Well, I suppose it is better to start at some point than never to start at all. Perhaps we can take some consolation in this thought. Students who have been exposed to the banking method of education for many years will find it unnerving to launch out on a new direction in the search for new knowledge, or new ways of interpreting cultural and political events. The fact is, we often become what we were thought and that is what we end up practicing because of our uncritical training. Sholle & Denski (1994) view this as the result of a number of factors in the educational system, for example, the separation of education from life; classrooms are setup into rigid patterns; classes are divided up into abstract subjects which have no connection to life:

> [P]edagogy takes predominantly a banking approach; the practices that knowledge applies to are held off in a distant future of adulthood; teachers set up a false authority for themselves through withholding any knowledge of the context of educational practice; success and "achievement" are expressed in grades as markers of competitive prowess; and so on (p.116).

This is the predicament in which students find themselves in their early years of schooling and they have accepted it because they had no say in the matter; they are their own accomplices in a classroom of silence and objectification through no fault of their own. Students have internalized the role of the underdogs who are waiting to be fed from the bowl of the teachers' reservoir of knowledge. The consequence is that media education becomes neatly canned in containers like chow. This is the professional methodology of media education. And we must not forget that this is the yard stick by which the good conduct or the lack thereof of good journalism is measured. It is frequently referred to as 'professionalism'.

These days everyone shouts for lack of professionalism when a journalist steps on his/her toes by revealing to the public the truth of the matter. Sholle & Denski (1994) are correct when they say that this professionalism, this pedagogy (if I may call it that) has nothing to do with empowering students to explore their own lives, to draw upon their own experiences and knowledge, and so connect their education with political practice, or to be critical and active citizens in a democracy. They are encouraged and rewarded when they become part of the reproductive, as oppose to productive, culture. In order for critical redemptive pedagogy to come about these disempowering practices must be reversed and discarded; we may need to sweep clean the attics of our minds. But I wonder whether that is really possible given that one of the most difficult things to do is to unlearn. (Every year around the middle of October I find myself 'instinctively' singing patriotic songs which I was taught at primary school in anticipation of Independence Day on the first of November.) Unlearning is very challenging but it can be achieved with sufficient self-determination.

I suspect that it is this type of disempowering media education that compelled Gilmor (2004) to lament the poor quality of journalism schools which have failed to incorporate the new developments in journalism into their curricula. He expresses a measure of skepticism about undergraduate journalism degrees. He is especially concerned about the state of journalism education and the lack of the state of the art techniques which have recently developed:

> Whatever your view of this endless debatable topic, the fact is that journalism schools are the main source of new staff. But we can't allow them to crank out new generation of reporters, editors, photographers, and broadcasters who don't understand, appreciate how the profession has changed. The problem is actually more serious among faculties than students (p. 131).

Gillmor (2004) further observes that there is a need for journalism schools to diversify their teaching methods:

> [T]o reflect the evolution from a lecture mode to a conversational mode. At minimum journalism schools should insist that students understand genuine interactivity, which is the basis for a conversation with the audience. They can start by making the conversation richer and fuller among faculty and students on campus; the lecture mode of education still has value in some circumstances, but only some (p. 132).

Gillmor (2004) is right. Media has changed significantly within the last five years. The citizenry no longer depends on the delivery of the daily paper or the television or the radio for the news. Many people are hooked up to the Internet and they can freely tap into any source that is news producing whether American, Canadian, Caribbean, European, or other. The Internet has made the world into a global village. People can reach other people whom they do not know and interact with them. People can discuss upcoming elections and voice their opinion on the issues with each other. Some people may not have access to television or radio station but they can stay in their living room or study and communicate their feelings through the Internet. In short, the Internet can be used to mobilize a wide cross section of the society. The point is succinctly demonstrated by Gillmor (2004) where he said that:

> In 2000, America saw the first serious demonstration of the Internet as a fund-raising tool. Republican challenger John McCain raised the then unprecedented amount of $6.4 million online in his campaign against George Bush. McCain lost, but the lessons of his efforts weren't lost on the next clutch of contenders. Internet fund-raising had become just one more arrow in the political quiver (p. 92).

Internet journalism is definitely the way to go and media educators must find a prominent place for it in their curricula not as an add-on. The curricular offerings must be diversified as well as the teaching methods. The Internet has opened up a whole new panorama of communication for the citizenry of which they will take full advantage as they become more and more computer literate. Through the Internet the citizenry will challenged their leaders and call them to account. Like Gillmor (2004), I believe this will create a greater participatory democracy:

> By 2004, American politics was approaching a tipping point. Enough people were online, and for the first time they had the tools to seriously shake things up themselves. And it was the Dean campaign that did the shaking. It's worth spending some time understanding how this happened, why it happened, and what lessons we can learn (p. 93).

It would seem that the effective use of the Internet in the last election in the United States was only the tip of the ice berg. The Internet has come of age and is sufficiently popular in the homes of Americans to be a medium that is frequently used for communication. What is even more fascinating is the openness and accessibility of the resources of the Internet which can be used to bring about meaningful structural, political, and cultural changes in the society. What seems to be happening here is the beginning of a universal conversation. I strongly suspect that Gillmor's (2004) prophecy that the role which the Internet played in 2004 was only the breeding ground or the foreshadowing of what is to come. The Internet has become an integral part of political campaigning, news reporting, and the general transmitter of important information; the writing is on the wall. The Gillmor (2004) prophecy came to pass in November 2008 in the Presidential campaign in the United States and in the eventual election of Barrack Obama as the first African American President. I have no doubt that there is more to come in the continued unfolding of the electronic media and the spin doctors will be in the vanguard of its utility.

SPIN DOCTORS, PERFORMERS AND POSERS

The television, radio news reporting, and calling programs have become the place where politicians and their cohorts spin and perform for the general public. They do not join in the universal conversation they simply trot out their stuff for the rest of us. Dressing up their political pathological lies and manipulating the public to good effects to serve their vested interest and their political ambition to seize power. Unfortunately many of us because we are so gullible are unable to see through this thin disguise of naked manipulation of the populace. Journalists have now become fully aware of the meaning of the word 'spin' and the performance which political leaders put on, on radio and television programs:

> Journalists become accustom to a process known as
> spinning. Wikipedia accurately describes this, in the
> context of public relations, as 'putting events or other facts,
> especially of those with political or legal significance, into
> contexts favoring oneself or one's client or cause, at least in
> comparison to opponents (Gillmor, 2004, p.184).

The news media and their public relations people have been spinning
the public for a long time, on the radio, in the printed press, and
especially the television which has become a crucial source for news
information. The public has an incredulous tendency to accept what
they see on the television screen as the gospel because it provides easy
answers. The enormity of public gullibility is absolutely astounding.
Lazy journalism is particularly responsible for this state of affairs
because many journalists seem to be more concerned with feeding the
public with what they want to hear instead of endeavoring to create
critical investigative journalism. They make a mockery of journalism
through their perpetual spinning.

So to make the performance more like TV land the actors are
called 'players', as though matters of state are just games that are
played by the politicians and the media. The word has acquired such
pejorative connotations that people who wish to be taken seriously in
public discourse should avoid it like the plague. De Zengotita (2005)
describes it as "savvy players who represent various identity and/or
interest groups through performance politics in a never-ending show/
game for a fan base of identifiers" (p. 139). It is all in the performance.
There is no serious moral commitment to any of the positions which
are advocated; whether this is on the issue of immigration, abortion,
gay marriage, minimum wage, or war. The players and the performers
are fully cognizant that it is the winning of the horse race that is really
important and winning is all that counts. "It follows that arguments
are just performances designed to influence naïve opinion. Players are
preoccupied with how to do that, with manipulating arguments and
other celebrated items – people, lifestyle, grooming, events, legislation,
anything that comes along – manipulating them for effect" (Zengotita,

2005, p.139). In other words, the players need to understand how to sex up the materials to obtain the desired spin and the greatest effect on the minds of the gullible public. In these performances, the journalists seem to have become the court jesters. De Zengotita (2005) says "It got called "spin," because the expression so precisely captures the improvisational feel of this interminable enterprise" (p. 139).

Given this state of affairs, it is important that journalism subscribe to a reasonable code of conduct which will exert restraint upon those who would seek to mislead the public by sexing up the information and spinning it to suit their vested interest in the news item. A code of conduct apart, journalism education must see to its students' critical awareness and savvy media literacy would be a good antidote for the public against the spin doctors.

MEDIA OBJECTIFICATION AND THE CONSTRUCTION OF REALITY

We now live in an age of hyper-commercialism which was brought to and imposed upon us by big media corporations. Advertising is a very important segment of big media because it is a significant source of revenue for them in particular and for profit oriented business in general. Much of the media has been taken over and corrupted by advertisement. Advertisement is able to exercise this pernicious hold on the media because for some corporations it is their big income earner. The unfortunate aspects of advertisement is its effective objectification of people, in particular women, and the (re)construction of reality; creating needs and desires for things which people do not need and can hardly afford. Advertisement effectively manipulates the public into thinking the way in which the makers of the product want them to think in relation to their product:

> Advertisement is anything but a benign process of
> communicating information about product prices and

attributes. And there is nothing "natural" about its
existence. Any effort to address the problem of the media
has to deal directly with the advertising and commercialism
(McChesney, 2004, p.138).

Kilbourne (1999) has demonstrated effectively the caricatures which
advertisements create of people and the unnecessary desires which they
inculcate in our minds. The harm of advertisement is that it frequently
tells us that something is wrong with us without furnishing us with
any evidence and offers us a false hope that a particular product is the
solution to the problem which we have, although the persons who
created the advertisement do not know the persons to whom they are
speaking. Many persons buy into the false impression because the
general public is so naïve and gullible. Kilbourne (1999) gives an apt
description of psychological manipulation of advertisement:

> Advertising encourages us not only to objectify each other
> but also to feel that our most significant relationships are
> with the product that we buy. It turns lovers into things
> and things into lovers and encourages us to feel passionate
> for our products rather than our partners (p. 27).

Kilbourne (1999) and McChesney (2004) are only two of the numerous
persons, especially feminists, who have pointed out that advertisement
thrives on creating a state of dissatisfaction in the appearance of
women; and men are increasingly being targeted as well. The striking
thing is that the advertisements are succeeding in converting their
target groups whether men, women, or children. Consequently life
has become a materialistic quest for more and more products which
manufacturers are only too happy to produce and dole out to meet the
public's insatiable appetite. This is the proverbial "rat race".

THE PROFESSIONAL LEASH

The current state of the media is due to the type of education which the colleges and universities provide for media workers. The notion of professionalism was concocted by the neo-conservatives who seek to gain absolute control of the media. By linking professionalism with journalism those who oppose a radical media are able to use it to rein in journalists who stray too far into the prohibited areas. This kind of control of the media has the undesirable effect of coloring or watering down journalism to suit the whim and fancy of those in power. The mantra is that journalists will report the news in a professional manner without any bias as trained professionals.

Therefore it would not matter who owned the media or whether the media get many advertisements or none. This would be a reality only in a fool's paradise. It is common knowledge that journalistic independence is at the behest of the owners of the media who sway economic and political power. This situation is a present and constant threat to journalism and by extension democracy. I am inclined to hold opinion with McChesney (2004) that the media system could not be democratic if journalists aligned their interests with the publishers, advertisers, and powerful government and business leaders and not the readers. If publishers could not be relied upon to put commercial and partisan biases aside to complete the work constitutionally guaranteed to the public, journalists would have to be entrusted with the right and protected in their employment by union contracts.

The pretensions of professionalism was therefore planted into the study of journalism so that anything that is done by officialdom and prominent public figures are accepted legitimate news even when they have been sexed up. People buy into the idea, but it is a cruel hoax because professionalism never really applied to journalism in the same way in which it applies to lawyers and doctors, for example. So the term professionalism was misleading because journalists are employees of some big media and the directorate of that corporation will make the determination as to what will make the news. Furthermore, the notion of professionalism in journalism prevented the journalist from taking seriously public criticism because it was not informed criticism. The object of all of these contrivances was the colonization of the media by corporatism for the purpose of controlling the masses and to keep them in abject subjugation so that the political objective and ideology of the neo-conservative elite may be freely propagated without let or hindrance.

Given this situation, I must concur with Sholle & Denski (1994) that media education can be liberated through the employment of a critical pedagogic approach in the education of journalists. De Zengotita (2005) also expresses the view that the transmission style of education should not be the main teaching approach but that the transaction/ transformation method should be employed as well to further the goals of a radical democracy. If this view is accepted then there is no need for the media educators to clamor and hanker to obtain recognition as a discipline or profession. It is what it is already; an instrumentality in the vanguard for the protection of democratic values which should not be water down by institutionalism.

> [M]edia education should not be a discipline to call attention to the fracturing of knowledge forms in postmodernism, but it is not to say that media education should simply be a hodgepodge of other disciplines. Media education then must reject two forms of discipline, the discipline of industrial modes of training and the discipline of the traditional university structure where the boundaries of fields serve to shut off the thoughts of educators within narrowly defined and standardized departments (Sholle & Denski, 1994, pp. 113-114).

Evidently, to put media education in its proper perspective would entail a very ambitious restructuring of the educational system. This of course, I am aware, is wishful thinking. But we can start with a dream to bring about meaningful and effective changes in education through a spirit of sincerity, courage, and hope. After all, President Obama's ascendancy was stirred in a dream of hope.

CONCLUSION

The media is one of the great pillars of democracy. Another is public education for the masses. I find it intriguing that the neo-conservative, reactionary right has made and continues to make Herculean efforts to gain full control of education and the media for the propagation of their ideology. This is a present danger which continues to watch and beset democracy and one that must be met head on. But the problem seems to be the lack of resources by those who are aware of the danger that is lurking behind the rhetoric of the far right and other political players. If justice is going to roll down like a river and righteousness like an ever flowing stream in a pluralistic democratic society, then the ascendancy of neo-conservatism must be neutralized and checkmated. A critical redemptive pedagogic approach in journalism education will go a long way in defeating the challenges of the neo-conservative right to impose their ideology on the media and education to the detriment of Africentism. Educators, especially Black educators, must persevere in the struggle for liberation of the instrumentalities of a non-idiotic education.

CHAPTER NINE

Radical Redemptive Education: Charting Freedom's Discourse

> An important goad of teaching about racial, ethnic, and
> cultural diversity should be to empower students with the
> knowledge, skills, and attitudes they need to participate in
> civic action that will help transform our world and enhance
> the possibility for human survival (Banks, 2003, p.21).

This chapter critically examines the application and importance
of creating curricular modules for the radical redemptive
pedagogy in adult education in the African Diaspora. The
curricular orientations that are advocated in this chapter reflect various
conceptualizations and (re)interpretations of the philosophy of freedom,
education, and democracy. Three modules: democracy and education,
multicultural education, and social reconstructionism are analyzed.
The theoretical concept of critical redemptive pedagogy for rescue and
redemption is further developed and advocated. The discussion and
analysis are aimed at explicating and clarifying the nexus between
democracy, racism and oppression and the quest of Black people to
liberate themselves from hundreds of years of oppression through the
medium of a critical redemptive education. The radical educational
transformation paradigm which is discussed in this chapter is an

exposition of the continuation of the struggle of people of African descent for rescue and redemption through education. The thrust of the discussion is to theoretically demonstrate how human kindness, flowering, and flourishing can be achieved in the context of a multicultural society in the African Diaspora through the medium of an education that is non-idiotic and liberatory.

PEDAGOGY FOR BLACK RESCUE AND REDEMPTION

Creating pedagogy for Black rescue and redemption must include the contribution of critical pedagogy in the fight for the liberation of oppressed peoples. Pedagogy of rescue and redemption has tremendous meaning and significance for Black people because it addresses Black protracted suffering from colonialism, slavery, White racism, segregation and de facto segregation. This is the Black search for hope and an identity that do not alienate us from our African origin. The concept is underpinned by critical theory together with a grass root Africentric philosophy of redemption. Many sources are used to explicate the curricular philosophy which this book advocates. This necessarily involves several disciplines: philosophy, politics, history, economics, in so far as these disciplines impinge upon the curricular philosophy that is discussed in this study. In creating pedagogy of rescue and redemption from the stand point of post-secondary curricular transformation in the context of post-colonial African Diaspora, the Swahili seven principles of *Nguzo Saba* are the yard stick which will be used to judge the redemptive value of the theoretical module. This is crucially important because the standards and criteria of the traditional Eurocentric curricular perspectives cannot be used to create the curricular orientation that is envisioned by this study for pedagogy of redemption. This philosophical approach will not belittle the Eurocentric culture as it relates to people of European descent, but the Eurocentric curricular model will be removed from its position of privilege and dominance, and placed as one of the several perspectives which are relevant in a pluralistic multicultural society. Table 4 is an illustration of the Africentric curricular module.

The overarching curricular orientation is based on liberation from oppression. The curricular discourses that are put forward remove the emphasis from teaching to learning, from teacher-centered to learner-centered. A redemptive pedagogy that makes the learner the focal point of the learning process, invites the learner to actively participate in his/her redemption from social oppression. An educator will receive tremendous assistance from a redemptive pedagogy in that it recognizes and understands the historical experience of African people in the Diaspora and the current problems which are faced by post-secondary education after hundreds of years of European domination through British colonial rule. One of such problems is the forging of an African identity for Black learners which will remove the ambiguity and ambivalence in the general Black population. Alleyne (2002) refers to this as the psychological reconstruction and rehabilitation process. Establishing a Black identity is an essential part of this process of redemption.

The pedagogy of redemption uses the two primary categories of: 1) educational goals and objective (cognitive skills), and 2) sociocultural goals and objectives (affective/behavioral skills) which are advocated by Colin and Guy (1998) together with "the Swahili *Nguzo Saba* as the normative framework for defining an Africentric cultural perspective" (p.44). The rationale for using these categories as the normative framework is:

> 1. the Nguzo Saba is an indigenous and, therefore, legitimate African value system;

> 2. it has gained growing awareness and acceptance among African Ameripean/African Americans in the United States through the ethnic celebration of Kwanzaa;

3. it addresses the major elements of a cultural system
by focusing on the essential elements of community and
identity, aesthetics, economics, politics, philosophy, and
religion (1998, p. 44).

The *Nguzo Saba* is used to analyze and evaluate each of the curricular
orientation that is advocated herein, namely, multiculturalism, social
reconstructionism and critical theory (see Table 4 below). This is the
yard stick by which I have measured each curricular orientation for
its adaptability to an Africentric philosophy relative to a pedagogy
of redemption in the context of the radical curricular transformation
paradigm. Pedagogy of redemption is crucial to make the link to an
African ideology and the education of Black learners. This is not a part
of the national consciousness in the Diaspora and it is not reflected in
the post-secondary curriculum, but this is what is urgently needed in
the post-secondary curriculum. Table 4 shows the theoretical concepts
that are compatible with radical redemptive education theory.

TABLE 4

REDEMPTIVE EDUCATION CURRICULA ORIENTATION

The Swahili Nguzo Saba Seven Principles of an Africentric Worldview	Critical Theory	Multicultural Education	Social Reconstruction	Radical Redempt. Education
Umoja (unity)	No	Yes	No	Yes
Kujichagulia (self-determination)	Yes	Yes	Yes	Yes
Ujima (collective workand responsibility)	No	Yes	No	Yes
Ujamaa (cooperative Economics)	No	No	No	Yes
Nia (purpose)	Yes	Yes	Yes	Yes
Kuumba (creativity)	Yes	Yes	Yes	Yes
Imani (faith)	No	No	No	Yes

Table 4 shows that while some of the other theoretical concepts share
some of the principles of *Nguzo Saba*, only the concept of radical

redemptive education is on all fours with the seven principles. This is the theoretical concept which must underpin the curriculum for redemptive education.

The term *curriculum*, according to the *Webster's College Dictionary* comes from the Greek word *curere* meaning to run a course, race, or career. When used in education it means a program of study. Miller & Seller (1985) see curriculum as "an explicitly and implicitly intentional set of interactions designed to facilitate learning and development and to impose meaning on experienc." (p.3). According toMiller & Seller (1985) the explicit aspect of curriculum, on the one hand, is expressed " in the written curricula and in courses of study" (p.3). On the other hand, the implicit aspect of the curriculum is seen in what is called the 'hidden curriculum', "… by which we mean the rules and norms that underlie interactions in the school. Learning interactions usually occur between teacher and student, but they also occur between student and student, student and subject matter, student and computer, and student and community.(p. 4).

In other words, there are two aspects to the curriculum, the explicit and the implicit, or the formal and informal. This line of reasoning is supported by DeMarras & LeCompte (1999) in their definition: "the term *curriculum* refers to the total school experience provided to students, whether planned or unplanned by educators. By conceptualizing the curriculum this broadly, we are able to include its intended as well as unintended outcomes" (pp. 223-24). The unintended outcome is 'taught' through the hidden curriculum that:

> Consists of the implicit messages given to students about socially legitimated or "proper" behavior, differential power, social evaluation, what kinds of knowledge exist, which kinds are valued by whom, and how students are valued in their own right. These messages are learned informally as students go about daily life in schools (p.244).

Similarly, for critical theorist, curriculum is far more than a program of study; it teaches a way of life, determines acceptable knowledge and

IVAN HUGH WALTERS

culture. "Curriculum favors certain forms of knowledge over others and affirms the dreams, desires, and values of select groups of students over other groups, often discriminatorily on the basis of race, class, and gender" (McLaren, 2005, p. 86). In other words, curriculum has an inherent bias in favor of the dominant group in the society, who produces the curriculum which in effect is a reproduction of their own cultural domain.

The existing post-secondary curriculum despite its pretensions of being inclusive has a mono-cultural orientation in favor of the dominant minority group in the Caribbean and the dominant group in America being tailored after the British educational system. The British influence is particularly evident in the curricula of the Caribbean educational institutions. Consistent with the critical theorists' definition of curriculum are two sides of curricular practices in the Caribbean, North America, and England: the overt curriculum and the covert or hidden curriculum. The overt curriculum tends to reinforce the status quo that favors the culture of the European descendants to the detriment of African descendants, in that it constructs and presents a Eurocentric version of knowledge as the legitimate version for all students. This is in the informal instructions which students receive in relation to authority, morality, religious doctrines. These are only incidental to the program of study but they provide very powerful lessons for students. In these circumstances the curriculum, contrary to popular sentiments and beliefs, is not politically neutral. In fact it is virtually impossible to create a curriculum that is apolitical.

Critical theorists view curriculum as a form of *cultural politics*, that is, as part of the socio-cultural dimensions of the schooling process which is integral to the continued existence of democracy. The term cultural politics permits the educational theorist to highlight the political consequences of interaction between educators and students who come from dominant and subordinate cultures (McLaren, 2005, p.88). Generally in the Caribbean there are two types of cultures: a "high" and a "low". The so-called high culture is associated with Eurocentrism. It is stagnant and non-creative. The high culture is riddle with sterility due to its reproductive nature. The low culture is popular, aggressive, creative, and dynamic and is associated with Blacks.

This popular culture has not altogether won the approval and recognition of the elite classes, but given the exogenous nature of the "high" culture and its association with the White elites, the popular culture is really the only serious claimant for the status of national culture (Alleyne, 2002, p. 99). Blacks are caught in the dilemma of working out how to vest this popular culture with national recognition and dignity. The situation is further aggravated by the right wing fundamentalist attitude of some of the denominations in Christianity which reject the popular culture because they consider many aspects of it to be crude, vulgar, and unchristian. These political contestations are brought into the classroom among the learners from the various socio-cultural backgrounds for exploration, discussion, and possible resolution. Here is where the importance of a redemptive pedagogy becomes crucially important. Reconstructive schooling in a democratic context requires the fair representation of stories of all cultures in the curriculum to create a *salvific multicultural education* which cultivates new skills and knowledge; an epistemology for empowerment. Gutek (1997) points out that:

> [A] Critical Theorist curriculum would use the students' unique multicultural experiences to develop new skills, and knowledge. Such a curriculum would stress (1) the study of the students' histories, languages, and cultures; and (2) an analysis of the persistent issues ... that empower some and disempower others (p.328).

In other words, the curriculum must reflect the stories and struggles of all peoples, and the issues that are of deep concern to them which put them in a place of advantage or disadvantage. Through the use of the language of critique, progressive educators can analyze ways in which the curriculum is used to reproduce and socialize students into the dominant culture. The task of the progressive educator, however, is to create alternative curricula, alternative instructional methodologies, and alternative ways of assessing students so as to empower them, whether in the context of school, the workplace, or in the public sphere. This is the utopian dream that is advocated in this book's pedagogy of redemption. The curricular practices in the Caribbean and America do not reflect the history of the struggle of Black people for liberation, nor do they address the persistent poverty and economic disenfranchisement of Africans in the Diaspora. This curricular imbalance needs to be corrected so as to shift the focus from preparing learners for the job market to one of deep political and cultural reflection for life in a multicultural democratic society. To this end, nothing short of radical transformation of the post-secondary education curriculum will suffice.

Teaching that is grounded in an Africentric curricular orientation can remove many of the stereotypes and myths about Black people that are still an active force in Caribbean and American societies. This of course will not be a panacea for all of our social ills, but it will go a long way in healing the nation and exploding myths and stereotypes. For instance, the myth that Africans had to be enslaved because they were uncivilized and lazy; that slavery would not only civilize us, but would also deliver our souls to God (Banks 2003). Banks (2003) and Nieto (1999) provide us with the detailed learning approaches that can be used to create multicultural learning communities and educators who wish to reform their teaching methodologies and content of their curricula will find them to be an invaluable source and treasure for their practice. Further assistance can be derived from Zemelman, Daniels & Hyde (1998) who provides us with the state of the art method of instruction which can be incorporated into progressive teaching of the Africentric curricula.

The progressive educator who adheres to an Africentric philosophy obviously cannot fit into the *modus operandi* of the banking educational construct and therefore must create a new learning situation which invites and accept the full participation of the students as both learner and teacher, and the same is also true for the teacher. Students must be actively involved in the teaching of intellectual skills just as the students who are in the "performance-oriented areas such as arts or sports" (Huba & Freed, 2000, p.35). Freire (1987) describes a liberatory education as the fundamental situation "where the teacher and the student *both* have to be learners, *both* have to be cognitive subjects, in spite of being different ... educators and students both to be critical agents in the act of knowing" (p.33).

This is the kind of dialogical approach which is required for the radical Africentric curricular orientations which give students a greater participation in the learning process by incorporating the voices of the students into the learning process so that students can take on the direct responsibility for their learning for their own liberation. "Making the classroom a democratic setting where everyone feels a responsibility to contribute is a central goal of transformative pedagogy" (hooks, 1994, p.39). In other words, the learning process is being democratized. The method of teaching here is being revolutionized to create a greater cohesion between the teacher, the subject matter, and the students. "Accepting the decentering of the West globally, embracing multiculturalism compels educators to focus attention on the issue of voice. Who speaks? Who listens? And why?" (hooks, 1994, p.40). The inescapable point which hooks is making here is the important role which the voices of the students play in the learning experience especially in a multicultural class because Black children have been socialized into a culture in which they are neither to be heard nor seen; the invisible student, the silent student, the objectified student. This is particularly so for Black women. Therefore it is imperative that Black men and women speak like thunder and lightning in their classroom. They must let their voices be heard because they are intelligent, because they have the intellectual capacity to expound and expatiate on science, mathematics, literature, arts, and creative songs and dances. They are capable of redeeming themselves from systems of domination.

The educator must cultivate in the students the intellectual capacity for critical thinking because teaching is not just the transferring of knowledge but the total involvement of every aspect of personal and societal living. This is the subjectification of the learners and the teacher. Freire (1998a) noted that in the context of true learning, the learners will be engaged in a continuous transformation through which "they become authentic subjects of the construction and reconstruction of what is being taught side by side with the teacher, who is equally subject to the same process" (p.33).

This means that the transformation which is being advocated here by Freire (1998a) is not just in terms of the teacher-student relationship. The context of this transformational learning is the social injustice which exists in the society. The source of the problem extends far beyond the classroom into the wider society. "Precisely because of that, the context for transformation is not only the classroom but extends outside of it. The students and educators will be undertaking a transformation that includes a context outside the classroom, if the process is a liberating one." (Freire, 1998a, p. 33) In other words, transformational learning does not only aim to change the instructional methodology in the classroom, but it brings with it an exponential effect which can be propagated throughout the society. Herein lies the pellucid distinction between liberatory education with its emphasis on democracy and the seeking of an egalitarian society, and traditional education, which seeks conformity. This mode of education is diametrically opposed to the traditional, conventional reproductive schooling which promotes inequality, competition, and segregation. This is why it is crucially important that the transformation which takes place in school reverberate throughout the entire society.

Transformative education in the context of multiculturalism with its emphasis on redemptive curricular orientation incorporates the voices of the students in the learning process. As a matter of fact, it is the responsibility of each student to make constructive contributions to the learning process because the students are no longer docile, passive listeners but have become critical co-investigators in the socio-political dialogue with the teacher (Freire, 1971). Redemptive education is part and parcel of oppositional politics and part of the *modus operandi* of the progressive educator's teaching to transgress the old institutions of neo-colonialism that enslave the minds of Diaspora people. This is the educator's methodology for challenging the limitations which have been placed upon education by the powers that be. This is the transformational utopian dream for redemptive education.

Redemptive pedagogy therefore pushes against the narrow boundaries which traditional education use to hem in knowledge and preserve it for the elites; it pushes against the grain of pedagogic deadwood and breaks through the stained glass windows of static, passive instructional methodology to liberate epistemology from the shackles of neo-colonialism. Redemptive pedagogy is vivacious, strong, resilient, and has the synergy which stoutly resists becoming the captive of any person or institution. When educators recognize the importance of redemptive pedagogy for the transformation of their noetic structure then they will be able to give to their students the education which they so richly and justly deserve in a multicultural context. While redemptive pedagogy focuses on things African, it does not seek to promote ethnocentrism. This is why it is to be understood as one of the aspects of multiculturalism. It recognizes and holds the tension which exists between the 'both /and' symbiotic concept. As Delpit (1995) suggests: "I believe in a diversity of styles, and I believe the world would be diminished if cultural diversity is ever obliterated. Further, I believe strongly … that each cultural group should have the right to maintain its own language style" (p. 39). Delpit (1995) makes the salient point here that demonstrates the importance of each ethnic group to the well-being of the society as the unity of diverse peoples. Among these many peoples are the Diaspora people.

REDEMPTIVE DEMOCRATIC EDUCATION CURRICULAR DISCOURSE

The democratic system is predisposed to the actualization of human rights for all individuals. Of course, this is not to say that there are no drawbacks in the democratic system. The fundamental rights and freedoms which are very similar to human rights are enshrined in most if not all democratic constitutions in the Commonwealth Caribbean,

United States of America, and including the unwritten constitution of England which has been bolstered by the European Human Rights Conventions and the Human Rights Act of 1998. These countries place the fundamental rights of its citizens in a position of pre-eminence in their domestic laws. The fundamental rights: freedom of speech, freedom of movement, freedom of conscience, the right to life, equality before the law are heavily entrenched in the constitutions and cannot be amended (except in England) through the ordinary legislative process. However, education in a democratic state when it is provided by the government seems to suffer from similar defects as in the totalitarian states. But is there a nexus between democracy and education? Because critical education is an aspect of political activism which involves critical reflection on political issues such as racism, oppression, discrimination, corruption and so on, there must be a connection between education and democracy. For an educator to exercise his/her intellectual capacity to reflect critically on hard social issues, she/he must do so in the context of politics, history, and philosophy. This is why a strong connection is made in this book between democracy and education. Dewey (1916) defines democracy in this way:

> A democracy is more than a form of government: it is primarily a mode of associated living, of conjoint communicated experience. The extension in space of the number of individuals who participate in an interest so that each has to refer his own action to that of others, and to consider the action of others to give point and direction to his own, is equivalent to the breaking down of those barriers of class, race, and national territory which kept men (sic) from perceiving the full import of their activity (p.95).

The kind of democracy which is conceived by Dewey (1916) portrays a political system in which people who live together are accountable to one another for their conduct. It is a political situation which provides freedom and at the same time requires restraint in terms of respect for the rights of the neighbor. A simplistic explication is that it requires personal accountability for individual conduct. The neighbor principle is important in a democracy because there are competing interests and each person must be mindful not to cause harm or to infringe upon the rights of his/her neighbor. Furthermore, if one really cares about the well-being of one's neighbor, racism and oppression would be less of a social problem because there is "associated living". We cannot, however, overlook the fact that democracy is practiced in the economic confines of capitalism which cherishes competition and this in turn spawns individualism rather than collective responsibility (*ujima*) and cooperate economics (*ujumaa*) for the general good of the community.

Be those facts as they may, the democratic society is obliged to respect the human rights of the students to a good education as set out in the Human Rights Convention not only because the country is a signatory to it, but even more important, because education is crucial for the flowering and flourishing of democracy as a form of associated living in a community where all persons are valued. Therefore, the coercive force of the school must be limited in a democratic society for the proper exercise of the freedom in terms of influencing the future of the students. In an authoritarian state the rulers determine the content of education because the state has arrogated to itself the privilege and prerogative of being the only entity that knows what is good for the citizens. This is not the philosophy that is practiced in democratic states which emphasize the freedoms of the individual citizen.

Therefore it follows, inexorably that the curriculum is not politically neutral but rather it is intricately bound up with many of the social issues which are found in a democratic system: social class, culture, gender, power. This is the position from which curriculum is normally written, but what enters the curriculum depends on who is writing it. As the matter now stands, in the classroom setting the dominant education discourses determine what books are used, which curricular approaches should be employed, and the values and beliefs that should be transmitted to students. This is what happens when the curriculum is designed by neo-conservatives. It is for this reason that good pedagogy must identify and discuss the political assumptions upon which the curriculum is based in order to transform the undemocratic arrangements of neo-colonialism which reek with social oppression. In this way educators can empower their students for meaningful social change through education in a democratic society. "Education proceeds ultimately from the patterns furnished by institutions, customs, and laws. Only in a just state will these be such as to give the right education; and only those who have rightly trained minds will be able to recognize the end and ordering principles of things." (Dewey, 1916, p. 97) In other words, neo-colonial education is reproductive of the social order and only those who receive critical training will be able to discern the purpose for which the educational system is designed. They are the ones who will be able to change it. The biblical statement is correct where it says if the blind leads the blind they both will fall into the ditch. This is why education should facilitate freedom of thought, freedom of expression and conscience. Education therefore, must create critical thinking faculties in citizens, place great premium on discussion and dissent. This is democratic space for democratic public discourse. Dewey (1916) observes that the devotion of democracy to education is a familiar fact. He further states that:

A society which makes provisions for participation in its good of all members on equal terms and which secures flexible readjustment of its institutions through interaction of the different forms of associated life is insofar democratic. Such a society must have a type of education which gives individuals a personal interest in social relationships and control, and the habits of mind which secure social changes (p.98).

Social changes are facilitated through critical thinking and critical thinking is imperative for the survival of a democratic society. It is only in a democratic society that citizens can exercise the form of critical thinking that is inherent to the survival of democracy. Here Dewey provides us with the intimate connection between democracy and education. This is the form of critical thinking which is advocated by Dewey (Spring 1994, p. 20). The tautology of this statement is evident, but the point is clear that critical thinking and democracy go hand in hand. As Springer (1994) puts it:

> [T]he form of critical thinking Dewey argues for is
> necessary for a democracy involves an understanding of
> social construction of knowledge and the ability to test and
> judge the value of new forms of knowledge. Consequently,
> history is at the heart of Dewey's instructional methodology.
> It is through the study of history that students learn how
> and why knowledge and institutions were created (p. 21).

This principle that knowledge is historically constructed is vitally
important, together with the intellectual ability to do critical analysis
of historical creation of knowledge. Knowledge is not sacrosanct, nor
is it etched in stone; it changes over time. An example of knowledge
mutability is the dogmatic positions which have been taken by the
Church for many years, such as the notion that the earth is the centre
of the universe. This myth was exploded by Galileo's discovery of the
solar system. This new discovery forced the Church to retreat in the face
of new scientific knowledge that belies its dogmatic teachings.

> [T]he citizens in Dewey's ideal democratic society both
> understand the social usefulness of their work and are able
> to relate theory to practice. In addition, they understand
> that knowledge and institutions are products of particular
> social conditions, needs, and they are willing to change
> when ideas and institutions become outmoded (Spring
> 1994, p. 23).

The social construction of knowledge is created in particular historical
circumstances. There is a nexus between knowledge and power, in
that those who have power can both create and decide what acceptable
knowledge is. The Europeans were able to enslave Africans because
they had the power to do it and they could justify it by producing
the knowledge that was required for its justification. McLaren (2003)
advises that knowledge be examined not only for the ways in which it
might misrepresent or mediate reality, but also for the ways in which it
actually reflects the daily struggles of people's lives. He further stated
that the "knowledge which is acquired in the classroom should help
students participate in vital issues that affect their experience on a daily

level rather than simply enshrine the values of business pragmatism" (p.85). The knowledge that the White minority in Barbados were able to hold on to their colonial position of power because they had the power to manipulate the political situation in the post-independence era to their advantage is a vital issue that should be debated in the classroom and the mechanism through which they were able to make themselves, as Beckles (1993) puts it is: "a silent and hidden force that successfully manipulated elements of the political directorate to its own end" (p.537). This is also another vital issue for classroom discussion.

The democratic empowerment through education which is advocated here seeks to eliminate social injustice and decrease the inequality in power that is prevalent in the societies in terms of wealth, social status, occupation, gender, race, housing, and economic opportunities. The irony is, although there is greater freedom in a democracy, there also seems to be greater injustice and inequality. Therefore, there must necessarily be a constant struggle for empowerment of ordinary folks to eliminate the social scourges.

In this context, the school, as a site of democratic struggle, should be shaped by attempts to promote justice and eliminate inequality of power. Critical pedagogy is a method that prepares all citizens for participation in the democratic state and prepares students to participate in this democratic struggle within the school and in other public spheres of life (Spring 1994, p. 25).

This is the posture which a progressive educator must take in the context of the African Diaspora. The students in post-secondary institutions must develop a critical awareness of the undemocratic control by the White elites of the economic activities in the Caribbean and North America; and their constant manipulation of political leaders to the disadvantage of Black folks. It is a vital as well as a demoralizing issue that in the Caribbean, Barbados being a typical example, "... the corporate power of these groups has never been challenged by an organized political force." (Beckles, 1996, p.537) This lack of political challenge to white corporate power is due to the unabashed co-option of political leaders. West (2004) describes it as:

> This illicit marriage of corporate and political elites – so
> blatant and flagrant in our time – not only undermines the
> trust of informed citizens in those who rule over them. It
> also promotes the pervasive sleepwalking of the populace,
> who see that the false prophets are handsomely rewarded
> with money, status, and access to more power (p.4).

The posture which is created in students of an Africentric redemptive pedagogy is crucial to the survival of freedom and democracy. In a very real sense we are our brothers' and sisters' keepers; the gatekeepers of citizens' freedom and human rights. This is why it is incumbent upon each one of us, in fact it is our moral duty to stand firm against injustice and oppression whenever they raise their ugly heads in our society. This is our collective work and responsibility (*ujima*) as required by the principles of *Nguzo Saba*. We are the guardians of our human rights, our right to a non-idiotic education. Through the methodology of Aficentric redemptive pedagogy students can obtain a voice in the vital issues that impact on their lives. They can obtain an understanding as to how the social construction of knowledge determines what they believe, and they can challenge the source and the truthfulness of those beliefs. Critical Africentrism forces students to confront racism, sexism, classism, corruption, and other social oppression within the society. The possible outcome of such critical dialogue is an understanding of their origin as a regime that was put in place by those who possessed power for the oppression of others. African people are in an especially strong position to pronounce against oppression and social injustice better than most persons because we have lived through various forms of discrimination and oppression. We must bear in mind that the only thing that is necessary for evil to triumph is for good men and women to do nothing. "To sit passively by while injustices are committed, or democratic institutions collapse, in the hope that others will step in, is to be a free rider" (Kymlicka cited in Parker 2003, p. 54).

Parker (2003) pointed out that the free rider's passivity catches up with him eventually and destroys him too, when no one is left to look out for him. It is this passivity, apathy, or fear that has placed

Diaspora people in the predicament that they are in today, because Black leaders were too timid to challenge White economic power when the opportunity presented itself for them to do so. This is mainly due to these leaders placing concern for their political career first rather than the long term interest of the nation. Black leaders have failed to implement cooperative economic (*ujamaa*) regimes in the Caribbean which would have had tremendous benefits for the people.

Parker (2003) poignantly describes this kind of attitude, the politicking of political leaders as "idiocy". This word he uses with its etymological meaning "Idiotic" in its origin is not what it means to us today, stupid or mentally deficient. This recent meaning is entirely and deservedly out of usage by educators, but the original meaning needs to be reclaimed. It is an ancient Greek term that shares with "idiom" and "idiosyncratic" the root *idios*, which means private, separate, self-centered – selfish. This conception of idiocy achieves its force when we contrast it with *polites* (political) or *public*" (p.2). With the use of this definition Parker (2003) sets forth an argument for the great importance of communal endeavor (*ujamaa*) to ensure that injustice and inequality are dealt with by the entire community because all is affected by the conduct of some. A democratic society must be sensitive to the needs of all members of that society, albeit that democracy literally means the rule of the majority, but good democracy does not encapsulate majority tyranny. Citizens of a democratic state are obliged to speak out against injustice and inequality, whether or not it affects us or our family, the minority or the majority. In any case, soon or later "they will come for us." He further demonstrates that there must be unity in diversity: "The interdependence of the *pluribus* and *unum*, diversity and liberty, and multicultural education and citizenship education" (p.2) The salient point that I wish to make here is that human rights must include a right to education, and education must include multiculturalism, and social justice education, an education that is not idiotic, a redemptive education. Spring (1994) refers to this as planting a wheel in the head. Spring (1994) admits that there are some wheels in the head that are necessary.

The right to an education which includes an education in human rights is fundamental to centering human relationships on a moral duty to protect and maintain everyone's human rights. Do human rights become a wheel in the head? Yes, they do become a wheel in the head, but it is a wheel that drives everyone to work for the necessary conditions that allow human action in a world of freedom and economic security (p.169).

Parker (2003) contrasts the "pluribus", the public life, citizenship with the "*unum*", the private and self-centered life which is sterile, bereft of human connectedness. To illustrate "the non-idiotic life – the citizen's life" (p.8), he cites the civil disobedience demonstration of Mohandas Gandhi and Martin Luther King Jr. as two examples par excellence. These two men were concerned for the public good, to end racism and injustice in their particular circumstances. If they were idiotic, concerned only with their own family, what Parker (2003) calls "amoral familism", they would not have taken the risk to challenge the status quo. Similarly, Rosa Parks refused to sit at the back of the bus because a Negro is just as much a human being as any Caucasian. The argument which Parker (2003) raises here is similar to the principles of *Nguzo Saba*. He emphasizes the *pluribus* over against the *unum*, while *Nguzo Saba* creates a communal humanitarian approach (*ujamaa*) in the interest of unity (*umoja*). This unity of humankind is captured in King's Birmingham Letter as cited in Parker (2003):

> Injustice anywhere is a threat to justice everywhere. We are caught in an inescapable network of mutuality, tied in a single garment of destiny. Whatever affects one directly, affects all indirectly. Never again can we afford to live with the narrow, provincial "outside agitator" idea. Anyone who lives inside the United States cannot be considered an outsider anywhere within its bounds (p.8).

Parker's (2003) opinion is corroborated by that of Spring (1994) that every citizen is morally obliged to stand and fight against unjust laws which promote injustice and inequality:

> All the members of society have an obligation to ensure
> that everyone is treated equally before the law and that
> everyone has the right to life, liberty, and security of person.
> Everyone would be called on to fight discrimination based
> on race, color, sex, language, religion, political or other
> opinion, national or social origin, property, and birth and
> other status (p.169).

I hold opinion with Parker that everyone must ensure that the human
rights of the others are protected against incursion by unscrupulous
persons and institutions. Democracy goes a long way in protecting
the fundamental rights of citizens as enshrined in the constitutions.
However, democracy alone is not enough. Citizens must be prepared
to speak out in their own defense and in defense of those who do not
have any voice, who can only groan under the burden of discrimination
and marginalization. Although democracy is crucially important for
educational flourishing, it does not guarantee protection of human
rights.

> Without a civic culture that commits all people to
> exercising a moral duty to protect civil rights, democracy
> can quickly slip into a form of government that strips
> people of their rights. Therefore, key to a democratic system
> that protects human rights is a civic culture based on the
> moral commitment of all citizens to defend the rights of
> all (Spring 2000, p.48-49).

I believe that all people can experience the good life through a
redemptive education which includes an education for social justice
that seeks to right the evils of racism, sexism, and classism which have
a debilitating impact on working class people. A redemptive education
is crucially important to their liberation. The citizens must be the
architects of their liberation and they can only do so if they become
fully aware of the harm which a reproductive, conservative educational
system inflicts upon them by denying them their full participation in
the national agenda, or from participating in the "different forms of
associated living," as Dewey (1916) puts it. Education should have an

emancipatory agenda, instead of churning out human capital for the job market, instead of using education to ply the corporate ideology. A redemptive education would create the condition that is conducive for citizens' self-determination in the wider society – the *kujichagulia* of the *Nguzo Saba* principles.

Advocates of redemptive education have an uphill struggle in raising the consciousness of Black people who have been marginalized by the ruling elites for the purpose of exploiting their labor, and other resources. It is not inconceivable that oppressed people sometimes put up stout resistance to change for their liberation because they have accepted and internalized their own oppression. This is why there is an obsequious state of mind, which makes Black people collude in their own subordination.

> People who have been socialized in an oppressive environment, and who accept the dominant group's ideology about their group, have learned to accept a definition of them that is hurtful and limiting. They think feel, and act in ways that demonstrate the devaluation of their group and of themselves as members of that group (Adams, 1997, p. 21).

It is not only the oppressed who are in need of liberation; the oppressors may be in an even greater need of liberation through democratic education especially those persons who wield power in the society. While it is imperative that we see to the education of the poor and the oppressed, we cannot afford to leave the members of the dominant group without education because this can make them all the more destructive. Therefore, those who are in positions of power are also in need of democratic enlightenment: "those who occupy the board rooms, legislatures, court chambers, and faculty positions at prestigious universities" it follows inexorably that all persons "if they are to walk the democratic path with diverse others, require a high-quality education for freedom, justice, and equality. This applies equally to the powerless and the powerful" (Parker, 2003, p.156). The creation of a democratic *productive* education is a prerequisite to the enjoyment of the good life Therefore, the right to an education ought to be a fundamental right which is enshrined in the constitutions as advocated above.

REDEMPTIVE MULTICULTURAL CURRICULAR DISCOURSE

The current neo-colonial, Eurocentric curricular orientation of post-secondary institutions in the Caribbean and the mono-cultural educational system that is predominant in North American need to be revamped, restructured and/or renewed so as to reflect a multicultural orientation. Students who are Africans and of African descent, Syrians, Europeans, Chinese, Arabs, Jews, and Indians need to learn more about the history, culture, and early civilization of their ancestors. This is where their roots lie and if it is not invested with pride and dignity, it will have a negative impact on their self-esteem and their children's. But this fact has been ignored for hundreds of years due to the Anglo-American colonialism and slavery. The curriculum has reflected the voice and the story of the dominant Eurocentric group in the society. The dominant group has always covertly and overtly advocated the doctrine of assimilation, social cohesion; the non-White population is expected to cohere to Anglophonic cultural values and systems of government. The predominance of the Westminster export model of governance has been transplanted to the Caribbean with minor indigenous modifications, but it is not indigenous. The Caribbean has assimilated many of the British colonial habits and customs and they proudly and unabashedly proclaim them to be its cultural heritage: "The Greco-Roman tradition is very evident in the democratic traditions and legal systems. It is evident also in the general intellectual, philosophical, artistic and aesthetic norms" (Alleyne, 2002, p.92).

Any attempt to incorporate elements of African culture is met with stout resistance, especially from the petty middle class. However, African folklore is used in plays and skits as entertainment for the polished middle class for their amusement. But African folklore is not being woven into the tapestry of the country's culture; that would be heretical, although African folklore is part of the popular culture. Both the political arrangements and the legal system are mimicked reflections of the Anglophonic mentality and habits; an almost unabashed consumptive acculturation/assimilation *modus operandi*. It's not unusual to find lawyers and executives in the Caribbean sweating like pot covers in the boiling mid-day sun all bedecked in jackets and ties, sometimes double breasted suits, and all. This is a typical assimilated culture. "The assimilationist idea envisions a society in which ethnicity and race are not important identities. Group identities and affiliations would be based primarily on such variables as social class, politics, education, and other interests" (Banks, 2003, p. 3). There is no melting pot here, only little England.

This is a profoundly demoralizing situation for those who have Africentric or Pan-Africanist orientations, and an almost insurmountable barrier to break down because it has been etched into the minds of many Black folks. This is a cultural prison which does not require lock and key because the people are their own gaoler. There is clearly an eminent need for cultural and social change. Some of this is already on the horizon and this is particularly reflected in the music to which the youths are drawn, namely reggae, rap, and dub. The multicultural curricular modules can make a significant contribution to the required meaningful social change for national upliftment and healing. Multicultural education has the capacity and the energy to transform the challenges of ethnic, cultural, and racial diversity that is obtained in the African Diaspora into educational and social opportunities for the promotion of proper attitudes, communal care, affection, and understanding; a communal love and appreciation for people of all races, cultures, religions, and life styles. This approach and outlook is multicultural *kainonia*. This can be reflected in educational institutions at all levels by including more information about ethnic groups in social studies, language arts, and humanities curricula. This would go a long way to achieving the kind of *kainonia* that strengthens and uplifts youths and adults in our colleges and other institutions of higher learning.

In order to facilitate this approach there must be a wholesale transformation of the curricula of these institutions. The steps which have been taken so far at the primary and secondary levels are encouraging but more radical changes are needed. As the matter now stands, the modicum of ethnic studies being offered is lopsided because it only includes minority White culture and a spattering of African culture. But there is no far reaching, systematic effort to make positive meaningful change to the post-secondary curricula.

The greatest potential of multicultural education is that it has the capacity to cater to all cultural diversities and to accommodate each of them equally so that all of their voices and stories can become an integral part of the *multicultural kainonia* which will serve as a vehicle for general curricular reform and transformation. Therefore ethnic content cannot be merely added on to the traditional curriculum, which already has a plethora of problems. This would not facilitate ethnic curricular progress. The demographical changes which are rapidly occurring in the national student bodies plead for a *multicultural kainonia* for the promotion of positive and meaningful social change for all students. Junn (in Halpern & Associates, 1994) reports that educators in the United States of America are taking the need for curricular transformation in colleges seriously and have prepared and/ or are preparing themselves to meet the challenges:

> In response, growing numbers of educators are now adding their voices to the urgent call to reformulate a new vision incorporating the values and principles of *diversity* (referring to differences of all kinds – cultural, social class, ableness) and *multiculturalism* (referring to more specifically to differences in culture) into the educational system (p.128).

This is the challenge for multicultural education: to deal with this racial, ethnic, cultural, gender and gender orientation diversity so that they become opportunities for learning about the importance of different cultural forms. Educators will require a change of attitude and new skills to deal with the new situation. It would be unwise, to borrow a theological metaphor, to put 'new wine into old wine skin.' Furthermore, I am inclined to hold opinion with Banks (2003) when he emphasizes the crucial importance of re-conceptualizing the American society. In juxtaposition with such a re-conceptualization is the creation of the new curriculum. This line of reasoning is also applicable to the Caribbean which is in a dire need to rid itself of its neo-colonial cultural deadwood and corrupt political entities.

A similar call must be made for the region. I believe that here we may have to 'reinvent the wheel'. This, of course, is an onerous and Herculean task, a utopian dream. But educators in the Caribbean have got to put their backs to the wheel and toil and toil to make the Diaspora a better place, to bring about cultural and gender equity. Liberated educators must also be courageous and strong if they are to surmount the colonial labyrinth that has been transplanted into the psyche of Diaspora people in the various societies. Banks (2003) holds the view that because the assumption that only what is Anglo-American is so deeply ingrained in curriculum materials and in the hearts and minds of so many students and educators, the educational system cannot transform the curriculum by merely adding a unit or a lesson here and there. This same line of reasoning is applicable to the Caribbean. There must be a transformation of the entire post-secondary curricula.

What is really required as the antidote for our Anglophonism is a serious, critical examination of the conception of the region as "third world" countries and the pejorative dependency that is associated with that concept which is perpetuated in the curriculum relative to the basic canons, assumptions, and purposes that underlie the post-secondary curriculum. In seeking to transform the curriculum, we must ardently keep our focus on the purpose for which we are promulgating a fundamental institutional transformation. That is, our commitment to take into account an inclusive approach to the educational experiences that create a conducive learning environment for interaction in the learning community for all learners irrespective of ethnicity, social class, life style, age, gender, disabilities. I believe that the transformation of the curriculum will lead to the transformation of the society exponentially and that will in turn lead to greater educational equity for working class people. Providing that the vision is pondered in our hearts and lived out in our daily lives, we will be able to actualize and bring to fruition the important goals of the multicultural curriculum utopian dream. This will cure the Eurocentric distortion and misrepresentation of African history, African culture, and early civilization. It will present students with new ways to view and interpret African philosophy, literature, music, dance, and art. Any goals that are less ambitious, while important will not result in curricular transformation or enable Black students to acquire a new conception of themselves, their history, and the world (Banks, 2003).

An equally important goal of the multicultural curriculum is the empowerment of students to live holistic lives with dignity and respect in much the same way as feminism has improved the lives of women everywhere. The teaching of diversity in terms of gender, race, ethnicity, and culture will empower both the educator and the student with the power, the knowledge, the skills, and the right attitudinal acumen to participate fully in civil action that will change our world and augment and/or accelerate the chance of our survival on planet earth. Perhaps we may not see this come to pass in our life time, but we must plant the seed of cross cultural communication so that our posterity will find shade under it in time to come. As Banks (1993) puts it:

> To realize such a lofty goal, members of the learning community must be prepared to wrestle with difficult reforms in two fundamental and complex arenas; reforms in curriculum (What constitutes 'accepted" academic acknowledge?), and reforms in the total school environment (How does the classroom and the campus climate recognize and honor diversity?) (p.129).

The curricular transformation which is being envisioned and advocated here calls for the acceptance by mainstream academic canonical knowledge of the more recent knowledge that is closely associated with marginalized people. This is an integral part of a curriculum which purports to reflect diversity. This is why it is imperative that:

> [A]n institution's formal academic curriculum should represent both mainstream academic knowledge and the more recent 'transformative academic knowledge', which consists of 'concepts, paradigms, themes, and explanations that challenge mainstream academic knowledge and expand the historical and literary canon (Banks, 1994, p.129).

In creating the conceptual utopian multicultural curriculum, people of color who have experienced oppression, prejudice and institutionalized racism must not only be portrayed as victims of a vicious system, of course, that they were and still are, but we must also extol their nobler virtues, their contribution to history, to the economy, to religion, and science. Banks (2003) admonishes us that we should ensure:

> [T]hat a balanced approach is taken and that people of color are not depicted only or primarily as victims. They should also be described as people who helped to shape their own destinies, who built ethnic institutions, and who played major roles in attaining their civil rights. It is necessary to teach such concepts as prejudice, discrimination, and racism. However, it is also essential to teach such concepts as protest, empowerment, interracial co-operation, and ethnic institutions in order to portray a full and accurate view of the experiences of ethnic groups (p.51).

In terms of political achievements, it is important to point out that African American obtained their civil rights without the shedding of blood (on the part of African Americans) but through the philosophy of non-violence as advocated and promulgated by the late Martin Luther King. King's message is a perpetual message for every generation, for every race. If we would only stop a little while and listen, listen carefully to it, we will see that it is a most worthy message. No less important are the political struggles of the Africans and their descendants in the Caribbean as portrayed by Beckles (1993) and Campbell (1985) and that of the African children in England (Christian, 2002).

The inequalities in the educational system will only be cured when educators and policy makers come to the realization that every child is worthy of love, affection, and kindness. The multicultural curriculum which we will create will incorporate all ethnic groups, so that the voice and the story of each group can be reflected in it without seeking to assimilate any of them: the promotion of unity in diversity. Assimilation has created more harm than good and should therefore be laid to rest, "because assimilation can act as a disincentive to learning, alienation, and marginalization may be the result" (Nieto, 1999, p.35). Multicultural education will avert the psychological damages which result from alienating students from their culture. Multicultural education makes provisions for programs that critique ethnocentrism or exclusionary educational practices which seek to relegate some citizens to the bottom of the social order. Colleges and universities will be challenged by the burgeoning multicultural education: this includes teaching about diversity, gender differences, similarities and gender equity. The faculties must be able to rise to these challenges.

The significance of a multicultural curriculum is in its ability to help students develop a positive sense of Black identity and strong racial and ethnic pride. It advocates awareness of diversity but not to the detriment of Black culture and it harbors within itself the potential for dispelling stereotypes. Junn (in Halpern & Associates, 1994) demonstrates that multicultural issues should not be limited to the faculty in the humanities, albeit a very important and fertile ground for discussing and promulgating new and novel ideas, but there is great latitude to incorporate the hard sciences. For example, biology can explain the genetics of phenotype and genotypes, whether or not genes substantially influence the development of homosexuality in men and women, whether a particular race has the propensity to develop certain diseases because of its genetic endowment, and so on. This approach can shed light on racial predilection and educability.

The fundamental curricular reform, based on the principle of redemptive pedagogy, which I am advocating here to facilitate multicultural development can only be actuated if educators are convinced that there is a dire need for multiculturalism in higher education. Educators must take a holistic approach to the subject because a fragmented approach just will not suffice. Additives to the current curriculum will consign multiculturalism and redemptive pedagogy to the periphery of the curriculum. The new curriculum may stipulate that multicultural studies be prerequisites, core, and/or electives. However, the better approach would be to make the whole curriculum multicentric: "Armed then with this spirit of grassroots change, individual educators may begin to make a difference by taking steps to re-conceptualize their curricula and pedagogy in furthering the mission of a truly inclusive education" (Junn, in Halpern & Associates, 1994, p.133). The salient point that is being made here is that a piecemeal approach to curricular transformation is self-defeating. It will take a grassroots orientation to dislodge the Eurocentric curricular orientation.

INSTRUCTIONAL METHODOLOGY FOR RADICAL REDEMPTIVE EDUCATION

Radical redemptive education adopts the democratic dialogical approach to instructional methodology. Radical redemptive education seeks to create classroom communities where the seven principles of good pedagogy are applicable:

1. respect for the voice of the individual;

2. promotes critical reflection;

3. accepts the personhood of every student regardless of ethnicity, class, sex or sexual orientation;

4. breaks down the barriers which are created by racism, sexism, and classism;

5. emphasizes social justice;

6. emphasizes African heritage; and

7. accepts difference in diversity.

These principles work together with those of *Nguzo Saba*. The purpose of these principles is to emphasize the removal of educational methodology from the traditional teacher-centered approach to the learner-centered approach. Through this methodology the redemption of oppressed and alienated people can be actualized and the oppressor can come to the place where s/he acknowledges his her transgressions and need for redemption (*metanoia*). Redemptive pedagogy requires the active involvement of students in the educational experience in the construction of new visions for the good life. Redemptive pedagogy promotes and advocates the partnership between the educator and the educand in the actualization of the educational objectives. Dewey (1938) was right when he says:

> There is, I think, no point in the philosophy of progressive education which is sounder than its emphasis on the importance of the participation of the learner in the formation of the purposes which direct his activities in the learning process, just as there is no defect in traditional education greater than its failure to secure the active co-operation of the pupil in construction of the purposes involved in his studying (p.67).

This view that the students must play an active role in his/her education is fully endorsed by the principles of redemptive pedagogic orientations. Radical redemptive pedagogy accepts the intricate connection between the three aspects of the learning experience: the teacher, the subject matter, and the learners. Both the teacher and the learners wrestle with the subject matter in constructing meaning for their lives and the world in which they live and have their being. Therefore radical redemptive pedagogy cannot be aligned to the traditional pedagogy wherein the educator who is centre of power, the creator and the repository of all epistemology. No longer can the educator be the subject matter, while the learners are the passive, empty vessels to be filled with the educator's knowledge. In this context "his (sic) task is to "fill" the students with the contents of his narration —contents which are detached from reality, disconnected from the totality that engendered them and could give them significance" (Freire, 1971, p.57). This method of teaching blunts the creative imagination of the students and stunts their intellectual growth and development. In other words the learners become mechanical zombies that do not learn but memorize and regurgitate. Thus creating and perpetuating the false consciousness of the learners. This is what Freire (1971) refers to as the banking system of education:

> Education thus becomes an act of depositing, in which the students are the depositories and the teacher is the depositor. Instead of communicating, the teacher issues communiqués and makes deposits which the students patiently receive, memorize, and repeat. This is the "banking" concept of education, in which the scope of action to the students extend only as far as receiving, filing, and storing the deposits (Freire, 1971, p.58).

In other words educators 'pour' the content of their knowledge into the heads of their learners, who are passive receptacles, and the learners are expected to draw on the deposit at some later date usually in the form of a direct assessment test to prove their learning or acquisition of the new knowledge. In this situation the teacher is the active agent while the learners are passive subjects. Interestingly, the only person who is learning in this situation is the teacher. It is the teacher who research, integrate, and teaches the material. "Since so many professors teach from that stand point, it is difficult to create the kind of learning community that can fully embrace multiculturalism" (hooks, 1994, p.40). hooks (1994) sees an interesting irony in this situation in that it is easier for learners to give up their banking system of education than their educators and learners are far more willing to face the challenges of multicultural education. Herein lies the work of the progressive educator because it is from this system of oppression that critical redemptive pedagogy seeks to liberate the minds of Black learners so that they can become co-creators of epistemology with the educator.

The progressive educator obviously cannot fit into the *modus operandi* of the banking educational construct and therefore must create a new learning situation which invites and accepts the full participation of the students as both learner and teacher, and the same is also true for the teacher. Students must be actively involved in the teaching of intellectual skills just as the students who are in the "performance-oriented areas such as arts or sports" (Huba & Freed, 2000, p.35). Freire (1987) describes a liberatory education as the fundamental situation "where the teacher and the student *both* have to be learners, *both* have to be cognitive subjects, in spite of being different. Educators and students both to be critical agents in the act of knowing" (p.33).

The traditional educational system is focused on teaching rather than learning, but the critical redemptive pedagogy requires a paradigm shift to focus on learning, that is learner-centered and dialogical in its approach to teaching and assessment. "To focus on learning rather than teaching, we must challenge our basic assumptions about how people learn and what the roles of a teacher should be. We must unlearn previously acquired teaching habits (Huba & Freed, 2000, p.3). The fact is that a progressive educator with a vision of the future must face his conditioning and be prepared to shift his/her paradigm. hooks (1994) stated emphatically that:

> [W]e must acknowledge that our styles of teaching may need to change. Let's face it: most of us were taught in classrooms where styles of teachings reflected the notion of a single norm of thought and experience, which we were encouraged to believe, was universal (p.35).

In other words, if the teacher is converted to change her/his style of teaching, the students will become the center of the learning experiences because teaching is not just the transferring of knowledge. The educator must cultivate in the students the intellectual capacity for critical thinking. Freire (1987) noted that in the context of true learning, the learners will be engaged in a continuous transformation through which "they become authentic subjects of the construction and reconstruction of what is being taught side by side with the teacher, who is equally subject to the same process" (p.33). Progressive learning involves the reconstruction of both the educator and the educand.

ASSESSMENT METHODOLOGY FOR RADICAL REDEMPTIVE EDUCATION

The Latin origin of the term assessment, *assidere*, literally means to *sit down beside*. Another way of thinking of assessment is the useful, careful judgment based on the kind of close observation that comes from "sitting down beside." Huba & Freed (2000) provides a broad definition of assessment that is most helpful:

> Assessment is the process of gathering and discussing information from multiple and diverse sources in order to develop a deep understanding of what students know, understand, and can do with their knowledge as a result of their educational experiences; the process culminates when assessment results are used to improve subsequent learning (p.8).

In other words, assessment is most effective when it reflects an understanding of learning as multidimensional. Traditional schooling emphasizes the assessment of: (1) logical and mathematical reasoning, and (2) linguistic abilities. Other abilities which do not fall within this parameter are precluded from the assessment process. When assessment focuses on these aspects of knowledge only, it sends the wrong message to students that only certain dimensions of learning are important. This message is most evident in traditional education which places a high premium on intellectual (academic) skills only relegating vocational skills to the bottom of the ladder. This message frequently emphasizes and elitizes academic knowledge. Under the Africentric curricular orientation other abilities and skills together with academic knowledge are treated as equally invaluable both to the learning process and to students. For this reason the Africentric curricular orientation seeks a new vision of assessment which includes assessment of the various abilities and skills whether in relation arts, technical skills such as carpentry, craft, motor mechanics, singing, and dancing. This means that students' learning outcomes will be based on a broader concept of intelligence, ability, and learning. Not only will logical and verbal abilities continue to be assessed because these are of vital importance, but a broad method of assessment will include the aforesaid areas together with the visual, auditory, kinesthetic, intrapersonal, and interpersonal abilities. This means assessing students' repertoire of learning strategies, skills in communicating with others, and knowledge as it is applied to day-to-day multicultural diversity.

Under the critical redemptive pedagogy, it is the duty of the educator to sit beside his/her students so as to make a fair and proper assessment of their work so that it becomes a collaborative reflection for both the educator and the learners. Huba & Freed (2000) describe assessment as the process for checking students' outcomes:

> When we assess our students' learning, we force the questions, "What have our students learned and how well have they learned it?" "How successful have we been at what we are trying to accomplish?" Because of this focus on learning, assessment in higher education is sometimes referred to as outcomes assessment or student outcomes assessment (p.8).

In other words, student outcomes assessment examines the success or failure of both the educator and the learners. Therefore, the assessment must be based on learning as knowledge and understanding, with a greater emphasis on understanding. The learning experiences are in turn based on metacognitive, philosophical, and multicultural perspectives. These perspectives suggest that meaningful learning occurs when the learner has a knowledge base that can be used with fluency to make sense of the world, solve problems, and make decisions.

It is important that learners develop a strong sense of self-determination, rigorous intellectual capabilities, and continually strive to acquire greater knowledge to be used as the tools for the social and political advancement of themselves and their society. Learners must have a repertoire of effective strategies for their own learning and for the ways and/or methods through which they share their learning with others and relate their leaning to the world. True learning will make learners empathetic to others who view the world and themselves from a perspective and/or point of reference other than their own.

Therefore assessment must do more than the traditional type of assessment because it is blindsided by its over-emphasis on academics as the hallmark of intelligence. This is why Huba & Freed (2000) do not give much credence to this form of assessment which comprised objectively scored paper and pencil test items like multiple choice and true/false questions because they typically test only factual knowledge but may not, or they are incapable of assessing students' understanding, or other aspects of students' understanding. An assessment for understanding must demand thoughtful and qualified responses to sometimes intricate issues such as the impact of slavery and colonialism on the present social and economic arrangements, the protracted impact of colonialism and slavery, the post-emancipation politics in the African Diaspora, of Black self-hate. This approach is the opposite of an assessment using unambiguous and non-problematic questions to test uncontroversial and discrete knowledge. In order to develop proper assessment strategies, the curriculum must have a good design. As indicated above, I advocate a preference for the backward design method. The method is only backward in so far as it does not follow the traditional procedures, but the implication of its name apart, it is very logical and commonsensical. As Wiggins & McTighe (1998) point out:

> [A] student's technical knowledge may sometimes be limited or even mistaken, but we could still conclude that he understands important things. Sometimes, a wrong answer can hide a great deal of understanding and vice versa; our assessments must make room for this difficult reality (p.81).

In other words, a different process, and a new language, to assess a student's capability for using and applying knowledge as well as understanding are needed. The education of an individual, understood in terms of developing abilities to use and apply one's knowledge and understanding cannot therefore be adequately assessed by traditional testing, as indicated above. Grading on a curve, which sorts students into groups for administrative purposes, says nothing about how each student is using his or her understanding, talents, or growing towards his/her potential. It does not reflect the development of higher order thinking, but it is perfect for the testing of rote learning.

Huba & Freedman (2000) advocate the "development and use of assessments like projects, papers, performances, portfolios, or exhibitions that evaluate higher order thinking and require students to directly reveal the very abilities that professors desire" (p.13). These types of assessments have intrinsic, qualitative values because through these means students are doing two important things: (1) demonstrating their learning, and (2) demonstrating their creativity. These finer qualities of higher order thinking cannot be demonstrated through the use of pencil and paper tests. This multidimensional assessment that is advocated by Huba & Freed (2000) is broad based, relevant to real life, process oriented and based on multiple measures which provide a rich portrayal of students' learning. Multidimensional assessment taps the power and diversity of active learning, creates multiple sources of information to support instructional decision making, and helps students become more reflective and capable learners. The multidimensional process is an integral part of learning and lends itself most ably to the observation of performances by the individual learners in action and judging them on the basis of collaboratively determined developmental criteria with feedback to the learners. Students' instruction will include mathematics, science, language, music, dance, drama, computer skills, games, cultural studies, and politics. Students' products will include, *inter alia*, performances, drama, exhibition, portfolios, discussions, debates, simulations, and research papers.

Under critical redemptive pedagogy, assessment must be comprehensive, seamless and ongoing instead of being done in periodic episodes, that is, in the middle and end of each semester. A comprehensive assessment system is a coordinated plan for periodically monitoring the progress of students both by the educator and by the students themselves, and both together in a variety of subjects. The rationale or basis for a comprehensive assessment in these orientations is that assessment is a process whose power is accumulative. Students' improvement is best fostered when assessment is based on a series of learning experiences which are assessment on a regular basis rather than periodical at the end of course or unit of study. The point is to monitor the student's progress towards the intended goals in the spirit of continuous assessment. The assessment process itself must be evaluated and refined because the system is not infallible and in order to keep current with new developments and trends in assessment.

It must also be borne in mind that assessment is not separate and distinct from instruction. On the contrary, assessment is integral to instruction and learning. The focus and purpose of assessment is on learning, on how it takes place, and how it can be improved, not on normative comparisons. This is why assessment must be a continuous process that drives instruction, instead of being done periodically. Furthermore, assessment does not bring an end to learning as is the case in the traditional system, but instead it provides information about how to continue to develop the students' skills, abilities, knowledge and understanding with respect to the course learning objectives. Therefore assessment is an active demonstration of students' understanding and ability to applying this understanding.

Because curriculum is the *grund norm* or matrix for assessment and instruction, the authentic, qualitative forms of assessments are pertinent to the radical curricular orientations which focus on students' learning outcomes. In this way learning will become more democratic and students will play a constructive role in their own education. Huba & Freed (2000) state that "we should design the curriculum as a set of interrelated courses and experiences that will help students achieve the intended learning outcomes." We can do this by "designing the curriculum by working backwards from learning outcomes helps to make the curriculum coherent" and holistic, a story that can be easily read and followed (pp.13-14). Wiggins & McTighe (1998) indicate that the backward design not only departs from the traditional curricular procedures but it also prefers the authentic, qualitative type of assessment.

> This backward approach to curricular design also departs from another common practice: thinking about assessment as something we do at the end, once teaching is complete. Rather than creating assessment near the conclusion of a unit of study ... backward design calls for us to operationalize our goals or standards in terms of assessment evidence as we begin to plan a unit or course (p. 8).

The point is to start with a conclusion in terms of what the students' learning outcomes should be for the lesson. This is important because the teacher instead of leaving the assessment for the end of the lesson begins with the assessment of the learning outcomes and this will serve as a guide for the instruction and the materials for the learning experiences.

Students will develop with the instructor relevant and meaningful assessments, and play an active role in developing rubrics and setting standards of performance for high quality work. In this way assessment will have a greater meaning for the learner than receiving a grade. Hence, the conviction that students' assessment must be a multidimensional process that is an integral part of their learning.

Assessment must be seen as valid, reliable, fair, and equitable. Validity is the extent to which an assessment measures what is needed for a particular purpose and to which the results, as they are interpreted and used, meaningfully and thoroughly represent the specified knowledge or understanding. Reliability is the consistency or stability of assessment results and the degree to which assessment is free from errors of measurement. Fairness and equity means that assessment procedures do not discriminate against a particular group or individual student(s), for example, students from racial, ethnic, or gender groups, or students with disabilities.

CONCLUSION

People of African descent continue the fight for equal rights and social justice. Democratic education is all about struggle against evil and unjustified misery with the view of humanizing our society. Democratic education can help to alleviate human suffering from social disaffection through the development of the intellect and respect for common human dignity, but it is not a panacea for all the social ills that exist in the society. History has shown that positive social change can be brought about through education whether gradual or magnitudinal. The success or failure of non-idiotic education depends to a large extent on shifting the educators' paradigm, developing new methods of instruction and assessment. Students can take the lead for social change from their educators, even when these changes are contrary to the expectation of their families. Students should be made aware of their right to an adequate, non-idiotic education. The theory of radical redemptive education can play a positive role in the redemption of students from the mono-cultural idiotic, Eurocentric education by which our epistemology has been victimized.

CHAPTER TEN

The Progressive Educator:
The Harbinger of Faith, Love and Hope

> It is a tragic yet revealing measure of the powerful threat that prophetic movements generate to note the serious ongoing efforts to silence the leadership of the liberation theology movement as well as the violent fate of other great prophets like Socrates, Jesus, Gandhi, and Martin Luther King (Purpel, 2004, p.94).

This chapter critically reflects on the history of the struggle of African people and people of African descent in the Diaspora who form the oppressed majority in the Caribbean and a significant minority in North America. Their quest is for their own rescue and redemption from socio-cultural and economic oppression. The oppression of African peoples has its basis in colonialism, racism, and slavery which were the social and legal practices of Europeans and their descendants in the Caribbean and United States. The connection is made with other African people in the Diaspora who are facing similar struggles in their particular social and political situation in the continued struggle for equal rights and social justice, for freedom and democracy. The main objective of the Africans struggle is to create a better life for themselves, their children, and generally the society in which they live.

The Chapter also draws on the demise of apartheid in South African and the African American Civil Rights Movement as paradigms in the reconstruction of race relations in the current struggle. The main objective is to briefly review the achievements which have been gained so far in the struggle for redemption and the transformation of the societies to which African people were transplanted through slavery. I advocate that there is an important role for the progressive educator in the advancement of the cause for redemption of the poor from oppression. I see the progressive educator as possessing the prophetic role of the harbinger of faith, love, and hope. These are sterling, moral and spiritual qualities to which all people who struggled, and those who continue to struggle against oppression have made a part of their repertoire and dream. Given that many of our political leaders have been co-opted into the service of White power with the object of obfuscating and bamboozling the people, the progressive educator must be the prophetic voice in this sociopolitical fermentation.

This perspective draws on the concept of the stewardship of the progressive educator. It is a tall order to fulfill and I wonder whether an educator has the capacity and political will to challenge *the status quo*. This calls for deep courage and tenacity. It is not a job for the faint-hearted. I shudder in my boots because I know the educator who dares, who has the audacity to challenge the pernicious, virulent White power puts everything on the line, especially in the Caribbean. This is why faith is vitally important if the prophetic educator is to be enabled to assist his people to rise above the squalor of poverty, oppression, and despair; if s/he is to be the voice of the one who cries out in the wilderness of oppression. The prophetic progressive educator must be armed with love, compassion, tolerance, and patience. I believe love is the most powerful human emotion and it is the key that will unlock the hearts of humanity to the true meaning of the equality of all men and women regardless of their ethnic origins. Love for our brothers and sisters as well as for the oppressor because they too are part of the human family despite their perversion. Hope is crucially important to the continuation of the struggle against oppression. The hope for a brighter tomorrow provides the energy and vitality to continue in the work which progressive educators are called to do. This is the *kerygma* of the progressive educator which s/he must teach for the redemption of both the oppressed and the oppressor.

TRANSFORMING THE NOETIC PARADIGM OF THE EDUCATOR

Given that most middle class educators are middle minded and embrace the fetishism of empire and colonialism, there must be some radical transformation of their intellect if they are to participate in the challenge for educational change. The fundamental curricular transformation from the traditional to a radical orientation which is advocated in this book cannot be actualized without the same or similar transformation of the educator, to do otherwise would lead to frustration and ineffectiveness. The reformation of the educator and the curriculum go hand in hand. That is to say, educators must be prepared to shift their paradigm; they must be prepared to accept the *keryma* of redemptive education. This is quite often easier said than done. However, educators who are interested in redemptive education can learn much from the writings of Freire (1998a) who has shown us the road to becoming caring and compassionate educators: the virtues of being a good teacher. He has shown us that we do not teach for ourselves or for an administration, but for our students' developmental well-being:

> When I enter a classroom I should be someone who is open to new ideas, open to questions, and open to the curiosities of the students as well as their inhibitions. In other words, I ought to be aware of being a critical and inquiring subject in regard to the task entrusted to me, the task of teaching and not that of transferring knowledge (p. 49).

In other words, the educator's work involves far more than the pen and paper transferring of knowledge, of perceiving her/himself as repository of knowledge which she/he must pour out into the empty vessels whom s/he is assigned to teach. The classroom is a site of contestations where both students and educators struggle for meaning to their lives and the world in which they live and have their being. Educators must be cognizant of the fact that students do not come to school empty, but that they have a bundle of experiences which they can use to facilitate the learning process, and also of which they are trying to make sense. The educator must condescend into the students' arena, he/she must step down from his/her intellectual pedestal to communicate and identify with the learners for effective and meaningful interaction in the learning experience. Freire (1998a) writes:

> It is important to insist on this point, to insist on this kind of teaching as necessary to being a teacher and as necessary to everyone in education. And to understand its ontological, political, ethical and epistemological, and pedagogical basis. It is also important to that it be something witnessed, lived (p. 49).

The good teacher lives his/her teaching as an integral part of his/her personality. Moreover, educators who are devoid of love and human compassion, who are unable to identify with their students' fears and aspirations, their circumstances, cannot be good educators and do much violence to the learning experience. Good educators care and care very deeply about the welfare and future of their students. Again I must perforce rely on Freire's (1998a) eloquence:

> How can I be an educator if I do not develop in myself a caring and loving attitude toward the student, which is indispensable on the part of one who is committed to teaching and to the education process itself? I can only dislike what I am doing under the pain of not doing it well. I have no reason to exercise my teaching function badly. My response to the offense committed against education is to struggle conscientiously, critically, politically, and in a

strategic manner against those who commit such an offense (p. 65).

The point which Freire is making here is that educators must be convinced that the fundamental curricular change which is envisioned by the radical redemptive pedagogy is important to them, their teaching, and it is capable of bringing about positive, meaningful social change for the healing and liberation of oppressed students. Barkan (1994) has advocated an interesting list of sixteen guidelines which educators could use for effective multicultural teaching which would be most helpful for all multicultural instructors. However, it is pertinent that an overarching plan be created that will deal with every facet of campus life – classroom, dormitory, recreation, social gatherings. Barkan's (1994) sixteenth guide line states:

> [W]e must recognize that the vital goal of a successful multicultural education is promoting and achieving unity with pluralism, inclusiveness not exclusiveness, and that the means to achieving this end must entail institutional as well as curricular change. One without the other will produce superficial changes, uncertainty, and instability and will convey to our students that in reality the status quo essentially endures (p.187).

Barkan's point is that a successful multicultural education requires a magnitudinal change in the repertoire of educators. Educators' traditional ways of doing business as usual cannot fit into this new ethos of schooling; educators must be willing to reform their ways of doing education. Educators if they are not already familiar with the different learning styles must learn or revisit them so as to maximize their students' cognitive skills. The three main instructional methodologies: transmission, transaction and transformation must also be revisited with the view of determining which methodology would work best in the new scheme of things. The principles of "Best Practice" as advocated by Zemelman, Daniels, & Hyde (1998) would be an invaluable asset to educators. Best practice views education and teaching from a whole new stand point which can be used by educators in developing new methodologies for their students' instructions.

When educators allow their pedagogy to be radically transformed through the acceptance that true democracy is a pluralistic and multicultural society, then the schools and colleges will be populated with multicultural students. Educators will then be able to give them the education they desire and deserve. The radicalising of the educators' pedagogy will transform the Black people's consciousness, which will foster a climate of freedom of expression as guaranteed under the Constitution for all peoples regardless of their race, gender, sexual orientation and politics.

The educators' reluctance to approach teaching from a standpoint that includes awareness of race, sex, class, and so forth, according to hooks (1994) is the fear that the classroom will become an unsafe place both for themselves and their students. No doubt the issues that are raised by topics like racism can really set tempers alight. This is why so much depends on the expertise of the educator. Educators cannot afford to allow the fear of passionate outburst to deter them from allowing students to vent their frustration and anger which they may have built up for many years, but it must be carefully managed. This can be the beginning of the students' deconstruction of what he/she has been taught for many years both directly and indirectly. This may also be the time of the students' reconstruction of self and the world in which they live. As hooks (1994) points out: "there is always a possibility that there will be confrontation, forceful expression of ideas, and, at times, conflict" (p.93). This is part of human interaction, of confronting and dealing with difference, and the many negative myths and stereotypes which they would have been taught about others and themselves.

The educator must be prepared to provide catalytic leadership for her/his students. The subject matters which are dealt with by multiculturalism are sensitive and must be handled with great care, patience, and diligence. Nussbaum (1997) expresses the view that "no topic divides American universities more painfully than the topic of race. In no area do we need more urgently to learn about one another, and in no other area are there so many barriers to that understanding" (p.150). The same observation is applicable to the Caribbean and other areas in the Diaspora. But as difficult as these issues are they must be dealt with up front, continued shadow boxing can only lead to further frustration and anger. I believe that Black enfranchisement must be dealt with by the White folks in North American, England, and the Caribbean in a constructive manner. I have also formed the belief that Whites folks are fully cognizant of the racial oppression which they use to maintain their privileged position, but they do not care because their greed for big profits has killed their consciences. So they wantonly disregard the need for fairness and economic enfranchisement of the Black folks. Black labour continues to be exploited for the enrichment of White folks, while the bulk of Black folks are forced to live on the bare necessities for their subsistence. The fact that the blood, sweat, and tears, of the ancestors of Black folks built the countries of North America, Europe, and the Caribbean means very little or nothing to them. The major concern is that Black labour be in abundance so that there can always be a surplus for exploitation to keep the cost of labour down. West (2004) puts it graphically and succinctly: "The Country gave birth to a new breed of plutocrats, the "robber barons," who ran unregulated monopolies and accumulated obscene financial fortunes" (p.51). These robber barons dominate the bulk of the economic activities in the country to the detriment of Black entrepreneurship. Beckles (1993) gives the Caribbean position:

In the 1920's, the merchant class, realizing the effectiveness of the planters' corporate innovation, responded by forming their own large-scale firm – Barbados Shipping and Trading Company Limited... signalled the origin of white corporate monopoly capitalism in Barbados, and a further stage in the successful economic domination of the colony by a white elite (p.531).

Beckles is here describing the method by which the White elite in Barbados grabbed hold of the reigns of corporate power in the early years of the last century and in this way they were able to entrench themselves into the core economic structure of the Island. According to Beckles (1993), the Whites further:

> [M]obilized their ideological argument that blacks had no propensity towards big business, and implemented policies designed to keep them out of the market economy. Blacks were effectively kept away from the centres of economic power in the private sector; they were rarely invited to sit as directors of corporate boards, or to serve as managers (p.536).

Through this ideological notion Blacks were render incompetent where good business acumen is concerned. Many of those persons who works in the private sector are made to feel that they are not part of the corporation because they work for and under the 'White man.' Those Blacks who managed to slip through the corporate guards do so at the behest of the white man's paternalism. This situation is vividly described by West (2004):

> The oppressive effect of the prevailing market moralities leads to a form of sleepwalking from womb to tomb, with the majority of citizens content to focus on private careers and be distracted with stimulating amusements (p.27).

This is the description of a sad human comedy.

Educators as organic intellectuals are one of the significant transforming agents in the society whose pedagogy is grounded in a political activism that is drenched in a desire to fight oppression, injustice, and bigotry in order to create a fairer and more compassionate world. Organic intellectuals, according to Brookfield (2005), are working class men and women who have acquired a discourse other than the one into which they were born who are capable of formulating and working out a strategy to rest power from the traditional intellectual. They are especially qualified for this purpose because they have their origin among the working class and are able to relate to oppression.

Organic intellectuals have the responsibility to help people understand the existence of ruling-class hegemony and the importance of replacing this with a proletarian hegemony. In order to do this, these intellectuals need a capacity for empathic identification with how it feels to be oppressed. They must inhabit the life world of the masses "feeling the elementary passions of the people, understanding them and therefore explaining and justifying them (Brookfield, 2005, p.109).

The orientation of the educator must be so transformed that she/he can identify with the pain and suffering of the down trodden masses so as to enable her/him to see the need to radicalize the curriculum so that the students from various cultural backgrounds can be taught their origin, their history and culture; they will advance the cause for harmony and unification through diversity. West (1993) provides Black critical intellectual catalysts with some sound advice as to their modus operandi when he writes:

> The most desirable option for people of color who promotes the new cultural politics of difference is to be a Critical Organic Catalyst. By this I mean a person who stays attune to the best of what mainstream has to offer – its paradigm, viewpoints and cultures of criticism (p.27).

But equally important to the development of critical intellectual faculties, is the need for the development of new methodology for liberatory education so as to accommodate the ways of learning of the students from various cultures. It is only by so doing that education can be meaningful and productive (as oppose to re-productive) for all students of whatever ethnicity. The critical organic catalyst in this context must have a radical orientation relative to her/his involvement in multicultural education. This is important because no matter how sincere a White teacher may be she/he cannot identify fully with Black oppression. They can sympathize, but they cannot empathize because Blacks come from a history of oppression and struggle, while Whites come from a history of dominance and privilege. Multiculturalism offers an education for critical consciousness as a means for the transformation of students' thinking so that they can become fully aware of their social situation but an even greater emphasis must be placed on the liberation of the educators for they are both the vision bearers and the vision keepers; they are the torch bearers of liberation. The light of the educator will illuminate the abyss of the dismal, oppressive society.

Educators have a profound influence on most of their students in terms of their expectation of them. The educators' expectation is a strong motivating force for them, but educators' ability to motivate students must be taken with a degree of caution because any one can easily blame the educators for students' lack of motivation and this would place an unreasonable burden on the educators, exculpating the home, the church, the society in general from their complicity in the students lack of motivation. In the post-secondary system students must take responsibility for their learning. However, the part of the educators cannot be overlooked because it is an integral part of the renewal process. Hidalgo (1993) points out that there is a need for educators' introspection to go back from whence they came, examine and re-examine what they were told and to put the appropriate value on their previous training and experience. The fact is that educators must first understand and know themselves before they can seek to understand or seek to change others. This is important because most educators were trained in a mode of the monocultural education of the Anglo-European brand which, when it takes root, penetrates and permeates heart, soul, and mind in an almost indelible fashion. Educators according to Hidalgo (1993) must therefore take an introspective retreat to discover who they are, where they came from and where they are going.

> This initial step in the process involves introspection. Educators need to ask themselves some fundamental questions: What framework do we bring into the classroom? How does our cultural perspective color our view of the world? Posing these questions helps (*sic*) educators analyze the deep rooted cultural features of their backgrounds. Educators may thus begin the process of understanding how our beliefs and behaviors are culturally based and how our system of beliefs is similar to or different from our students' beliefs (p. 99).

In other words, teachers must know themselves, their background, and their cultural heritage and the manner in which these impact on them. The educational process of liberation must commence with the educator first transcending his/her own domestication and becoming fully converted to the need to liberate the learning process: the blind cannot lead the blind or they will both stumble into the ditch. Freire (1985) calls it "conscientization." If the educator decides in favour of the transcendence of her/himself, then she/he will be able to condescend to the level of the ordinary students and so reach out to them and identify with them, with the view of engineering their liberation. In essence the educator has to live the profound meaning of Easter (Freire 1985). Educators must become *eastered* intellectuals through the death of their colonial intellect and the resurrection of their new intellect through a radical redemptive pedagogy.

The primary object of the liberating educational practice is the conscientization of the learners, the educator having previously gone through the profound conscientization process of intellectual resurrection. Both the educator and the learner together create a critical, analytical bulwark mentality that is as sharp as a two edged sword that breaks through the pretensions of conservative educational practices, its myths and legends to reveal them for what they really are – Eurocentric hegemonic ideology which is neither the beginning nor the end of things. The critical mind view is sharp, astute, alert, and both the educator and the learner are cognizant of what is happening in their environment, of what is at stake.

Conscientization of educator and learner makes a radical change in their circumstances – an outward and inward transformation of their lives. Through conscientization men and women face the moral demand for truth, righteousness and social justice. Through their transformation they are enabled by the power of love and a keen desire for justice and equity to bring upliftment to the oppressed Black people in the African Diaspora. The educator and the learner become imbued with a genuine concern for truth, righteousness and justice, which are demonstrated through their love for and service to humanity.

The educator must begin with his/her personal social construction with the object being to carry out an effective 'spring cleaning', to clear out all the cobweb and clutter that are in the attics of his/her mind. The educator must challenge his/her own upbringing and traditions with a view to dismantling the monocultural reproductive education which was inculcated in him/her from childhood. Hidalgo (1993) points out that when asked to define themselves ethnically and culturally, some educators have a very difficult time. He finds that many of them lack an ethnic consciousness. He avers that this difficulty often stems from previous schooling and socialization since the Anglo-European perspective in schools defines Black culture as being insignificant.

It is on this basis that Hidalgo (1993) invites educators on an introspective retreat. This retreat which is being advocated here cannot be accomplished solo. It must seek to bring together educators of the various ethnic backgrounds in fellowship to share and discuss their beliefs, childhood, and experiences as educators. If educators are able to relate to persons who are different culturally, they will be better able to deal respectfully and affectionately with the multiplicity of cultures which they will meet in their classrooms.

The educators' introspective retreat will not be a glorified seminar drenched in superficiality and artificial platitudes. It must be genuine and go deep down to the core; it may even be cathartic. After locating ourselves within a particular family and neighbourhood, questions related to the individual should be considered. The questions to think about may include:

> What is our cultural heritage? How does our cultural background influence how we perceive and understand others? What are our values and beliefs? How do our values influence our behaviour toward children? How does our socio-economic class frame our view about children in poverty? What is our definition of normal? How do we think about differences in children, and do we implicitly relate difference to deficiency? Do we believe there are gender differences in certain types of cognitive or physical

abilities? Do we think all children can learn? (Hidalgo, 1993, p. 102).

These are the questions which will confront the teacher who is willing to make the change. There are no easy answers to these questions. They touch upon many issues that we may not even be able to talk about easily, specifically, our values. This is why we must take the introspective retreat with a critical friend for moral support. Through this journey we can clarify our values and our goals for our ministry of teaching and edifying poor ordinary people in the manner that was done by Jesus Christ, Martin Luther King, Jnr., and Paulo Freire. They have indeed left us the road map for us to follow on this journey which will reveal our implicit cultural and social constructions. Because some aspects of our culture are so ingrained into our psyche, this kind of transformation is imperative for personal healing and soul cleansing.

Educators, especially educators of color, must accept themselves as they are with their ethnicity; they must see themselves as worthy people both in their individual and private capacity and as educators, despite the negativity that is prevalent in their environment. Educators who are White and Eurocentric must endeavour to tear away the shrouds of fear that are instigated by prejudice which is evident in their culture, so that they can empower themselves to be able to sympathize with people who are culturally different.

Educators need to go beyond a cognitive awareness of the influence of culture to an affective understanding. Knowing something in the abstract is insufficient to the awareness we seek. We have to be able to empathize with the experience of others. Knowing about inequality in the abstract, believing in the principle of equality, is only the first step towards multicultural awareness needed in classroom (Hildalgo, 1993, p.104).

The point is that educators cannot, especially those of color, afford to subscribe to the 'melting pot' notion. This is a myth that encourages non-White people to surrender their ethnicity so that they can be acculturated, absorbed into Eurocentrism in return for membership in main stream society. This is an exploded myth that must be jettisoned. The so-called melting pot is not a combination or a synthesis of the several cultures but the acceptance of Anglo-European culture to the detriment of the people of color. A person of color can never fully embrace the culture of another without becoming a pretender or a schizophrenic or both. Cultural pluralism may be compared metaphorically, according to Sleeter & Grant (1994) to a:

> patchwork quilt; an array of materials and objects of various sizes shapes and colours. Each ingredient is interdependent on the others, but each is still unique; and each ingredient together, therefore forms a collective total that is distinguished by its difference and diversity (p. 170).

The point is that the value and importance of cultural diversity must be promoted for a harmonious existence in a pluralistic society. It is possible to achieve unity in diversity as demonstrated by Nieto (1996).

PROPHETIC BLACK EDUCATORS AS INTELLECTUAL FREEDOM FIGHTERS

The post-emancipation struggle against institutional racism took on a different tone with the commencement of the Civil Rights Movement in the United States of America, South Africa, and the Caribbean. While slaves were prepared to take up arms against their white masters to obtain their freedom, the black people in North America for the most part followed the path of non-violence, although Malcolm X was prepared to use "any means necessary" to set his people free; for him and many other Black leaders were faced with the ultimatum of either liberty or death. The people of South Africa under the leadership of Mandela (1994) took the same stance of either freedom or death. They armed themselves and fought fire with fire and steel with steel to liberate themselves from White oppression. The spirit of insurrection and rebellion moved through the islands like wild fire. "There were rebellions in Barbados in 1816 (involving 13,000 slaves), in Trinidad in 1819, 1827, and 1829, and in Antigua in 1831" (Campbell, 1985, p.28). The Black people in the Caribbean were prepared to use whatever weapons whether real or improvised (sticks, staves, hoes, cutlasses) to challenge their White oppressors' enslavement of them, albeit that these rebellions were ineffective and short lived. Campbell (1985) presents the determination of the slaves in Jamaica:

> To demonstrate their will to be free, the slaves in Jamaica organized the biggest slave revolt in the Western part of the island when over 20,000 rose up and for two weeks set free the slaves in the parishes of Trelawney, St. James, Westmoreland, Hanover and St. Elizabeth (p. 28).

Physical armed resistance was mounted in 1937 by the working class Blacks in Barbados who were absolutely fed up with their economically deprived status. They were mobilized by Clement Payne to rise up against three hundred years of White oppression. Beckles describes the rebellion:

> Armed with stones, bottles, sticks and a host of other such inefficient instruments, workers attacked the new centre of ruling class power – the commercial district of the city. It was a war on the corporate symbols of white power (Beckles, 1993, p.531).

The Black people in Barbados had had enough of White oppression. But this rejection of White power did not last for very long because no sooner were the Blacks back under the yolks of White oppression that:

> Labour leaders soon rejected the ideas of 1937 and Clement Payne as hero; their subservience to white economic power emerged as the order to (sic) the day; the logical consequence was the fragmentation of national consciousness (Beckles, 1993, p.531).

Many Caribbean leaders emerged out of this struggle to lead the fight for Black folks to be free to live in dignity and peace just as White folks as equal members in their society. One of these leaders was a Baptist preacher, Sam Sharpe:

> Sharpe was holding forth on the evils of and injustices of slavery, and then binding his followers with an oath telling them that 'if black men did not stand up for themselves and take their freedom, the whites would put them out at the muzzle of their guns and shot them like pigeons (Campbell, 1985, p.29).

Prophetic criticism can be a very effective tool if it is used properly. During the post-slavery period Black leaders mushroomed over night: Bustamante, Manley, Marcus Garvey in Jamaica, Adams in Barbados, Bradshaw in St. Kitts, Bird in Antigua, to name a few. Prophetic criticism is still relevant to the struggle against oppression today. West (1993a) has given us some apt instruction when he writes:

> Prophetic critics and artists of color should be exemplars of what it means to be intellectual freedom fighters, that is, cultural workers who simultaneously position themselves within (or alongside) the mainstream while clearly aligned with groups who vow to keep alive potent traditions of critique and resistance (p.27).

This is a crucial point that West is making here that intellectual freedom fighters can draw from the mainstream things that are useful to the struggle but they still keep faith with the resistance struggle. This is great food for thought. The prophetic intellectual is encouraged and motivated by the struggles of resistance to White domination by their ancestors.

West (1982) shows that the vast majority of Black people in the United States of America were politically powerless in that they did not have the right to vote. They were economically exploited and socially degraded and humiliated by the pernicious system of segregation.

During this period the wanton lynching of Black people by White people was not uncommon. Consequently, many of the poor Black people migrated to the cities of the North in the hope of finding a better future for themselves and their children away from the system of segregation. However, in the North they were compelled by the same forces of racism, albeit in a different guise, to live in abject poverty. These squalid conditions led to the race riots of 1919, 1943, 1964, 1967, and 1968 as recorded by West (1982).

There were many radical Black leaders during this period. For example, there were Marcus Garvey and Malcolm X, but the most significant was Martin Luther King Jr. Together with his White allies he was able to motivate and mobilize a movement against institutional racism through the method of non-violence resistance to oppression.

King had formed the considered opinion that non-violence was the proper approach because he saw White people not as enemies but as brothers and sisters who had become perverted by greed and an insatiable lust for power and domination. He was therefore committed to non-violence so as to win over White people by appealing to their consciences and common humanity. He was cognizant of the fact that change will not come overnight because the White oppressors were not going to present equality to Negroes on a platter. He said (as cited in Washington, 1986):

> I do not want to give the impression that nonviolence will work miracles overnight. Men (sic) are not easily moved from their mental ruts or purged of their prejudice and irrational feelings. When the under-privileged demand freedom, the privileged first react with bitterness and resistance (p. 39).

The point which King is making here is that peaceful methods of protest and criticism of White power will not easily dislodge it. But those who are in the struggle for equality and justice must work persistently and arduously to bring it to fruition. The approach of King in resisting oppression is not unlike that which is recommended by West (1993) for intellectual freedom fighters; the tactics are different perhaps, but the opponent remains the same. The end result of King's struggle against racism was a successful battle for Black civil rights: integrated transportation, eating and recreational facilities, and greater than all of these, he secured the right of Black people to vote. Black people now have some political power. Both the social and political impotence of Black people had been ameliorated, but they had not been cured. The power of racism dies hard. King himself paid a very high price. He paid the ultimate price of sacrificing his own life that his people may be free. He truly followed in the footsteps of his Lord, Jesus Christ.

The work of King paved the way for the subsequent rise of the Black Power Movement. In Barbados while there has not been any open rebellion since 1937, the resistance continued and found some support in the Black Power Movement. As indicated above, several Black leaders came to the fore, namely Grantley Adams, Errol Barrow, and Tom Adams. These leaders in the early days continued the struggle for Black economical and political enfranchisement. Political enfranchisement was achieved in the 1960s with the granting of universal suffrage. Independence was negotiated with and granted by England in 1960's and after. However, White power still remains in firm control of most of the economic activities in the Caribbean because the Black leaders capitulated to White pressure and since then continue to be the captive of White power. The social and economic arrangements in Barbados form a typical example. Beckles (1993) recounts:

> Barrow's policy on land reform was cautious and limited ...
> He stressed government partnership rather than confront
> them with reform, or state ownership... only attempts at
> transforming race and managerial relationships in the work
> place, were confined to the need for black tellers in the
> Bridgetown commercial banks (p.533).

The point here is that Black leaders had the opportunity to level the playing field in the late 1960s but many of them squandered the opportunity and betrayed their people's hope for economic enfranchisement. There were no substantial efforts by most of the Black political leaders to reform the colonial arrangements which they had inherited from Britain that have been in place since the days of slavery. However, it must be pointed out that Burnham in Guyana and Manley in Jamaica did make some changes to the economic arrangements which they had inherited. These changes for one reason or a number of reasons failed miserably. The failure in the Jamaican and Guyanese political and economic arrangements in the post independence era was orchestrated by external interference. The economic and social circumstances of Black people have only been ameliorated. Although Black people have the reins of political power, the economic power is still controlled by both local and expatriate Whites, albeit that Blacks form the bulk of the middle class. Blacks continue to be the underdogs. I am supported in this opinion by Beckles (1993): "No campaign was launched to address or redress unequal resource ownership. This was the second major betrayal of the civil rights movement – capitulation in the face of consolidated mercantile power" (p. 533). The situation today has not changed much. This is the social and economic milieu in which the prophetic liberator is called to work.

However, the quest for liberation continued to be informed by the legacy of Black Power Movement. The Black Power Movement had both a political side and a theological side in Black Theology. Both the theological and the political were intertwined. White theology failed and continues to fail to provide any adequate or sufficient account to explicate and/or justify on reasonable grounds the oppression of Black people. As a matter of fact, racism was embedded and deeply entrenched in the main Christian churches. The churches, in spite of their avowed commitment to the Gospel of Christ, sided with the oppressors against the oppressed; even although the Bible is replete with examples of God's activities in favor of the poor. For many church leaders there was much profit to be gained from wining and dining with capitalism. Religious commitment to God or human kind was secondary. It is of interest to note that the Black folks who had ardent belief in God did not inherit the resources of the land.

The fact is that Black people theological reflection cannot be the same as White people because they do not share the same experience, even though they may have the same points of reference in the Bible and Jesus Christ. When the master and the slave pray, could they possibly be referring to the same person? When the slaves spoke of Jesus Christ, they did so against a background of pain, suffering, and despair. The master spoke of Jesus from a background of plenty, ease, and comfort. The slave master presented a Jesus who wanted to make the slaves better slaves in the service of their masters. This was rejected by the slaves because it was contrary to the Scripture and their African heritage.

> There is no truth in Jesus Christ independent of the oppressed of the land – their history and culture. And in America, the oppressed are the people of color – black, yellow, red, and brown. Indeed it can be said that to know Jesus is to know him as revealed in the struggle of the oppressed for freedom. Their struggle is Jesus' struggle, and he is thus revealed in the particularity of their cultural history – their hopes and dreams of freedom (Cone, 2003, pp. 31-32).

The point here is that educators in the Black religious tradition cannot identify with the political, social, and economic system of oppression; this would be otiose and repugnant to the fundamental calling of Christianity to make the liberation of the poor the center of its message and work.

Cone (2003) effectively demonstrates the connection between oppressed people and God. Nowhere in Scripture does God side with the rich against the poor. Her/His intervention into the lives of men and women normally takes the form of deliverance from oppression. The mission of the prophets was to the poor and anti-establishment oppression. God can easily identify with the poor in American, African, and Caribbean and he is able to do this because s/he loves justice or s/he has a working class background. In fact their relationship with him/her is recounted in many of the Negro Spirituals.

Therefore the prevailing status quo can be challenged on moral grounds because it practices corruption and abuses the poor. God (whatever the Divine Personality may be conceived to be) has given us his/her laws, the laws of nature, to guide us, not to enslave us. That law may be summed up in one sentence: love your neighbour as yourself. Such an understanding of the law of God would make the learner keenly aware that the law of God is far more than a mere multiplicity of statutes, ordinances, legal and juristic prohibitions. God's law seeks to foster relationship with him/her, with us, we among ourselves creating bonds of compassion, understanding, love and justice.

The ethical principle that one should love one's neighbour as oneself is evidently multicultural, given that the neighbour is all inclusive; putting all races on an equal footing. It is not sexist: seeking to promote one gender above the other. It is democratic in the sense that it makes all men and women under it morally accountable. It promotes the inalienable equality of all men and women regardless of their race, political status, or their socio-economic class. Rich and poor alike are equal and equally accountable for their conduct. However, despite this inherent equality, Divine solicitude bends towards the poor, the oppressed, the weak and afflicted, those who are victims of sexual and racial discrimination, towards the needy and those who have no helper. It is for them and on their behalf that God intervenes into history.

It is important that liberated educators construct a theology that provides a wholesome interpretation of Black experiences. The liberated educator does not accept soft-minded religiosity because it embraces all kinds of superstitions. The minds of soft-minded religionists are constantly invaded and haunted by all kinds of fears which range from Friday the 13th to a black cat crossing their path. Soft-mindedness carries an undue gullibility which is exemplified in their fatalistic acceptance and internalisation of the domesticating educational practice of White domination. They easily accept the spiritualization of the Black struggle to a future in the sweet by and by instead of a here and now demand for equality and social justice.

The educator who seeks to liberate the learner must be vehement in his/her outrage and brutally outspoken. She/he must expose what those who benefit from the *status quo*, the important people, are doing to the little people. She/he must do this because the little people have no voice – they can only groan under their oppression. In other words, the liberating educator is called to be belligerent, and yet he/she is expected to be kind and humane in dealing with other human beings because each man, each woman, is a brother/sister. This is the proper posture demanded of the liberating educator: to challenge forcefully and forthrightly the moral and social bankruptcy of the neo-colonial social order, of school and schooling, through critical redemptive pedagogy.

The liberated educator must bear in mind the observation of West in his talking book with bell hooks that there is a price to be paid by any intellectual who challenges the status quo of capitalistic dominance. He pointed out that intellectuals who are critical of capitalism have not been popular even among Black people:

> The problem is that any critic of capitalism in the United States is marginalized, and therefore it's very difficult for them to speak a language that is intelligible to large numbers of people. That is the major challenge (West & hooks, 1991, p.44).

Educators who are willing to teach politically will be sacrificed because their critical teaching rejects the privatized, competitive ethic of capitalism, the foundation of White privilege. White privilege and its acculturated Blacks will react by seeking to destroy the educator who threatens their continued existence. The liberated educator is thus caught between a rock and a hard place. S/he must work for money because it is important for daily survival:

> But that does not release us from continually checking the violence we do to others and ourselves by working in ways that violate our souls. Nor does it relieve us from wondering whether preserving integrity is a luxury. What brings more security in the long run: holding this job or honouring my soul?" (Palmer, 1998, p.30).

Freire & Shor (1987) point out that the educators who accept the challenge of social transformation have a dream of changing their society but they have many obstacles which they have to face:

> As I said before, the educators who support the status quo are swimming with the current, but the ones who challenge domination are swimming against the current. Diving into this water means risking punishment from the powers that are in power (p.177).

This is a sober warning to progressive educators that they must count the cost before embarking on this journey of transformation because it is a lonely place.

> [B]ecause of this the progressive educator has to create in herself or himself some virtues, some qualities which are not gifts from God or even given to them from reading books… learning the concrete limits for his or her action, getting clear on the possibilities, not too much behind our limits of necessary fear and not too far ahead." (Freire & Shor,1987, p.177).

The salient point here is that the progressive educator must be very shrewd in his/her action. S/he must be prudent, and wise in his or her advocacy of liberation; bearing in mind that those who are in power are the Eurocentric acculturated Blacks, the ardent supporters of the *status quo* and they will not brook any departure from it nor will they use punishment sparingly.

TEACHING LOVE AND RECONCILIATION IN THE PROPHETIC EDUCATIONAL MINISTRY

The struggle for freedom and democracy in North American and the Caribbean is not dissimilar because in both situations, it is the same historical struggle against colonialism, slavery, racism and sexism. The people of India and Latin America also had the same struggle against

European domination in their countries. The picture that emerges here is one of perennial contests against European domination by peoples who are peacefully pursuing a simple way of life. People who are being dominated seldom seek to subjugate and harness the labor of others for their own aggrandizement. It is no wonder then, that Cone (2003) sees God as being partial to the oppressed peoples; and the prophetic traditions portray God as the deliverer of the downtrodden peoples.

European domination, despite its apparent adherence to Christianity, has caused enormous suffering throughout the world. Within the last fifty years several nations and peoples have resisted and triumphed over Eurocentric domination. The main challenge for redemptive pedagogy is finding a way forward so that both the former oppressor and the oppressed can peacefully and equitably co-exist in one society. The relevant prophetic message for North America, the Metropole, and the Caribbean must be one of love and reconciliation through repentance. This approach was advocated in South Africa following the demise of the apartheid regime. However, it is important to bear in mind that reconciliation can only be effective if it is preceded by repentance. This is illustrated by the work of Bishop Tutu (1999) and the Truth and Reconciliation Commission of South Africa. Mandela (1995) advocated reconciliation between the Blacks and Whites of South Africa without diminishing or playing down the atrocities of the past:

> I told white audiences that we need them and did not want them to leave the country. They were South Africans just like ourselves and this was their land too. I would not mince words about the horrors of apartheid, but I said, over and over, that we should forget the past and concentrate on building a better future for all (p. 614).

This is the better approach because vengeance will only beget more vengeance. I do not believe that we can forget; but we can forgive, we can reconcile. The buck must stop here, even if it means that the initiative has to come from the very people who were so terribly wronged. If we follow the primitive principle of "an eye for an eye," the whole world, according to Gandhi, will soon be blind. As Bishop Tutu (1999) pointed out the world was expecting a ghastly blood bath in South Africa but it did not happen. The world expected that after the election of a democratic government, the Black people who ascended to public office for the first time in that country's history:

> [W]ho for so long had been denied their rights, whose dignity had been trodden underfoot, callously and without compunction, would go on the rampage, unleashing an orgy of revenge and retribution that would devastate their common motherland (p. 260-261).

None of these bloody expectations came to pass. This is a living testimony to the glory of Black humanity. Instead the world witnessed an amazing scenario in which the perpetrators of heinous crimes against Black humanity and heritage confessed their inhumanity to the victims, and the victims told their heartrending stories and their willingness to forgive the perpetrators of sordid atrocities. I respect the position offered by Mandela (1995) except that we will not forget White atrocities, we will not seek revenge either but we will not pretend that it never happened. If we pretend that it never happened it will come back to haunt us.

This is not just the isolated story of South Africans, it is also the story of the Black people in the Diaspora who have struggled and continue to struggle for equal rights and justice. Black people often seem to take the position of no revenge against those who enslaved and oppressed them. Even Toussaint, the leader of the Black Revolution in Haiti refused to take revenge on the White slave owners. He preferred to "treat them with the utmost forbearance, being helpful by an unwarped character which abhorred bloodshed of any kind. 'No reprisals, No reprisals' was his constant adjuration to his officers after every campaign" (James, 1963, 156). The point is that Blacks must not seek revenge. They must be willing to work with Whites because all persons are important to the society and all can co-exist equally in the absence of greed and avarice.

The progressive educator must be a prudent critic of the status quo. As the Bible asserts, he/she must be as wise as a serpent but as harmless as a dove. He/she can afford to take this posture because justice will come whether it takes a year, or two, or three. Justice will come. African slaves did not lose hope that freedom will come, perhaps not for them but for their children. Mandela endured the vicissitudes of nearly three decades of imprisonment and King and Malcolm X were prepared to pay the ultimate price of sacrificing their lives because they envisaged that down the corridor of time justice will come to their people.

THE PROPHETIC EDUCATOR TEACHES HOPE FOR TOMORROW: ENDINGS AND BEGINNINGS

The struggle for liberation continues to progress in small, but very important strides. The progressive educator has a crucial role to play in keeping the struggle alive and to awaken each generation with the need for continual critical reflection and reinforcement. Liberatory education is pertinent to social and political activism. An educated people can learn how to harness its political powers and how to use it to its own advantage. Political power is not the birthright of any social group, but those who possess it will not deliver it to others wrapped in neat packages, with ribbons, bows, and all, like a Christmas gift. Political power is a social force which can be used by any well organized social group.

All people of African descent in particular, and generally all peoples who struggle against oppression must enthrone education in their homes. Social and political power can only be harnessed and used wisely by those who are educated. Through education oppressed people can be the instrumentality of their own liberation. This is clearly demonstrated in the work of Freire (1992) in Brazil and Chile. We can learn much from his experiences. The best education will not come easily. We must be prepared to sacrifice, to forego, and to postpone some of the material things which are necessary for a comfortable existence. Our education must be rooted and grounded in a multicultural philosophy which places an emphasis on radical curricular transformation and on Black redemptive pedagogy. The combination of socio-political actions with educational competence can make an enormous impact on the political life of the country to bring about meaningful and structural changes. It therefore behooves the educated Black men and women who become lawyers, educators, doctors, businessmen/women, writers, entertainers, union leaders and so on not to withdraw from socio-political life and become indifferent to the society's need for their contribution. They cannot afford to adopt a marginalist nor an assimilationist attitude to their society, but instead to combine the attitudes of the exceptionalist and the humanist to foster proper growth and development in their society (West, 1982).

The levers of power which Black people need to take advantage of are ideology, economics, politics, and culture. These they must transform into working class hegemony. Euroentric ideology has a hegemonic hold on the society, this will not be easily dislodged nor pacified, but Black people can offer a feasible alternative in multiculturalism, the implementation of which would augur well for the societies as a whole throughout the Diaspora. However, many Blacks have bought into the Eurocentric hegemony especially those who are better educated because they crave for and identity with White middle class values and status symbols. Instead of providing leadership for the Black communities they spurn them. An earnest effort must therefore be made to win back the hearts and minds of Black defectors. The struggle of the African National Congress (ANC) in South Africa and the Civil Rights Movement in the United States of America and the Caribbean are worthy examples for the Black struggle today for economic enfranchisement in the Diaspora. The ANC has brought about the demise of the apartheid regime in South Africa. The civil rights protests have forced White America to rethink its democracy and redraw the rules: "As a consequence of the vigorous Negro protest, the whole nation has for a decade probed more searchingly the essential nature of democracy, both economic and political. By taking to the streets and there giving practical lessons in democracy and its defaults, Negroes have decisively influenced white thought" (King, as cited in Washington, 1986, p. 304).

The economic control of America is vested in the Eurocentric culture. The business activities of Afro-Americans are miniscule and perhaps not even measurable. I find this to be ironic because America is not only one of the largest economies, but a leading economy on the world stage. But this vast economic activity excludes Black and other minority businesses, tokens apart, to a large extent. No doubt the business activities of minority businesses are crucial to the continued existence of the minority peoples, especially the poor. While the minority may not have the controlling powers of the economy, there is another way in which they are very significant to the economy; that is, they have the power of the purse. They can either shop at white controlled businesses or not. We have seen how this type of protest can impact heavily on the profit of businesses whose life blood is big profits. Spending power apart, large numbers of Afro-Americans are employed in the big industries. These provide bargaining strength in the community.

Despite formidable obstacles it has developed a corps of men (sic) of competence and organizational discipline who constituted a talented leadership reserve, who furnish inspiration and who are a resource for the development of programs and planning. They are strength among the weak though they are weak among the mighty (King, as cited in Washington, 1986, p.304).

The corollary to the economic and political predicament of African Americans is the situation of Blacks in the Caribbean. The story of lack of micro or macroeconomic power of Blacks in America is similar to those for Blacks in the Caribbean. The difference in the two situations is an unabashed irony that the Blacks in the Caribbean make up the vast majority of the population, while the White, Syrian, Lebanese minority makes up a small percentage, yet the minority economic power is deeply entrenched in most of the countries even though in some places, it is 'invisible'. This is staggering by any measure. It is profoundly amazing that since the 1937 flare up, there has not been any significant political action to attempt to change this magnitudinal economical power imbalance in the region. This must be an example par excellence of the working of Eurocentric hegemony. It is almost embarrassing, to put it mildly, that Black people could be so docile.

The political power of the Afro-Americans and other minority peoples lies in the principle which was ardently advocated by Nelson Mandela of 'one man (sic) one vote'. This position was taken by Mandela (1995) because he had the assurance that the share number of Blacks in South Africa in a free and fair democratic election would bring the African National Congress into power. The population of Blacks and other minority peoples continues to increase, particularly in the Latino population by birth and migration. Many of the minority peoples now live in several of the big cities in America while the white population flees to the suburbs. This has political significance given that the large cities can impact on the political direction which the state takes and that can in turn impact on the presidential elections. The cities are teeming with young minority men and women who are at the voting age. It is conceivable that in the near future the political direction of the cities will not be decided in the boardrooms of corporatism but in the bulging, overcrowded ghettoes of the cities.

This prospect of a greater say for minority peoples in America is refreshing, but in the Caribbean, this kind of consideration is not necessary because as in the case of South Africa, we have the majority, we vote for the government of our choice, but alas! The governments of the day since 1937 seem not have neither the sagacity nor the will to pursue a policy of Black economic enfranchisement. Therefore, it is conceivable that the boardrooms of corporatism will continue to give political direction for the country to the elected officials.

At present many Black youths are infected with political apathy because they see political involvement as empty rituals. Here the work of the progressive educator is cut out for him/her to motivate and mobilize the youths who are in his/her charge to a higher level of political activism. The educator must seek to *conscientize* the youth to realize that united and organized pressure can bring tremendous improvement in their social circumstances. The result of the 1960s protests in the United States of America is a leading paradigm for oppressed people's protest. It shows that when oppressed people are united they can become a powerful political force. Meaningful and structural changes will only be effected by persons who have been educated for social transformation. Racism is tenacious but it is not unassailable. It can be dislodged, but only if there is combined concerted effort for social action with educational competency. It will not be moved by men and women who cannot organize themselves as a unified force to combat the evils of racism in the society. The lack of organization was one of the debacles which was faced by the Black leaders during the 1960's and is still present with us. The Haitian Revolution of 1791 to 1803 succeeded because Toussaint skillfully organized the ex-slaves and impressed upon them the need to fight for their freedom, and the timing was right. The Revolution brought into being the first independent Black Republic in the Caribbean (James, 1963). This is another Africentric paradigm for Black people in their struggle for liberation, although the current political upheavals in that country make it very unattractive.

We must teach hope to the children of Africa and other minority children who have to endure a ghetto life while their contemporaries enjoy the good life in the suburbs. We must teach the children to take heart and not to fear because deliverance will come. African children have waited a long time, centuries to have their humanity recognized, but we must be patient; we must continue to shout and sing *hope*. The social situation of the children of Africa and other minority peoples has improved significantly since the 1960's, but even greater improvement is needed. "Lack of education, the dislocation and urbanization and the hardening of white resistance loom as such tormenting roadblocks that the goal sometimes appears not as a fixed point in the future but as a receding point never to be reached." (King, as cited in Washington, 1986, p.13) Black people have been holding on for a long time for improvement in their socio-political and economic circumstances. We must avoid reaching the point where the proverbial straw breaks the back of the camel. The metaphors are used to guide our vision for the future are not perfect, but they encourage and urge us on. The cause of justice will come to fruition.

Justice for black people will not flow into society merely from court decisions nor from fountains of political oratory. Nor will a few token changes quell all the tempestuous yearnings of millions of disadvantaged black people. White America must recognize that justice for blacks cannot be achieved without radical changes in the structure of our society. The comfortable, the entrenched, the privileged cannot continue to tremble at the prospect of change in the status quo (King, as cited in Washington, 1986, p. 314).

In other words, radical structural changes which are required for the transformation of the society will only be realized if oppressed peoples continue the struggle for liberation. A critical examination of past experiences of Black and White peoples, and our common humanity, will help to facilitate peace and harmony in the world in which we live. This is the kind of hope that is cherished and advocated by West (as cited in Cowan, 2003):

> [H]ope is deep and enduring and provides and intent for pursuing the quest for justice in society, against what may appear insurmountable odds. West's hope is built on a deep and tragic sense of history and so does not seek a quick overnight solution (p.34).

West is right in that oppressed people must live with hope but they must also bear in mind that justice will not come overnight. The path of travel is between optimism and pessimism – progress will be made but paradise will still be in the distance.

It is against this background of struggle and resistance by oppressed people that the progressive educator's attention is required to make it an integral part of her/his educational practice. I agree with Freire (1992) that we cannot avoid our "slavocratic past." It is and will continue to color our view of the cultural politics and economic activities of the world. The liberatory educator must be fully cognizant of this and fully accept it. Struggle and resistance will always be a part of the life of people who are oppressed by the prevailing socio-political structures of modern societies. Oppressed peoples have practiced a political dialectic which allows them to survive. African slaves obeyed their masters because disobedience brought swift death. But when they saw the opportunity for rebellion they took up arms against their oppressors. A typical example is the Haitian Revolution as recorded by James (1963).

As Freire (1992) asserts:

> After all, by adopting such behavior, the slaves survive. And it is from learning experience to learning experience that a culture of resistance is gradually founded, full of 'wiles' but full of *dreams*, as well. Full of rebellion, amidst apparent accommodation (p.92).

This is the lesson which the progressive educator must share with the educands. The same struggles by oppressed people for dignity and respect, for homes, employment, cultural and educational equality are still pervasive today. The lack of proper medical facilities; the failure to take full advantage of the educational facilities and programs that are available for the children in the inner city schools have a debilitating impact on the social and cultural development of Black children, especially. In the Caribbean the struggle is along a somewhat different plain, in that much has been done in terms of the educational advancement of the Blacks. Education is free from primary to tertiary in some countries and there is compulsory education from five years to sixteen years in most, if not all, countries in the region. However, the transfer from primary to secondary school follows the traditional Eurocentric Eleven Plus Examination which annually relegates the bulk of the primary school children to the newer secondary school and to a life of second class citizenship, while those who are perceived to be intellectual go the elitist older secondary schools with the prospect for a good life. The experience is not unlike that which is portrayed by Hesse (1906) in *Beneath the Wheel*. This method of school transfer is one of the hangovers from the neo-colonial past, but one that is so deeply entrenched in the psyche of Caribbean educators that there seems to be no way out.

The progressive educator who subscribes to the philosophy of multiculturalism can bring hope to children who live in apparently hopeless situations. I must concur with Freire (1992) that:

> It is our task as progressive educators to take advantage of this tradition of struggle, of resistance, and "work it." It is a task that, to be sure, is a perverted one from the purely idealist outlook, as well as from the mechanistic, dogmatic, authoritarian viewpoint that converts education into pure "communication," the sheer transmission of neutral content (p. 92).

The concerns of the progressive educator will lead him/her to critically reflect on the evils of racism, poverty, marginalism, and materialism and seek to create ways and means by which they can be ameliorated, if not obliterated. This is a risky activity because it pushes against the nerves of the *status quo* which will reveal the systematic weaknesses that are embedded in the society and challenge the society to radical reconstruction as the real issue which it must face in order to redeem itself from further human denigration. The progressive educator will, must prophesy deliverance to avert social catastrophe. This is the prophetic role of the educator. He/she must educate the educands to challenge those who have failed to care for the plight of the poor, who have been heartless and blinded themselves with the immoral notion that the poor is comfortable in their misery. The society's redemption lies in caring, compassion, commitment, and hope for a better future for poor people. As Purpel (2004) points out: "Educators are primarily moral, political, and cultural agents with the responsibility of grounding their specialized insights in a cultural, political, and moral vision. An educator without some kind of moral and cultural grounding is either tragically alienated, cynically deceptive, or naively shallow." (p.203)

The point which Purpel & McLaurin (2004) make is that educators have a vocation and a moral duty to call the society to change its ways, and to continue the struggle to create a vision for the future so that we will not all perish. The prophetic ministry of the teacher reminds us that we either learn to live together as civilized human beings or we perish together as fools. The educator as an intellectual freedom fighter roars against poverty, injustice, and hunger that are part and parcel of the social, economical, political wickedness which is the progeny of capitalism, with which the poor wrestle daily. This calling is based on a higher principle which makes the educator beholden to no one. The call is vividly and tantalizingly describes by Purple & McLaurin (2004):

> This ministry (education) involves the dimensions we have described – sharp criticism, dazzling imagination, a sacred perspective, commitment to justice and compassion, hope, energy, and involvement. Freedom does not come, according to the prophets, from adaptation, accommodation, and acceptance, nor does it emerge out of numbness and callousness to injustice. Freedom for the prophets emerges from caring, and lies in hope, possibility, and commitment (p.93).

In other words, the educator is a prophet in his or her own right with a calling, a commitment to justice, and deep respect for freedom. Having this kind of vocation, the educator must *a fortiori* be a political activist. In this entire milieu, the educator is the catalyst that will trigger the change; this is why they have the awesome responsibility of raising the level of consciousness of the masses. In the pursuit of this ministry there are certain attributes which are indispensable to the educational practice of the progressive educator. These attributes are not inherent in the personality of the progressive educator; they "are not attributes that we can be born with or that can be bestowed upon us by decree or as a gift…they are developed through practice in concurrence with a political decision that the educator's role is crucial" (Freire, 1998, p.39). The attributes which Freire (1998b) have identified are: humility, lovingness, courage, tolerance, and patience-impatience. These are the attributes which progressive educators must carry within their persons as they pursue their educational ministry in the cultural politics of the African Disapora.

CONCLUSION

This Chapter critically examined the perennial struggles of Black people in the United States of American, England, and the Caribbean. Black people have had to struggle against slavery, colonialism, genocide, apartheid, segregation, and such other sordid inhumanities which are created by White ingenuity. The fight for equality and justice is still a fact of life for Black people everywhere. The socio-economic circumstances of the Blacks in the Caribbean are not unlike those of the Blacks in North America and the England. The significant difference is that in the Caribbean the Black majority is dominated by a small minority. The socio-cultural and socio-economical situation of Black people in the Diaspora must change. The progressive educator has a significant role to play in the cause for the advancement of meaningful change.

The progressive educator must be in the vanguard to bring about change. The progressive educator has a prophetic educational ministry, a calling and duty to teach the *kerygma* of redemptive education. The progressive educator must have the faith and the belief that right will triumph over might. Slavery has fallen, apartheid has fallen, and *de jure* segregation has fallen. Some progress has been made in the removal of the white-walled labyrinth of Eurocentric oppression, but comparatively speaking, this is miniscule. The great avalanche is yet to come. The progressive educator must teach the peasants, the poor and the despised to fight for human justice, the brotherhood/sisterhood of all humankind, of white, yellow, brown, and black; peace and abundance for all of humankind. The progressive educator must not shrink from the formidable tasks that rest on her/his shoulders. The progressive educator must teach the gospel of nonviolence. The progressive educator must teach the oppressed educands that there is hope for a brighter tomorrow because there is love, forgiveness, and reconciliation in the heart and soul of each human person. The progressive educator through his her kerygmatic pedagogy of redemption aspires to highest social goods of social harmony, friendship, community in diversity – the *summum bonum* of human strivings. Go softly – I can hear angels speaking: The American electorate has elected an African American to be their President. Is this the beginning of the great avalanche?

> Soft as the voice of an angel
> Breathing a lesson unheard,
> Hope, with a gentle persuasion,
> Whispers her comforting word.
> Wait, till the darkness is over,
> Wait, till the tempest is done,
> Hope for the sunshine tomorrow,
> After the shower is gone.
>
> Whisper, whispering Hope,
> Oh how welcome thy voice,
> Making my heart in its sorrow rejoice.

References

Adams, M., Bell, L. A., Griffin, P. (1997). *Teaching for diversity and social justice: A source book.* Lodon: Routeledge,

Alleyne, M. C. (2002). *The construction and representation of race and ethnicity in the Caribbean and the world.* Kingston, Jamaica: UWI Press.

American Declaration of Independence, 1776.

Anderson, J. & Byrne, D. A.(2004). *The Unfinished Agenda of Brown v. Board of Education: John* Wiley & Sons, Inc.

Apple, M. W., & Carlson, D. (1998). *Power/knowledge/pedagogy: The meaning of democratic education in unsettling times.* New York: Westview Press.

United NationsCommittee for The Elimination of all Forms of and Racial Discrimination (CERD): Barbados Report 2005:.

Banks, J. A. (1975/2003). *Teaching strategies for ethnic studies.* New York: Allyn and Bacon.

Barkan, E. R. (1994). Strategies for teaching in a multicultural environment. In D. F. Halpern & Asso ciates, *Changing college classrooms: New teaching and learning strategies for an increa singly complex world* (pp.175-190). San Francisco: Jossey-Bass.

Beckford, G. L. (1972/1999). *Persistent poverty: Underdevelopment in plantation economies of the third world.* Bridgetown, Barbados: UWI Press.

Beckles, H. (1993). Independence and social crisis of nationalism in Barbados. In H. Beckles & V. Shepherd(Eds.), *Caribbean freedom: Economy and society from emancipation to present* (pp.528-539). Kingston, Jamaica: Ian Randle.

Belle, R. H. (2002). *Understanding african philosophy: A cross cultural approach to classical and contemporary issues*. London: Routledge.

Belle, L. A. (1997).Theoretical foundations for social justice education. In M. Adams, A. Belle. & P. Griffin (Eds.), *Teaching for diversity and social justice* (pp.3-15). New York: Routledge.

Berliner, D. C. & Biddle, B. J. (1995). *The manufactured crisis: Myths, fraud and the attachk on Ameri ca's public schools*. New York: Addison-Wesley Publishing Company Inc.

Boland, O. N. (1993). Systems of domination after slavery: The control of land and labour in the British West Indies after 1838. In H. Beckles & V. Shepherd (Eds.), *Caribbean freedom: Economy and society from emancipation to the present* (pp.107-123). Kingston, Jamaica: Ian Randle Publishers.

Brighouse, H. (2000). *School choice and social justice*. New York: Oxford University Press.

Brookfield, S. D. (2005). *The power of critical theory: Liberating adult learning and teaching*. San Francisco: Jossey-Bass.

Browne v. Board of Education of Topeka, 347 U.S. 483 (1954).

Campbell, H. (1997). *Rasta and Resistance: From Marcus Garvey to Walter Rodney*. St. John's: Hansib Publication Limited.

Canadian Charter of Rights and Freedoms.

Committee on the Elimination of Racial Discrimination (CERD) Report (Barbados)

Clarke, A. (2003). *Growing up stupid under the Union Jack.*

Clarke, E. (1957). *My mother who fathered me*. Kingston: The Press, University of the West Indies.

Chubb, J. E. & Moe, T. M. (1990). Politics, markets, & America's schools. Washington, D.C.: Brookings Institute.

Civil Rights Act of 1866.

Civil Rights Act of 1875.

Civil Rights Act of 1964.

Clarke, A. (2003). *Growing stupid under the union jack*. Kingston, Jamaica: Ian Randal.

Cobley, A. G. (2000). The historical development of higher education in the anglophone Caribbean. In G. D. Howe (Ed.), *Higher education in the Caribbean: Past, present and future directions* (pp.1-23). Kingston, Jamaica: UWI.

Cohen, C. & Sterba, J. P. (2003) *Affirmative Action and Racial Preference: A Debate*: Oxford University Press.

Cohee, G. E. & Kemp, T. D.(eds.)(1998). *Feminist Teacher*. Feminist Teacher Editoria Collective.

Coleman, R. (ed.)(1992). Resolutions of the twelve Lambeth Conferences 1867-1988. Toronto. Anglican Book Centre

Committee for Public Education v. Nyquist 413 U.S. 756 (1973).

Colin, S. A. J., III & Guy, T. C. (1998). Africentric Interpretive model of curriculum orientations for course development in graduate programs in adult education. *PAACE Journal of Life Long Learning, Volume 7*, (pp.43-55).

Colin, SA. J. (2002). Marcus Garvey: Africentric adult education for self-ethnic reliance. In E. A. Peterson (ed.), *Freedom road: Adult education of african Americans*. Malabar, Fl. Krieger (rev. ed)

Community College Act, Chapter, Barbados.

Constitution of Barbados (1966)

Constitution of the United States Amendment XIII and *Amendment XIV*

Cone, J. H. (1975/2003). *God of the Oppressed.* New York: Orbis Press.

Cowan, R. (2003). *Cornel West: The politics of redemption.* MA: Blackwells.

Counts, G. S. (1932/1978). *Dare the School Build a New Social Order?* Illinois: South Illinois Univer sity Press.

De Zengotita, T. (2005). *How the media shapes your world and the way you live in it: Mediated.* New York: Bloomsbury.

Delpit, L. (1995). *Other people's children: Cultural conflict in the classroom.* New York: New Press.

DeMarrais, K. B. & LeCopte, M. (1999). *The way schools work* (3rd ed.). New York: Longman.

Diop, C. A. (1974). *The African origin of civilization: Myth or reality?* Chicago: Lawrence Hill.

Dewey, J. (1938). *John Dewey: Experience and education.* New York: Touchstone.

Dewey, J. (1916). *Democracy and Education.* New York: Barnes & Noble Books.

*Dred Scott v. Sandford,*163 U.S. 537

Ellis, P. (2003).*Adult Education in Barbados.* Bridgetown: UNESCO.

Elementary and Secondary Education Act,2001.

European Convention on Human Rights

Executive Order 10925 (Pres. J. F. Kennedy, 1961).

Fanon, F. (1963). *The wretched of the earth*. London: Clays.

Fisher, L. E. (1985). *Colonial madness: Mental health in the Barbadian social order*. New Jersey: Putgen University Press.

Freire, P. (1971). *Pedagogy of the Oppressed*. Connecticut: Bergin & Garvey.

———— (1985). *The politics of education: Culture, power, and liberation*. New York: Bergin & Garvey.

———— (1998a). *Pedagogy of freedom: Ethics, democracy, and civic courage*. New York: Row man & Littlefield.

———— (1998b). *Educators as cultural workers: Letters to those who dare teach*. Colorado: Westview Press.

———— (1992). *Pedagogy of hope*. New York: Coninuum.

Freire, P. & Shor, I. (1987). *A pedagogy for liberation: Dialogues on transforming education*. Connecticut: Bergin & Garvey.

Freedmen's Bureau Act1865.

Gill, B. P., Timpane, P. M., Ross, K. E. & Brewer, D. J. (2001). *Rhetoric versus reality: what we know and what we need to know about vouchers and charter schools*. Santa Monica, California:Rand.

Gillmor, D. (2004). *We the media: Grassroots journalism by the people, for the people*. Cambridge: O'Reilly.

Giroux, H. A. (1985). Introduction in P. Freire, *The politics of education: Culture, power, and libera tion* (pp.xi-xxv). New York: Bergin & Garvey.

Giroux, H. A. (1988). *Teachers as intellectuals: Towards a critical pedagogy of learning*. Connecticut: Bergin and Garvey.

Gratz Et Al v. *Bollinger Et Al,* 539 U.S. 1.

Grutther v. Bolliger Et Al, 288 F. 3rd 732 (2002)

Goodridge, S. S. (1984). *A companion to liberation theology.* Bridgetown. Cedar Press

Gore, J. M. (1993). *The Struggle for Pedagogies: Critical and Feminist Discourses as Regimes of Truth.* Routledge.

Guarasci, R. & Cornwell, G, H. (1997). *Democratic education in an ae of Difference: Redefining citizenship in higher education.* San Franciscos: Jossey-Bass Publishers.

Gutek, G. L. (1997). *Philosophical and ideological perspectives on education.* MA: Allyn & Bacon.

Hardiman, R. & Jackson B. W. (1997). Conceptual foundations for social justice courses. In Adams, M., Belle, A. & Griffin, P (Eds.), *Teaching for diversity and social justice* (pp.16- 29). New York: Routledge.

Harry, B. (1992). *Cultural diversity, families, and the special education system: Communication and empowerment*: Teachers College Press.

Hesse, H. (1906). *Beneath the wheel.* New York: Fisherman.

Henig, J. R. (1994). *Rethinking school choice: Limits of the market metaphor.* New Jersey: Princeton University Press.

Hidalgo, N. M. (1993). Multicultural teacher introspection. In T. Perry & J. Fraser (Eds.), *Freedoms' plow: teaching in the multicultural classroom* (pp.99-108). New York: Routledge.

Hirsch, E. D. Jr. (1996). *The schools we need and why we don't have them.* New York: Anchor Books.

hooks, b. (1994). *Teaching to transgress.: Education as the practice of freedom.* New York: Rout ledge.

hooks, b. (1990). *Yearning: Race, gender, and cultural politics.* Boston: South End Press.

Hoyos, F. A. (1979/1995). *Barbados: A history from the Amerindians to independence.* London: Mac millan.

Huba, M. E. & Freed, J. E. 2000). *Learner-Centred assessment on college campus: Shifting the focus from teaching to learning.* Boston: Allyn and Bacon.

Huitt, W. & Hummel, J. (2003). *Piaget's theory of cognitive development. Educational psychology interactive.*ValdostaStateUniversity. Retrieved12/1/2004from valdosa.edu/whuitt/col/cogsyss/piaget. html.

Hurtado, S., Milem, J., Clay-Pedersen, & Walter, A. (1999). *Enacting diverse learning environment,* volume 26, No. 8 George Washington University, Washington.

James, C. L. R. (1963). *The Black Jacobins: Toussaint L'Ouverture and the san domingo revolution.* New York: Vintage Books.

Junn, E. N. (1997) Experiential approaches to enhancing cultural awareness. In D. F. Halpern and Associates, *Changing college classroom: New teaching and learning strategies for an increa singly complex world* (pp.128-164). San Francisco: Jossey-Bass.

Kilbourne, J. (1999). *Can't buy my love: How advertisement changes the way we think and feel.* New York: Simon & Schuster.

Kohli, W. (2000). Teaching in the danger zone: Democracy and difference. In D. W. Hursh & E. W. Ross (eds., *Democratic social education: Social studies for social change* (pp.23-42). New York: Falmer Press.

Kozol, J. (1990). *The night is dark and I am far from home.* New York: Touchstone.

——— (1991). *Savages Inequalities: Children in America's Schools.* Harper Perennial.

——— (2005), *The shame of the Nation: The restoration of apartheid schooling America.* NewYork: Crown Publishing.

Lamming, G. (2000). *Coming, coming home: Western education and the Caribbean intellectual coming, coming, coming home.* Philipsburg: House of Hehesi.

Law v. Nicholls, 414 U.S. 563.

Liner,D.(2002).ThetrialofGalileo.htt://www.umke.edu/faculty/projects/trials/Galileo/gallileoaccount.html

Mandela, N. (1994). *Long walk to freedom: The autobiography of Nelson Mandela.* New York: Little, Brown and Company.

McChesney, R. W. (2004). The problem of the media: US communication politics in the 21st century. New York: Monthly Review Press.

McLauren v. Oklahoma State Regent, 539 U.S. 637

McLaren, P. (1995/1997). *Critical pedagogy and predatory culture.* New York: Routledge.

———(2005). Critical pedagogy: A look at the major concepts. In A. Darder, M. Baltodano,& R. D. Torres(Eds.): *Critical pedagogy reader* (pp.69-96). New York: Routeledge Falmer.

Miller, J. P., & Seller, W. (1985). *Curriculum: Perspective and practice.* New York: Longman.

Nieto, S. (1996). *Affirming diversity: The sociopolitical context of multicultural education.* New York: Longman.

Missouri Ex Rel. Gaines v. Canada, Registrar of University of Missouri, Et Al, 305 U.S. 337

Neill, M. et al (2004). *Failing our Children: How "No Child Left Behind" Undermines Quality and Equity in Education*: National Centre for Fair and Open Testing. *U.S. Department of Education, Office of Elementary and Secondary Education, No Child Left Behind: A Desktop Reference, Washington, D. C., 2002.*

Nieto, S. (1992). *Affirming diversity: The sociopolitical text of multicultural education*. New York: Longman.

Nieto, S. (1999). *The light in their eyes: Creating multicultural learning communities*. New York: Teachers College Press.

Nussbaum, M. C. (1997). *Cultivating humanity: A classical defense of reform in liberal education*. Massachusetts: Harvard University Press.

Palmer, P. (1998). *The courage to teach: Exploring the inner landscape of a teacher's life*. San Fran cisco: Jossey-Bass.

Parker, W. C. (2003). *Teaching democracy: Unity and diversity in public life*. New York: Educators College Press.

Patai, D. & Koertge, N. (2003). *Professing feminism*. New York: Lexington Books.

Plessy v. Fergusson, 163 U.S. 537

Population census 2005:Government of Barbados.

Public Order Act, Chapter 169A, Barbados (19).

Purpel, D., & McLaurin W. M. (2004). *Reflections on the moral & spiritual crisis in education*. New York: Peter Lang.

Rawls, J. (1971). *A theory of justice*. New York: Harvard University Press.

Richards, J. J. (1993). Classroom tapestry: A practitioners perspective on multicultural education. In P. Perry & J. W. Fraser (Eds.),*Freedom's plow: Teaching in the multicultural classroom* (pp.47-64). New York: Routledge.

Re Codringtion, USPG v. Attorney-General (1970) 16 WIR 87.

Sholle, D. & Denski, S. (1994). *Media education and the (Re)production of culture.* Westport: Bergin & Garvey

Shops Act, Chapter 356A, Barbados.

Sleeter, C. E. & Grant, C. A. (1993). *Making choices for multicultural education: Five approaches to race, class, and gender.* New York: McMillan.

Spring, J. (1999). *Wheels in the head: Educational philosophies of authority, freedom, and culture from Socrates to human rights.* New York: McGraw Hill College.

———— (2000). *The Universal Right to Education.* New Jersey: Lawrence Earlbaum Associates.

Sweatt v. Painter, 339 U.S. 629 (1950).

Tutu, D. (1999). *No future without forgiveness.* New York: Doubleday.

Tyler, R. W. (1949). *Basic principles of curriculum and instruction.* Chicago: University of Chacago Press.

United Nation Convention for the Elimination of all Forms of Racial Discrimination (1965).

United Nation Declaration on Human Rights

University of California v. Bakke, 438 U.S. 265 (1978

Washington, J. M. (1986). *A testament of hope: The essential writings and speeches of Martin Luther King, Jr.* San Francisco: Haper & Sons.

Welch, L. B. (ed.) (1992). Perspectives on minority women in higher education. Connecticut: Praeger.

West, C. (1982). *Prophesy deliverance: An afro-american revolutionary Christianity.* Philadelphia: Westminster Press.

———— (1993a). *Keeping Faith: Philosophy and race in america.* New York: Routledge

———— (1993b). *Race Matters.* Boston: Beacon Press.

———— (2004). *Democracy Matters: Winning the fight against imperialism.* New York: Penguin Press.

West, C. & hooks, b. (1991). *Breaking Bread: Insurgent black intellectual life.* Ontario: Between the Lines

Whitepaper on Education Reform, Government Printing Department 1995.

Wiggins, G. & McTighe, J (1998). *Understanding by design.* Alexandria: ASCD.

Williams, C. (1987). *The destruction of black civilization: Great issues of a race from 4500 B. C. to 2000 A. D.* Chicago: Third World Press.

Witte, J. F. (2000). *The market approach to education: An analysis of America's first voucher program.* New Jersey: Princeton University Press.

Woodson, C. G. (1933). *The miseducation of the negro.* New Jersey: African World Press.

Zemelman, S., Daniels, H. & Hyde, A. (1998). *Best practice: New standards for teaching and learning in america's schools.* Portsmouth, NH: Heineman.